I0130295

THE RACE FOR CITY STATUS

How Doncaster became one of
Britain's newest cities

Jim Carley

Fisher King Publishing

THE RACE FOR CITY STATUS
How Doncaster became one of Britain's newest cities

Copyright © Jim Carley 2024

All rights reserved

Print ISBN 978-1-914560-99-6
Ebook ISBN 978-1-916776-00-5

No part of this publication may be reproduced or
distributed in any form or by any means, or stored in a
database or electronic retrieval system without the prior
written permission of Fisher King Publishing Ltd.

The right of James Carley to be identified as the author of
this work has been asserted by him in accordance with the
Copyright, Designs and Patents act, 1988.

Thank you for respecting the author of this work.

Published by Fisher King Publishing
fisherkingpublishing.co.uk

For Anne, George, & Alice,
Mum, Dad, & Tricia

And for all the amazingly wonderful people
of the great city of Doncaster.

Just once in his life,
A man has his time,
And my time is now,
I'm coming alive!

St Elmo's Fire (Man in Motion) –
Atlantic Records,1985
Music & Lyrics by
David Foster & John Parr

Contents

First Things First

It was Thursday 19th May 2022, a warm and sunny day by all accounts. I had taken my team, the people who work for my small business, to the Mount Pleasant Hotel, just south of Doncaster in South Yorkshire. It's a very pleasant four-star hotel, which started out as a converted farmhouse in the 1930s, and which has been since been expanded to offer more than 60 en-suite rooms, a variety of function spaces, an artisan brasserie, a small spa, and some nicely landscaped gardens. As a business, we are a team of professional proposal writers, and we were having an off-site team building day. It was the type of event where, as you might expect, we were engaged in activities and discussions all geared to making our small business even better. There were fourteen of us, including some recent new starters, and the purpose of the day was also to help integrate these new faces into the group. The morning had gone well. Just after finishing a more than pleasant lunch in the hotel's restaurant, I stepped outside the main entrance, where there's a quaint little pagoda and a pond full of koi carp, to check my messages. That is when I got the call from Dan Fell, the Chief Executive of Doncaster Chamber. There was only really one reason why Dan would be calling, and that would be to share news about the Platinum Jubilee Civic Honours competition, the contest for towns across the UK to win the much-coveted title of city status. But this wasn't just any news, this was the most important news that I'd been waiting on for the past six months. This was *the* news, and for Doncaster it was very good news indeed.

Dan said something to me along the lines of 'we got it', to which I immediately blurted out some choice language and punched the air. We then spent a few moments verbally slapping each other on the back. He wanted me to have heard the news in person from him, which I certainly appreciated. After the call, I firstly quickly dialled my wife, Anne, to share the news with her. She had, after all, put up with my insufferable journey into city status geekdom over these past months, and had more than earned her place at the top of my list. Then I hurriedly went back to the hotel reception and purchased some champagne to be delivered to our meeting room. Back in the room, with the team distracted on another activity, I surreptitiously wrote four words in large letters on the back sheet of the flip chart. Then, at the end of the day, with my team bemusedly eyeing the tray of glasses and champagne that had just arrived in the room, I spun the flip chart around, revealing the final page, and the words I had written: *Doncaster is a CITY!* It took a micro-second for them to process it, which also probably tells you something about the dreadful quality of my handwriting, but the reactions were priceless. The corks were popped, and we raised a toast. We had been part of something remarkable.

But let's not get too far ahead of ourselves. I should really start by properly introducing myself. My name is Jim. Well, technically it's James, but only a select few relatives still call me that. Even if you live in Doncaster, you have very likely never heard of me, nor would I have expected you to. When people ask me what I do for a living I tell them that I'm a bid writer. That is usually met with a shrug and a blank expression. What's a bid writer? I've never met one of those before. You are not alone, most people haven't. As career paths go it's a very select field, and many of us in this trade found our way here by accident. So, I start to explain that I write proposals aimed at winning competitively tendered contracts. If the blank expression is still there, and it usually is, I know I need to elaborate a little further. So, I go on to explain that, say for example, a local council has put out a tender for something that it wants to buy, say a contract to fill in some potholes or to empty the bins, I would write a proposal on behalf of a supplier to help them win that contract. That's my job. I am a writer of bids, or you might call them proposals, or tenders. That starts to make some sense, but at this stage I can tell that the person I'm talking to has, most likely, already lost interest. It's not the kind of job title that naturally encourages follow up questions. Such is the plight of being a bid writer. How I envy doctors, accountants, and solicitors who, by virtue of just stating their job title alone, offer immediate clarity of their vocation without the need for further explanation.

I've been a bid writer for my sins for 25 years now. For the past 15 years I have managed my own small bid writing company. Across my career I have written, and more importantly won, a lot of bids. I've written bids on behalf of both national corporations and the smallest local enterprises. I've written bids for contracts valued from a few thousand pounds to tens of millions. I've written bids for contract opportunities in Europe, Australia, and the Middle East. I've been hired to write bids by everyone from the son of a former British Prime Minister to one of the reality TV stars from *The Real Housewives of Cheshire*. I have written bids in response to all manner of policy initiatives that have come, gone, and, in many cases, been long since forgotten. But writing a bid to elevate a town to become a city? That is truly a little bit special, something historic, a once in a career opportunity! If 71 AD is etched in the history books as the year that the settlement of Doncaster was first established, then 2022 will be etched alongside it as the year it became a city. I was very privileged to be the Project Director for Doncaster's successful bid to become a city, writing and producing the official application on behalf of the borough. It was, without doubt, a massive honour to have been part of this most special of projects. This book attempts to retell the story of that bid.

When I first told Anne that I was writing this book she asked me 'is it going to be funny, or is it going to be dull?' I think that question was a reflection on the choice of subject matter, a book about cities and how they come to be, rather than a general statement on my ability to write (or at least I hope so). She paused for a moment before concluding, with a tone of glass-half-empty gloom, that 'it's going to be dull, isn't it?' Fortunately, I was not crestfallen; my wife always helps to keep me appropriately grounded. Whilst it's true that critics are unlikely to say that this book is a side-splitting, laugh-out-loud, rollercoaster ride of belly aching hilarity, I hope nevertheless that it makes you smile more than once. As I've written the book, I've reflected a lot on our relationship with places; the places where we were born, the places where we grew up, the places where we fell in love, and the places where we live now. It's a theme that resonates strongly with me, having lived roughly half my life in the south of England, and then the second half in the north. The people of Doncaster might well raise a toast to their newfound city status, and have a refreshed sentimentalism about their community, but why should anyone else really care? Most people in Britain haven't been to Doncaster, and most of those who haven't perhaps never will. The places we care about the most are the ones which we have the most personal connections with. Everywhere else is just somewhere else. But places, and the stories which resonate from them, are also the very things we all have in common. Every city, every town, and every village are each the setting of their own compendium of stories. It's a factor of Britishness which I think we can all connect with.

Many of us have a love-hate relationship with these very places that arguably should be the most important to us. Even though most of us live contently in towns and cities, we often regale in telling each other how truly bloody awful we think they all are. The singer Coleen Nolan, for example, was criticised in 2015 after she referred to her hometown of Blackpool as being a 'binge drinking hell-hole'[1]. But Coleen is far from alone in making less than gratifying remarks about her town. It is not uncommon for towns and cities to earn disparaging nicknames, whether they warrant them or not. Take, for example, the

---

unflattering unofficial alter-egos sometimes attributed to nearby Skegness (Skegvegas), Scunthorpe (Scumthorpe), and Pontefract (Ponte Carlo), as just a few examples. Doncaster, like so many of these places, has its fair share of detractors, and many of those live in Doncaster itself. The website ilivehere. co.uk runs an annual poll to identify Britain's "crap towns", attracting some 50,000 voters each year. Aylesbury in the leafy former county of Buckinghamshire surprisingly topped that poll in 2022, with Doncaster ranked 46th, which feels vaguely respectable under the circumstances. I think that we British seem to relish these types of polls. Our default is to call out the worst things around us, rather than the best.

At the same time, and as something of a cultural oxymoron, we are also fiercely proud of these very same towns and cities. Just look at the terraces of any given football club on a Saturday afternoon, awash with scarves and shirts in club colours, and a deafening weekly chorus espousing the virtues of the locality, whilst ridiculing the locality of the away team. And whilst Blackpool may have lost its shine for Coleen Nolan, there are plenty of celebrities who wax lyrical about their home towns. Take Doncaster's own Louis Tomlinson, formerly one fifth of the globally successful boy band One Direction. Tomlinson is fiercely proud of Doncaster, having filmed one of his pop videos here, and he once famously even tried to buy the football team. He said that 'I always ask how my friends from Doncaster, who know nothing about music and fashion, would interpret an outfit or a song or whatever. That has always really helped me, because if you get to a stage where you disconnect from those friends from home, other people don't really dare go there.'[2] So, even if the idea of reading a book about Doncaster doesn't immediately float your boat, I hope this story will nevertheless make you reflect further on the place where you come from, whether that be a village, town, or city, and what that place means to you. It may not be quite as terrible as others might have you believe.

Whilst a select handful of British towns have been elevated to become cities over recent years, almost none of them took the time to record how, specifically, their city status was achieved. The only book I am aware of was written by Dr John Hulbert, the former Provost of Perth in Scotland, which tells the story of how his town won city status in 2012[3]. But there is no equivalent book which tells the story of how Wolverhampton, or Preston, or Sunderland won their city status, which I can't help but think is a bit of a shame. Whilst I was writing this book, I was lucky enough to make the acquaintance of the writer and broadcaster Simon Fanshawe, who was the chairperson of Brighton & Hove's successful city status bid in 2000, coinciding with the Millennium celebrations. Simon shared several reminiscences with me, such as the idea to photograph 100 residents as part of their campaign, each person born in a different year of the twentieth century, reflecting the theme of the millennium. He

---

2   https://www.bbc.co.uk/programmes/
     articles/42pPbMLyQzl4LpddpyfHqNF/9-stars-who-seriously-love-their-
     hometown

3   *"Scotland's oldest and newest city: How Perth regained its city status and
     why it matters"*, Hulbert, J, Luath Press, 2016

recounted the touching story of the moment that the 99-year-old gentleman at the photo-shoot, the oldest member of the ensemble, was handed the youngest member to hold, a newly born baby. A large tear ran down the old fella's cheek. A century of Brighton & Hove's history captured in a single moment, and a wonderful story. I am sure that there were so many more intriguing stories like this behind all those bids, many of which may well be lost forever.

Indeed, the attainment of modern-day city status is a subject upon which surprisingly little has been written at all. The only other specific book I am aware of is the catchily titled *City Status in the British Isles, 1830–2002*, by John Beckett, recently retired Emeritus Professor of English Regional History at the University of Nottingham, first published in 2005. If you are, like me, a city status nerd, it's well worth a look. But Beckett's book, as thorough as it is, was written from an outsider's academic perspective of local political history. Whilst he recounts what some of the bids said, and the political pathways they had to navigate, he doesn't take you inside the campaigns of the city candidates themselves. Given the grand tradition of British towns chasing and competing for cityhood, this wider vacuum of literature is surprising. But Doncaster's story is one which deserves to be told and preserved. Decades from now, and long after my own time is over, I'd like to think that this story will still have its place. Perhaps there will be a classroom of inquisitive youngsters a century from now studying the history of Doncaster, and a threadbare copy of this book will be pulled from a dusty shelf in a school library (if school libraries are still a thing by then, which they probably won't be, but anyhow). The book will tell them the story of how and why the people of Doncaster went to bed one night in a town and woke up the next morning in a city. What might they make of that?

But why Doncaster? We were not the favourites in this contest, and many may have raised an eyebrow at our success. How could a northern, traditionally blue collar, post-industrial borough like Doncaster come out on top against towns which many may believe were more deserving of the accolade? Well, I'll do my best to explain that as we go along. I've endeavoured to give an honest and full account of our campaign. Although we were successful, there were a few inevitable bumps in the road along the way. In admitting to this, I've not attempted to sugar coat events. Everybody involved always had the best interests of the campaign at heart, but the campaign wasn't a full-time job for any of us, and sometimes our collective eye wasn't always on the ball. The bid writing textbooks paint a picture of the perfect proposal process and can lead you to think that writing a winning proposal is the most stressless and seamless of things, but in practice bid rounds rarely go off without incidents. Similarly, Doncaster has some rough edges and a few skeletons in its cupboard. To understand our success, you can't really tip toe around these home truths; you need a handle on both the rough and the smooth. So, this account is warts and all; celebrating everything we got right, but not being afraid to tackle the occasionally unwelcome elephant in the room and to discuss the things that we might have done a little better.

Whilst the focus of my story is Doncaster, I'll also tell you a little bit about the other towns and localities who we were bidding against. After all, this was a competition, and you can't have a competition without competitors. It would be a bit like commentating on just a single horse in the Grand National, or I should probably say the St. Leger Stakes. Notably the towns of Blackburn, Colchester, Reading, Middlesbrough, and Wrexham, as well as the district of Medway in Kent, had all, like Doncaster, chalked up three previously unsuccessful city status bids in previous Civic Honours competitions. No-one in that group wanted it to be four failed bids on the bounce. The competition, as such, was stiff, and the stakes were high. Keeping a watchful eye on our competitors, and attempting to second guess their strategies, was all part of the game plan. Alongside these towns, we will also visit a few other places along the way. After all, to really understand cities and what makes them tick, it would be a little short sighted to limit our field of vision to the British Isles alone.

To be clear though, this isn't a history book, or at least it is not a conventional history book. I'm not going to attempt to recount the comprehensive life and times of Doncaster and, besides, dozens of books have already been written about that. Some of them focus on Doncaster's railway heritage, or its former trolleybuses, or its coal mines, or the relative ups and downs of Doncaster Rovers on the football pitch, but between them they cover most of the bases. There is, of course, lots of history in this book. You can't be a city without having a bit of history, and a generous dollop of that was scooped into

Doncaster's successful city status bid. There are multiple dates which have punctuated the Doncaster story, some of clear historical resonance, such as 1194 when King Richard the Lionheart granted Doncaster its first Royal Charter, all the way through to slightly more enigmatic milestones, such as 1973, the year the BBC first filmed the classic Ronnie Barker sitcom *Open All Hours* in the town. The core timeline for this story is far more specific though. It begins at the launch of the Civic Honours competition in the summer of 2021, through to the announcement of Doncaster as a new city and onward to the historic arrival of our letter's patent, the official document from the monarch confirming city status. It's amazing, when I think back, just how much we achieved in a little over a year.

It was a period that would leave its own mark on history, not just for Doncaster. The Civic Honours competition began in the wake of the global Covid-19 pandemic that had affected every household in Britain, all too tragically in too many cases. Covid-19 had, very literally, changed our way of lives, introducing lockdowns and social distancing measures on a scale never seen before, with a legacy that will be with us for years to come. But this was also a time when we had enjoyed the unbridled summer celebrations of the Queen's Platinum Jubilee itself, and the magnificent celebrations staged in London, followed all too shortly afterwards by the profound collective national grief felt by her passing. It was a time that we experienced a stifling cost-of-living crisis with record breaking energy prices and spiralling inflation. We saw the unravelling of the 'partygate' scandal which eventually led to the resignation of Boris Johnson as Prime Minister, as well as the heroic resistance of the Ukraine as it was faced by the hostile invasion from Russia. Perhaps most pertinently to this story was the horrific murder of Sir David Amess, the Southend-on-Sea politician and advocate in chief of city status for the Essex town he represented. All these things provide a backdrop for this story, and the context of public and political sentiment which our campaign had to navigate its own way through.

The book also provides an opportunity for me to share some insights about the art, or perhaps more rightly the science, of writing and winning proposals. As with the history of Doncaster, a lot has already been written about this too. Most of these books are, however, "how to do it" guides, focused more on the theory of proposal writing, perhaps more so that the application. Shipley Associates, a communications consulting company heralding from the suburb of Bountiful in Utah, just north of Salt Lake City, are widely regarded as the go to global authority on proposal writing. In 1988 the company first published its 96-step process for a business development lifecycle, more typically referred to simply as the Shipley process. With 96-steps, you can imagine it is, ironically, not the lightest of reads, but it has nevertheless stood the test of time. But the Shipley process is not, in my humble opinion, a panacea for every proposal. Alongside Shipley there have been a wide variety of inspirations and influences which have shaped my own bid writing philosophy over the years, and many of these were brought to bear on the Doncaster bid. I hope that by using Doncaster's bid as a case study, I can convey some of the nuances of good proposal writing which, without doubt, were integral to our success. If you happen to be a local authority officer contemplating a city status application some years from now, then I hope that you will find several writing hints and tips herein to stand you in good stead.

This book is also unashamedly an opportunity to tell you a little of my own story and how it converged with that of Doncaster's. As a bid writer for a living, who finds himself writing something or other almost every day, I've enjoyed this rare opportunity to write something in my own words for a change. A happenstance chain of events took me from a childhood upbringing in rural Kent, steering me into my career as a bid writer, and dropping me into the right place at the right time to play my part in the city status bid. Fate or coincidence, who really knows for sure? There is a lot of me in Doncaster's bid though, and, vice versa, a lot of Doncaster that has become an inherent part of who I am today. So, this is an alternative history book, a guide to proposal writing, and something of a personal memoir, all wrapped into one. It is my own personal playback of the Doncaster city status story, a love letter of sorts dedicated to Yorkshire's newest city. I may have missed some aspects of the story experienced by others; I wasn't always in the room for everything that happened. I hope that, nevertheless, and on behalf of everyone who was involved in the campaign, I have done the story justice.

So, without further ado, let's get to it. Whilst the settlement of Doncaster was originally founded by the Romans, I'm going to start my story a lot further down the timeline of history. I'll begin with the birth of a very important little girl, who arrived at the peak of the Art Deco movement and the blossoming of the jazz age, in the decade affectionately known as the roaring twenties. A little girl of such importance, whose personal seal of approval was ultimately required if Doncaster was ever to become a city. A little girl who, as a child, had very little idea of just how important she would grow up to be. Whilst I never met her in person, she has been an inspiration for this book, and is unquestionably the star of the show.

Long to Reign Over Us

In the small hours of the morning on the 21st of April 1926 a baby girl, weighing in at exactly 6 lbs, was born at 17 Bruton Street in Mayfair. Notwithstanding its prime location, a thoroughfare to Berkley Square, the address was comparatively unremarkable. Indeed, it is far from being the most obvious address from where you would have expected a baby of her family and lineage to have arrived. A palace, perhaps. At the very least a grandeur estate, a fine country house, or a well reputed hospital. But 17 Bruton Street was instead a slightly more modest townhouse and the then home of the Earl and Countess of Strathmore, the little girl's maternal grandparents. Despite the importance of their granddaughter, the house itself was torn down relatively shortly after her birth in the 1930s. It was replaced by Berkley Square House which, when opened in 1938, had the rather less endearing claim of being one of London's first major reinforced concrete buildings. The girl grew up to become one of the most famous and instantly recognisable women in the world, yet as a child her pathway to prominence was far from certain. It would take the abdication of her uncle in 1936, and the untimely death of her father in 1952, which would thrust her firmly into the nation's spotlight. She was christened Elizabeth Alexandra Mary Windsor. You will know her better as Her Majesty Queen Elizabeth II.

Queen Elizabeth was the first and only British Monarch to celebrate a Platinum Jubilee, marking an illustrious reign of 70 years (70 years and 214 days to be precise). King Louis XIV of

France is the only monarch to have reigned a sovereign country for longer than her, in his case an impressive 72 years and 110 days between 1643 and 1715. King Rama IX of Thailand and King Johann II of Liechtenstein are the only other two monarchs in history to have celebrated a Platinum Jubilee; it is a very exclusive club. Elizabeth was only 25 when her father, King George VI, who was still himself a comparably young man of only 56, died of a coronary thrombosis, catapulting her to the crown. It must have been a daunting prospect for someone of such a young age, only having married Prince Philip four years earlier, and now with two very young children, Prince Charles and Princess Anne, already in tow. Yet Elizabeth was always steadfast in her duty and her service to her country, qualities that perpetually endeared her to the public. In a speech made on her 21st birthday in 1947 she famously said: 'I declare before you all that my whole life, whether it be long or short, shall be devoted to your service and the service of our great imperial family to which we all belong.' Her life was indeed long, and her declaration made that day was unfalteringly kept throughout it.

Everyone born in Britain since around the end of the Second World War, which is pretty much everyone in Britain today, grew up and lived their life up with the constancy of Elizabeth as their Queen. She was our Queen in the 1950s, when ITV made its first broadcast, when the first stretch of British motorway was opened, and when Calder Hall became Britain's first nuclear power station. She was our Queen in the 1960s, when the last British prisoner was hung for murder, when abortion and homosexuality were legalised, and when she presented Bobby Moore with the Jules Rimet Trophy after England's famous World Cup victory at Wembley. She was our Queen when we voted to join the European Economic Community in 1972 as well as when we voted to leave the European Union in 2016. She was our Queen when British scientists first discovered DNA, when the world's first test-tube baby was born in Oldham, and when Tim Berners-Lee, a computer scientist from London, invented the World Wide Web. She was our Queen when her cousin, Lord Mountbatten, was murdered by an IRA bomb, and when her daughter-in-law Diana, Princess of Wales, had her fatal car crash in the Pont de l'Alma tunnel in Paris. She was our Queen during the Great Smog of London, the Suez Crisis, the Three-Day Week, the Falklands War, the Miner's Strike, the Poll Tax Riots, the Foot & Mouth outbreak, the 7/7 Bombings, and the 2012 London Olympics. Across her 70 years as our Queen, she was served by no fewer than 15 different Prime Ministers, and was, at one time or another, the Head of State for 32 different Commonwealth realms. Mother of 4, grandmother of 8, and great grandmother of 13 (so far). She had a life fully lived by every standard, and then some.

Amongst her many passions, the Queen was well known for her love of horse-racing. She is synonymous with Royal Ascot, where she arrived each year along the track in horse-drawn landaus and spent the day watching the racing from the Royal Enclosure. The Queen first rode a horse at the age of three and was said to be immediately besotted with them. 'My philosophy about racing is simple,' she once said in a BBC documentary. 'I enjoy breeding a horse that is faster than other peoples. And to me, that is a gamble from a long way back. I enjoy going racing, but I suppose, basically, I love horses, and the thoroughbred epitomizes a really good horse to me.' Her interest was may more than a casual dalliance. The Queen had almost 2,000 winners as a racehorse owner, a record few other owners can match, with her jockeys always wearing purple, gold, and scarlet. And horse-racing is where the bond between the former monarch and Doncaster was at its strongest.

Doncaster racecourse is the home of the St Leger Stakes, the oldest of Britain's Classic flat races, first ran in 1776, and a firm favourite with the Royal family over the centuries. The St Leger Stakes are run over 1 mile, 6 furlongs, and 132 yards (just shy of 3km), also making it longer than the other four Classics; the 1,000 Guineas and 2,000 Guineas at Newmarket, and The Derby and The Oaks at Epsom. It is a signature, must attend event for Doncaster. As Charles Dickens, who came to the St. Leger in 1857, described it:

No labourers working in the fields; all gone 't'races.' The few late wenders of their way 't'races,' who are yet left driving on the road, stare in amazement at the recluse who is not going 't'races.' Roadside innkeeper has gone 't'races.' Turnpike-man has gone 't'races.' His thrifty wife, washing clothes at the toll-house door, is going 't'races' to-morrow. Perhaps there may be no one left to take the toll to-morrow; who knows? Though assuredly that would be neither turnpike-like nor Yorkshire-like. The very wind and dust seem to be hurrying 't'races,' as they briskly pass the only wayfarer on the road. In the distance, the

Railway Engine, waiting at the town-end, shrieks despairingly.
Nothing but the difficulty of getting off the Line, restrains that
Engine from going 't'races,' too, it is very clear.

Almost a century later, in 1953, Queen Elizabeth II went "t'races". She was seated alongside Sir Winston Churchill, watching on as her own horse, Aureole, came home to claim third place in the St. Leger. Perhaps though her most memorable visit to the racecourse came in 1977 during her Silver Jubilee celebrations. The race meeting that she attended that year was in July, but another of her own horses, Dunfermline, would fittingly triumph in the St Leger Stakes a few months later. It is one of the most significant race wins achieved by any of the Queen's own horses. In all the photos I've seen of the Queen on her visits to Doncaster racecourse she always had a beaming smile. True that the Queen tended to have a beaming smile in most photos, regardless of where she was, what she was doing, or who she was doing it with, but I'd like to think those days out at Donny races still held a special significance.

A much lesser-known fact about Queen Elizabeth II was that she also bestowed the official designation of city status on more British towns than any other monarch who came before her. Alongside her record-breaking reign, her record of making cities is one which may also never be broken by a future British monarch. Beginning with Southampton in 1964, she had conferred the same honour upon no fewer than 17 different towns prior to the start of her Platinum Jubilee year in 2022. That translates to almost a quarter of all the cities in Britain at that time. In the century or so prior to the coronation of Queen

Elizabeth II, city status was most typically achieved by local mayors making their case to the Home Office, who were then the de facto arbitrators of cityhood on behalf of the crown. The practice was fraught with accusations of bias and party-political horseplay, and encouraged a free-for-all in terms of towns continuously lobbying to become cities, making the whole system far from ideal. Then, to mark the Queen's Silver Jubilee in 1977, the idea of having a celebratory contest to determine the next British city was put to Her Majesty. She approved of the idea, and the first ever Civic Honours competition was held. The principle is like the recognition afforded through the public honours system, where MBEs, OBEs, knighthoods, and damehoods are handed out to the most deserving of citizens. The Civic Honours competition, however, would recognise places instead of people. Nine candidates were invited to participate in that very first competition: Brighton, Blackburn, Croydon, Dudley, Newport, Sandwell, Sunderland, Wolverhampton, and the eventual winner, Derby. The competition was deemed to be a success, and the practice of Civic Honours competitions has been followed ever since.

It has been customary for Civic Honours competitions to coincide with each of the Queen's major milestone jubilees. The competition held for the Ruby Jubilee in 1992 saw the accolade go to Sunderland. Five cities were established, and notably at least one from each of the home countries, through the Golden Jubilee competition in 2002. Preston in England, Newport in Wales, Stirling in Scotland, and Lisburn and Newry in Northern Ireland were all winners. Following them, Chelmsford, Perth, and St. Asaph were elevated for the Diamond Jubilee in 2012. The only break in tradition came in the year 2000 when, rather than coinciding with a jubilee, a special Millennium competition was held. That saw Brighton & Hove, Inverness, and Wolverhampton all join the exclusive cities club. Let's not forget that the Queen was the evaluator in chief across all these competitions. Obviously, she didn't read and score every written proposal put forward, but the sign-off on the winners always sat with her. I can't really imagine a higher standard than having the Queen as adjudicator in chief! Given her illustrious wave of city making over the decades, it was inevitable that a further city status competition would be run for the Platinum Jubilee in 2022.

And so, it came to be. The Platinum Jubilee Civic Honours Competition was launched on 8th of June 2021[4]. The competition was open to any local authority in the UK, as well as, for the first time, Crown Dependencies and British Overseas Territories. A second competition to bestow a Lord Mayoralty or Provostship upon an existing city was also launched. In firing the metaphoric starting pistol, Chloe Smith, Minister of State for the Constitution & Devolution, declared that 'The Civic Honours competition is an opportunity to promote your hometown and win an honour for it that will last for all time. I encourage entries from local authorities in every part of the UK, from vibrant towns and cities with distinct identities, history, and sense of community'. The Culture Secretary,

---

4   https://www.gov.uk/government/news/prestigious-civic-honours-to-be-awarded-by-her-majesty-the-queen-for-first-time-in-10-years - 8th June 2021

Oliver Dowden, added that 'It's a great opportunity for towns and cities in every corner of the country to showcase their heritage and tell us more about the people and places that make their local area so unique - and a fitting tribute to Her Majesty's reign in her Platinum Jubilee year'. Although they were just words in a press release, you could almost imagine a rendition of *Land of Hope & Glory* playing in the background. The pomp and circumstance of it all! Which town wouldn't want to put itself forward for such a coveted prize?

Far away from Whitehall, the 8th of June 2021, the day that the Platinum Jubilee Civic Honours competition was launched, began for me pretty much like any other Tuesday. I got up early, had my usual breakfast of a bowl of cereal and some fresh grapefruit. I sleepily flicked through the morning headlines on my phone, which were dominated by Britain's vaccination programme and our steady progression out of Covid-19 lockdowns. Scrolling down there was a story about some hoo-hah bubbling up in Moscow owing to the release of the latest Ukrainian football shirt, the design of which featured an outline of the Ukrainian border including the Crimea peninsula which Russia had annexed in 2014. It came across as a seemingly minor diplomatic fracas and not all that significant at the time. I finished my breakfast and headed round the corner to the leisure centre in Retford for the 6.45am spin class. That may sound like a brutal start to the day, but for me it's just part of a weekly routine that I don't really need to over think, I just turn up, get on an exercise bike, and pedal. I don't want to deceive you into thinking that I was some sort of silver fox with a ripped six-pack, far from it, but I was equally in not too shabby condition for a man who was, at that time, 48 years old. After forty-five minutes of huffing and puffing on the bike, I was back home, showered, dressed, back in the car, and driving to my office in Doncaster in time for our daily 9.00am team call.

After a largely unremarkable morning, I headed off at lunchtime to Castle Park stadium, home of the Doncaster Knights rugby union team. The stadium can cater for 5,000 fans, most being seated in the imposing, all seater West Stand, albeit on a quiet Tuesday lunchtime in June the fold-down seats were all conspicuously empty. The West Stand is also where the hospitality suites are to be found, looking out over the terraces and the pitch, and where I would be spending the rest of my day. The reason for my visit was for a Networking Lunch & Away Day Afternoon for staff and board members of the Doncaster Chamber of Commerce. As the owner of a Doncaster based business, I had joined the board in 2019, albeit most meetings I had attended so far had been video calls held over Zoom or Microsoft Teams. The reason for this, of course, was the Covid-19 pandemic, which had outlawed in-person business meetings for most of that time. The gathering at Castle Park was therefore significant, as it was the first time that many of us had been physically in the same venue together for over a year. Certain restrictions were still in place, like wearing face masks around the building, and all being sat in an appropriately socially distanced formation. The early summer weather was kind to us though, and the terraces provided a welcome break out space, keeping our discussions going in the sunshine as the groundsmen tended to the pitch below. The small talk was largely focused on Covid-19, comparing notes on how our different businesses had weathered the storm. The main agenda focused on where we wanted to be as a Chamber, what our routes to success looked like, and what actions we wanted to take away from the session. It was good to have the time to get into the weeds of some of these issues and set out our stall for the year ahead.

The topic of the city status didn't come up on that afternoon. With the competition having only just been launched, the news hadn't yet trickled down and, even if it had, the significance of the opportunity for Doncaster probably wouldn't have struck us at the time. None of us knew at that point that Doncaster was going to enter the competition. None of us knew that a photo of the West Stand, where we were sat chatting and enjoying a coffee, was going to feature in that bid. None of knew that Dan Fell, the Chief Executive of the Chamber, was going to Chair the campaign, and none of us knew that I was going to be the person who would ultimately write and produce the written application. And, of course, none of us knew that we were going win and that, less than a year later, Doncaster was going to be announced as a new city. Like Frodo Baggins and his friends in *The Lord of the Rings*, we had no idea that we were about to embark on an epic journey to our own metaphoric Mordor and back. Instead, we sipped on our coffee, talked shop, and enjoyed the sunshine.

As for the Queen herself, well she had more important business that day too. Whilst the Civic Honours competition was being launched in London, and the Doncaster Chamber board were chewing the cud at Castle Park, Her Majesty was over on the other side of the Pennines in Manchester. She was on route to ITV Studios to visit the set of the long running soap opera *Coronation Street*, which was celebrating its sixtieth anniversary, an equally impressive landmark[5]. She visited the famous cobbles and The Rovers Return, perhaps the most famous fictional pub in the country, to meet the cast. The red carpets were out, and the cast and crew were enthusiastically waving Union Jacks. She was wearing one of her colourful trademark outfits, with a matching hat. Bill Roache, who had played the character of Ken Barlow in the soap since 1960, was one of the actors she met. The Queen had asked how the crew had managed to keep filming during the Covid-19 pandemic, saying: 'It's really marvellous you've been able to carry on.' Roache had replied with a laugh: 'Well, ma'am, you're the one who has carried on.' In that respect, he couldn't have been righter.

The world still feels a little strange with Queen Elizabeth no longer in it, following her death in September 2022. She wasn't just *a* Queen; she was *the* Queen. Whilst one of her final acts was to grant city status to Doncaster, the responsibility of dispatching the Letters Patent, the official documents of cityhood, would fall to her son Charles, in one of his first acts as monarch. Having sung *God Save the Queen* as our national anthem for the whole of my life up to that point, the reprised

---

5   https://www.bbc.co.uk/news/uk-england-manchester-57764192

lyrics of *God Save the King* still feel a little awkward in my mouth. The incoming bank notes, coins, and stamps with a new face on them seem a little strange and unfamiliar too, as did the appearance of Charles giving a King's Speech on Christmas Day. In some ways it felt to me as if Elizabeth would simply always be here, but Kings and Queens don't live forever. The Carolean age has begun, a term taken from the Latin word for Charles, and notably first coined by Liz Truss; perhaps the only legacy of her 44 days as Prime Minister. For me though, winning city status in Queen Elizabeth's final Civic Honours competition somehow gives it just a little more kudos. Doncaster is not just a city; it's a Platinum Jubilee city, and, for me, that is just about as cool as a cucumber sandwich served at a Buckingham Palace Garden Party.

Thank you, your majesty, for choosing Doncaster. We are honoured.

Doncaster for Beginners

A few days before Easter in 2022 I happened to be in Amsterdam. I was attending a conference taking place at the Beurs van Berlage, the imposing historic former stock exchange in the heart of the city, built in 1903, which is now primarily used as a meeting and events venue. The conference in question, Bid & Proposal Con Europe 2022, or BPC Europe for short, brought together practitioners in the field of proposal writing, people who write bids and tender responses for a living, applying their craft to win new contracts from their organisations. People like me! The conference was organised by the auspiciously titled Association of Proposal Management Professionals, or APMP, the closest thing us bid writers have to a professional institute. The programme was, as you might expect, geared to the interests of this discerning audience, a variety of talks primarily about the art of proposal writing. This included a workshop I was delivering, a case study all about Doncaster and its bid to become a city. Most of the time bids are wrapped tightly in commercial confidentiality clauses and non-disclosure agreements, meaning that good case studies are rarely shared. It was something of a luxury for me to therefore have a bid project which I could talk about openly and in detail. I had a small yet select audience in my breakout room, of various nationalities. After a brief show of hands, it transpired that only two of them had ever been to Doncaster, and several more had never previously heard of the place. It looked like I had my work cut out!

Most people in Britain are not well travelled within their own country. A survey in 2019 revealed that around 6% of adults in the UK, some 3.5 million people, had never once set foot in London[6]. For comparison, that is more than the entire population of Wales! It therefore stands to reason that the proportion of Brits who have never once set foot in Doncaster is manifestly higher. That's not a Doncaster thing per se, I am sure that the same is true for pretty much every British town or city. I'm well-travelled, probably a lot more than most people, but I've never been to Burnley, or Harlow, or Yeovil, or Kilmarnock, or a load of other places. I may, quite probably, never go to any of those places. It's nothing personal, but the reason or opportunity may just simply never arise. Similarly, whilst most of us have a level of familiarity with place names, knowing exactly where these places are, and what goes on there, is quite another matter. If I gave you a blank map of Britain, and invited you to accurately put a pin in each of Burnley, Harlow, Yeovil, and Kilmarnock, could you do it? No, I doubt I could either. In reflecting on this it occurred to me that you, my reader, may very likely also be someone who has never stepped foot in Doncaster before. So, in a similar fashion to my audience in Amsterdam, let me introduce you to Yorkshire's newest city.

Let's start with its name. Doncaster, in many respects, isn't a pretty word. Phonetically it's pronounced as don-caa-ster, as opposed to don-car-ster; a common mispronunciation typically made by southerners (like me), in the same way that

---

6   https://www.thesun.co.uk/news/9797900/london-expensive-crowded-tourists/

we pronounce the "a" sound differently in words like bath, path, and grass to our friends in the north. Don derives from the name of the river and Caster derives from the Roman word Castrum (and latterly the Old English word Ceaster), which means fortification. It literally translates to the fort on the river Don; you can't get a plainer speaking, to-the-point, Yorkshire name than that. Despite the simplicity of its meaning though, it's a name that doesn't smoothly trip off the tongue, however you pronounce it. Doncaster is a determined, sturdy word, with roughly edged syllables, butting up against each other, and lacking a certain phonographic harmony. If a city can literally grow into its name, then Doncaster is perhaps a textbook example. Even if you haven't been there, the very name of Doncaster conjures up an image of a hardened, uncompromising, and industrious place that rightly belongs somewhere in the weather-beaten north. It's a name that wantonly spurns the daintiness of titles like that of a Princes Risborough, and shamelessly cares little for the tweeness of an Ashby-de-la-Zouche. Doncaster's name instead revels in its enduring hardiness. It's a proper, no-nonsense, warm beer drinking place name.

In Britain we apply affectionate labels to people from different places; Cockneys from London, Scousers from Liverpool, Brummies from Birmingham, Geordies from Newcastle, and so on and so forth. There isn't a universally accepted equivalent for Doncaster, but the term Doncastrian is perhaps the closest. A few people prefer Doncasterian (with an 'e'). The term Donnyite also comes up, as does Donconian. Maybe now that it is a city one of these options will more decisively rise to the top and see off the others. Donny, Doncaster's shorthand nickname, is perhaps a little more familiar. Ironically though it's a name that never appeared in the city status bid. The Project Board thought that Donny was a little too colloquial and self-deprecating as a shorthand name, and that it may portray a misplaced tone of joviality, even though it's the name by which many refer to the town. Looking back, I think we got that wrong. I would like to have found a place for Donny somewhere in the bid as it is, without doubt, as much a part of Doncaster's identity as, say, Pompey is to Portsmouth's.

Identity, when it comes to city status, is key. One of the application requirements of the city status bid was to demonstrate that your locality had a distinct identity, and I think that ask of distinctiveness is critical. In my chat with Simon Fanshawe, he recounted how he was often asked by contemporaries from neighbouring towns as to how they could become the next Brighton. His advice was to rethink the question and deliberate instead about how they might better define themselves as the current Eastbourne, or Hastings, or wherever. And he was right. Consider for a moment the romanticism of Paris, the glitziness of Las Vegas, the samba-beat of Rio, or the earnest hospitality of Dublin. All have a certain distinctiveness. Being a big town simply isn't enough, a great city must have a definable character and individuality, but sometimes that's a hard thing to draw out. In an era of identikit shopping malls, drive through coffee shops, endless miles of dual carriageways and roundabouts, and swathes of modular new-build housing estates, the distinctiveness of Britain's towns and cities is increasingly starting to blur. Pitching Doncaster as the next Sheffield or Leeds wasn't going to cut it. If Doncaster truly had the distinctiveness that the title of city demanded, then it would be something that we would need to carefully identify, tease out, and present.

So, let's put Doncaster on the map. If you draw a line between London and Edinburgh, and then draw a further latitudinal line across England aligned roughly with the centre of Manchester, then Doncaster is the point where the two lines will cross. The city is nested at the southern tip of Yorkshire, England's largest historic county, and often referred to as God's Own County. Whilst thoughts of Yorkshire conjure up images of rolling dales, stone walls, and heather ladened moors, Doncaster is at the comparatively flatter end. If you were hoping for the type of landscapes made famous by James Herriot or the Bronte sisters, you'll be a little disappointed. Doncaster sits alongside Sheffield, Barnsley, and Rotherham in completing the South Yorkshire sub-region. As you cross the border from Nottinghamshire to the south and enter the outlying enclave of Bawtry on the old Great North Road, the first address you come to is No. 1 Yorkshire. At 219 sq. miles, Doncaster is the largest metropolitan borough in England. Whilst the core area, what you would have previously called the town, has a population of around 110,000, the wider borough pushes that figure to over 300,000. To bring that figure to life and give it impact, as we presented it in the bid, around 1 in every 220 people in Britain live in Doncaster. Makes it sound big, doesn't it!

As we also put it in the bid, Doncaster embodies the welcoming spirit of Yorkshire, a place where front doors were historically always left open, where the kettle is on, where neighbours are always welcome, and where the local community looks out for its own. Yorkshire is in many respects a bedrock of England's overall identity, and the warmth of Yorkshire underpins every facet of life in Doncaster, not least in terms of how the people speak. The Yorkshire dialect is often derided, but I personally find an endearing charm in a community which routinely drops its Hs; uses its own shorthand words like nowt and owt; and applies a common elision where the determiner "the" is replaced with a "t" sound (e.g., I'm off t'races). The word "off", as in that example, routinely replaces the word "going" and the word "us" routinely replaces the word "our" (e.g., where's us car?). Sentences are often laced with wonderful colloquial phrases like "there are no two ways about it". I also love the fact that a "village" is used in everyday parlance as a standard unit of measurement, i.e., to get t'garden centre need to go three villages up, down or over. Puritans may deride all this as poor English, but I love the fact that Yorkshire has its own unique take on our language. It's integral to the character of Doncastrians, who are characteristically a friendly, welcoming, plain speaking, no-nonsense, proud, and occasionally stubborn people. They say it how it is!

Doncaster arguably doesn't have the historical quaintness of, say, Bath, Oxford, or Durham. It doesn't have nationally significant landmarks like London or Edinburgh, nor does it have the commercial pull of Birmingham, Manchester, or Glasgow. At a mere 160 feet tall. St. George's Minster, Doncaster's tallest building, is less than one sixth of the height of London's Shard. Doncaster is not a city of high-rises and skyscrapers. It doesn't have ideas above its station. I don't say that in any way to degrade Doncaster, but rather to present it authentically and truthfully. But whilst Doncaster is not overstated, it still has everything you would expect from a fledgling city. Its centre has a sizable retail and hospitality district, home to many familiar high street brands, an award-winning market, and a choice of affordable eateries and bars. Orbiting this is an assorted mix of suburbs and, beyond a clearly definable green belt, smaller outlying towns. It conforms to a classic hub and spoke city model. It's ensemble of historic properties, including Consibrough Castle, Brodsworth Hall, and Cusworth Hall, each present an enjoyable and educational day out, and The Yorkshire Wildlife Park has rapidly grown to become one of Doncaster's best loved attractions, attracting some 800,000 visitors per year. Then of course there is the St. Leger Festival, attracting 60,000 racegoers over four days every September. Whilst it may not be an obvious city break destination, Doncaster still has a lot to offer.

The origins of Doncaster date back almost 2,000 years. In 71 AD Caesar Vespasianus Augustus, or Vespasian to his friends, was at the helm of the Roman Empire. If the busts of Vespasian sculpted at the time of his reign are accurate, he was a relatively flat headed bald man who didn't smile very much. By the time of his reign the Roman Empire covered almost the entirety of the Mediterranean coastline across Europe and Africa, fully occupying the totality of modern-day Spain, Portugal, France, Greece, and Turkey. Rome was also in command of all but the North West of England, with ambitions to conquer Wales (Cambria) and Scotland (Caledonia) too. You can imagine that Vespasian had his hands full in managing such a vast empire. Much of his short reign was pre-occupied by the First Jewish-Roman War, which a year earlier, in 71 AD, had seen the Siege of Jerusalem, ending with the Roman's devastating the city, and brutally killing most of its residents. Ironically though as Vespasian was busy obliterating one city, on the other side of Europe his troops were tentatively nurturing the early foundations of another. The river Don was, more or less, at the front line of the empire in Britain as the Roman's sought to push further north, which very likely explains why they decided to build a small fort there. It originally took the name of Danum, after the river, and a modest settlement began to grow around it. It wasn't all that much of a place at the time, and only a small section of Roman wall still survives, but this is where the story of Doncaster first began. The Roman's stayed around in Doncaster for about 300 years, before their empire began to collapse in on itself, and they all hotfooted it off back to Rome.

In 828 AD the Historia Brittonum (History of the Britons), supposedly collated by a Welsh monk named Nennius who had way too much time on his hands, was published. The book gives an epic account of the history of the British Isles, and lists Doncaster, then known as Cair Daun, as one of the 33 Anglo Saxon cities of its day. Before we take that as validation of Doncaster already being a thousand-year-old city, we should note that the Historia Brittonum contains plenty of more fanciful content. Nennius claims, for example, that the legend of King Arthur is one of historical fact, meaning that any wider substance placed upon his book requires a small pinch of salt. Having seen off the Romans, Doncaster at that time was enduring the Vikings, a rowdy bunch of Norse troublemakers, who perpetually raided, pillaged, and were being an all-round nuisance. At the Battle of Doncaster in 868 AD, the army of the Viking Lord Ivar the Boneless was defeated by an allied Anglo-Saxon, Welsh, and Irish army led by King Ethelred of Wessex. Britannia 1, Denmark 0. There are various theories as to why Ivar was known as the Boneless, such as him having some form of brittle bone condition, having missing limbs, or just being very thin. Some stories have him being carried on a shield at the head of his army owing to his disability, whilst others claim that he was perfectly able bodied. Whatever the truth, it's a name that is both swanky and terrifying in equal measure, and what he lacked in bones he more than made up for in fury and wrath. Despite Ethelred's victory, Doncaster spent many years under Danelaw, part of a swathe of eastern and northern England controlled by the Vikings. It wasn't until after the Normans invaded England in 1066 that the Vikings were seen off in their longboats back across the North Sea once and for all.

Highlights of the Middle Ages include the annexing of Doncaster by King David I of Scotland under the Treaty of Durham in 1136. Giving Doncaster away was part of a trade-off made by England's King Stephen in the hope of keeping the intruding Scots firmly north of the border. It must have been a very curious negotiation for Doncaster, of all places, to be on the table. King David signed the Treaty, but it didn't stop him from trying to invade again three years later. Either that or he was just trying to get to his newly acquired lands in Doncaster, which were at least a full weeks' ride from Scotland on horseback. In my head I imagine him repeatedly asking, 'are we there yet?' like a frustrated toddler. The Treaty remains the stuff of local folklore, as it was never repealed, meaning that Doncaster is still, at least on parchment, a ward of Scotland. Further on, in 1336, Doncaster had its very own bona fide royal birth. Prince William, the second son of Edward III, was born at the royal hunting lodge which used to stand at Hatfield Chase. Sadly, however, young William's life was short lived, and he died as a baby. There are various other battles, historic buildings being built, bestowments of charters, and other general historic goings-on during the Middle Ages, but it all starts to get a little bit samey. So, let's instead skip ahead to the nineteenth century and the industrial revolution, the period which has arguably most heavily influenced Doncaster as it is today.

Between the 1850s and the First World War, no fewer than eighteen coal pits opened across the borough, part of the wider coalfields seam that transcends Yorkshire, Nottinghamshire, and Derbyshire. That's roughly one pit for every 12 sq. miles of the borough, literally one in every community. A life down the pit was therefore a default career destination for generations of young men, following their fathers, and their father's fathers. The 1850s were also the decade when the Doncaster Railway

Works, also known as The Plant were established by the Great Northern Railway. Some of the most famous steam locomotives ever engineered would roll out of those sheds, including *The Flying Scotsman* and *The Mallard*, the latter still holding the world record for the fastest speed ever achieved by a steam train (126 mph in 1938). Both were engineered by Sir Nigel Gresley, the grandfather of steam and an adopted Doncastrian icon, even though he was a Scot (King David would be proud). In tandem, coal and rail redefined the identity of Doncaster. New streets of Victorian and Edwardian two-up two-down red-brick terraces, with their outhouses and snicket alleyways, spread out from the town centre, forging new suburbs. Doncaster evolved seamlessly from being a small town, to becoming a large one. These terraced houses still account for around a quarter of Doncaster's housing stock more than a century later. It was a working man's town, with life centred around the Miner's Welfare Clubs that formed the heart of each community, alongside the bustling market which thrived in the town centre.

To give a true sense of Doncaster in the heyday of coal, I should perhaps pass over to a true Doncastrian who experienced it first-hand. Kevin Keegan, the football legend who won 63 England caps, scoring 21 goals, and captaining the side on 31 occasions, was born in Armthorpe in 1951. His father was a Doncaster coal miner, and there is a wonderful paragraph in Keegan's autobiography which neatly captures life in the town from the perspective of a child growing up here in the fifties and sixties[7]. It goes like this: 'Dad never drank at home, and we didn't keep beer in the house, but he loved to pop down to the Liberal Club. Mum would join him on Saturdays to play bingo and Doncaster, a horse racing town, did have its occasional highlights. When I was older, I saw The Four Tops at the Co-op Emporium and the town came alive when it was St Leger Festival Week. It was such a big week for Doncaster, they even closed the pits. There was a free entry to the course and if you were from a mining family and, for a kid, there was hardly anything more thrilling than running over to the rails to see the horses flashing by with the incredible noise they made and the blur of colours and numbers.'

Like many industrial northern towns though, Doncaster's prosperity was living on borrowed time. The railways went electric, and the age of steam ended. The pits began to close, most notably driven by the policies of Margaret Thatcher's government and her will to break the unions. By the mid-1980s, fuelled by the pit closures, some communities in Doncaster were experiencing staggering unemployment rates of over 20 percent. Ageing former miners were blighted by long-term illness, including coal workers' pneumoconiosis, commonly known as black lung disease, which occurs when coal dust is inhaled over many years, scarring the lungs. It's a horrible, incurable disease which leads to breathing difficulties and ultimately heart failure. If you were lucky enough to avoid that, you may just as equally have suffered from vibration white

7   "My Life in Football: The Autobiography", K. Keegan, Pan Books, 2018, Page 27

finger, brought on from excessive exposure to vibrating power tools, damaging the nerves, joints, and blood vessels in the hand. South Yorkshire had become one of the most disadvantaged regions not just in Britain, but in Western Europe. Doncaster's economic reliance on coal cannot be understated. There was no tailor-made industry to replace it. Too many third and fourth generation miners were stalwart union men, too long in the tooth to even entertain the idea of doing any other job. Even if they weren't, the poor health of many meant that their working lives were prematurely cut short. Doncaster's fortunes were at an all-time low and the road to economic recovery would be long and hard.

To an outsider of sorts such as I, Doncaster can sometimes feel conflicted about its mining history. Whilst coal is hardwired into Doncaster's cultural DNA, it is also a past chapter that some want to disassociate with. Footage of striking miners and picket line scuffles from the 1980s are misaligned with the modern-day image that Doncaster wants to present. This was a poorer, harder, grittier version of Doncaster. Several communities are still pre-fixed as "former mining" towns and villages, even though many of the pits closed some 40 years ago. The black soot doesn't easily wash out. But coal mining is also, arguably, one of the most distinctive aspects of Doncaster's identity, and it was something I wanted to celebrate within the bid. Whilst the pits are gone, The Hatfield & Askern Colliery Band survives as a leading local brass band and several non-league football sides, such as Rossington Main FC and Armthorpe Welfare FC, started out as local colliery teams. The Rich Seam monument, sculpted by artist Laurence Edwards and completed in 2021, stands in the heart of Doncaster. The artwork comprises of a 6-foot-tall bronze miner stood between two walls. Portraits of forty local miners, support staff from the pits, and their descendants, are all carved out in niches in the sculpture's walls. The pit wheels from Denaby Main and Askern are mounted for prosperity at these former mine sites, and many of the pits have been repurposed today as country parks. Everywhere you go in Doncaster, the legacy of the coal mines is never far away.

Nostalgia aside though, Doncaster needed a future beyond coal, and in this regard its saving grace was its location. It was already home to a key interchange station on the East Coast Mainline, with direct rail connections across the north. The medieval Great North Road evolved to become the A1 in the 1920s and has since been progressively enhanced as a primary trunk road from London, through Doncaster, to the North East and Scotland. By the end of the 1970s the M18 had also been built, linking Doncaster to Sheffield and the M1 to the south, and to the M62 and the Humber ports to the north. All imports coming through the major ports of Hull and Immingham, and trucked towards London, the Midlands, and the South East, now pass through Doncaster. RAF Finningley, on the outskirts of Doncaster, served as an Airforce base between 1915 and 1996. It was redeveloped and reopened as Doncaster Sheffield Airport in 2005, catering to the short haul and commercial cargo markets (albeit the fate of the airport is something we will return to). Then in 2006 work began on developing Doncaster's iPort, a massive multi-modal rail freight interchange. Within the space of just a few decades, Doncaster had become idyllically placed as a transport, distribution, and logistics hub. Household brands with major distribution bases in Doncaster include Amazon, Next, Asda, The Range, Tesco, B&Q, and BMW. Ikea's Doncaster distribution centre is its largest premises in the UK, at 1.3 million sq. ft., equivalent in size to 17 football pitches.

Not everyone celebrates this though. Logistics, warehousing, and distribution may account for a growing swathe of Doncaster's jobs, but these are also sectors that are characterised as being of low skill and, relatedly, of low pay. Some worry that Doncaster may ultimately morph into a single giant warehouse. Home delivery is a marketplace that has boomed in the wake of the Covid-19 pandemic, when we all got far more comfortable with shopping at home, but it's also put far more pressure on the prospects of the High Street. Debenhams and BHS, previously two of the UKs largest department store chains, have both now closed their doors, including their prime units in Doncaster. Relying solely on the logistics boom is precarious, but Doncaster isn't a one trick pony. Whilst a lot of British manufacturing has been displaced to Asia's tiger economies in recent years, Doncaster is making a fightback. It is still home to a vibrant engineering and support sector to the railway industry nationally and internationally. More recently it's also become home to a variety of emergent technologies, including clean hydrogen power and eco-airship manufacturing. Over the past decade the borough has benefited from over £150m in new investment, including its redeveloped Civic & Cultural

Quarter, a University Technical College, and the regenerated Danum Gallery, Library, and Museum (DGLAM). Doncaster isn't perfect, and it faces a future that is not without risks. It is perhaps not a model city, but it is holding its own.

Doncaster isn't the next Sheffield or Leeds, and it certainly isn't a Paris, a Vegas, a Rio, or a Dublin, but it does have a story, a character, and a distinctiveness of its own. If Preston, Wakefield, Peterborough, and St Albans could all be cities, then why on earth couldn't Doncaster join them on that pedestal? We were no less deserving by any measure. If you're not from Doncaster, you may still never get around to visiting it, or necessarily be able to put a pin in it on a map. That's okay. I hope, nevertheless, that you at least now have a slightly better idea of where it is, where it came from, and what it is all about. I hope too that you will agree that Doncaster had an appropriate back-story upon which to build a winning bid. We had a starting point, but how exactly do you go on from there to win city status? For that you need to understand how exactly a Civic Honours competition works.

The Rules of the Game

Around 6,000 miles or so south from Doncaster you will find Lake Nakuru National Park, a UNESCO World Heritage Site which sits in the Great Rift Valley that cuts its way through the temperate highlands of Kenya. Lake Nakuru, the large soda lake from which the park takes its name, is home to an array of African wildlife, including lions, zebras, and rhinos, but is perhaps most famous for its swathing legions of flamingos that forage on its shores, blushing the water pink when they gather. Idyllically named lookout points such as Baboon Cliff could easily provide a backdrop for a scene straight out of *The Lion King*. A short distance away is the Menengai Crater, the second largest surviving volcanic crater in the world, with a forested caldera covering around ten square miles. It stretches out as far as the eye can see and plunges straight down to a forbidding depth of around 500 meters at its rim. Both impressive natural sites can be found on the outskirts of Nakuru, a burgeoning metropolis which is already home to over half a million Kenyans and growing rapidly. Established by the British during the colonial era, Nakuru's population descends primarily from the native Kikuyu and Kalenjin tribes-people. It's a predominantly low-rise spread of interconnecting townships; the tallest building is only 12 stories high. Despite this, Nakuru has two well respected universities, is home to the headquarters of Kenya's four largest retail supermarket chains and is a trade centre for agriculture. Coffee, wheat, barley, and maize are amongst the crops harvested by the many outlying local farms. At Nakuru's heart there is a bustling central business district, including the Maasai Market where tourists bargain with curio owners to purchase souvenirs, carvings, and jewellery. It is a vibrant and captivating place that arguably embodies modern Africa.

In December 2021 something significant happened in Nakuru, albeit it wasn't something that you will have heard about on the BBC *Six O'clock News*. Back in the UK, Doncaster and the other competitors vying for city status from the Queen were finishing off their bids, administering the final rounds of proof reading, and getting ready to submit. Over in Africa, however, Nakuru was about to leapfrog over all of them. On the 1st of December, following the approval by the Kenyan senate earlier in the year, Uhuru Muigai Kenyatta, the President of Kenya, issued a charter conferring city status on Nakuru, making it only the fourth city in Kenya after Mombasa, Kisumu, and the capital Nairobi. For a short moment at least, Nakuru was the newest official city in the world. But the Governor of Nakuru didn't need to enter a competition to win this honour, beating off lesser rival towns from elsewhere in Kenya. The process was far more procedural. Kenya has a piece of legislation called the Urban Areas and Cities Act. Section 5.1 of this Act determines that an urban area may be classified as a city if it satisfies a set of defined criteria. These criteria include having a population of at least 500,000 residents, having capacity to generate sufficient revenue to sustain its operation, and, quite importantly, having capacity for functional and effective waste disposal. Nakuru, having invested in ticking all these boxes, and having its credentials properly validated, was duly awarded the accolade of cityhood. And Kenya is supposedly a third world country!

The word "city" derives from the Greek word "polis", which itself has influenced the actual names of many cities including Napoli (Naples), Minneapolis, and Indianapolis. Cities were, in many respects, far more important in the past than perhaps they are now. In the Middle Ages the city-states of Athens, Sparta, Corinth, and Carthage were major independent sovereign cities, and respective focal points of political, economic, and cultural life. Prior to the creation of a unified Italy in 1861, the Italian peninsula was similarly divided into a network of independent metropoles such as the Duchy of Milan, the Lordship of Bologna, and the Republic of Siena. The gravitas of such city-states is perhaps most familiarly illustrated in Shakespeare's *The Two Gentleman of Verona*. The two gentlemen in question are Valentine and Proteus, who, after travelling from Verona to Milan to broaden their horizons, end up getting into a bit of a pickle with the Duke of Milan over their respective amorous intentions towards his daughter. Unimpressed, the Duke banishes Valentine from the city, such was his power, and Shakespearean high jinks then ensues, before everyone ultimately ends up living happily ever after. The world map shifted radically in the latter 19th century, with city-states giving way to the nation-states which we are now more familiar with. Whilst many modern cities, including the likes of London and Manchester, still hold a level of devolved self-governance, these still ultimately sit below their respective national governments. Only a select few places, such as Monaco and Singapore, exist today as truly independent city states. The Duke of Milan has been replaced with a mayor, but he doesn't have the power to banish his daughter's suitor from his city just because he doesn't quite like the cut of his jib!

There is no singular international norm when it comes to defining a city. In 2020 the United Nations came up with its own definition, largely to support consistency and comparison in international economic policy making. This definition is based on the relative degree of urbanisation, whereby a city must have a population in its centre of at least 50,000 people, and at least 1,500 inhabitants per adjoining square kilometre. In other words, it's a measure of both population scale and density. If applied as an official yardstick in Britain, our smallest cities, such as Wells, Ely, St. Asaph, and St. Davids, would all lose their status overnight. In contrast, Middlesbrough, Reading, Bolton, Stockport, Luton, and a host of other places would be immediately promoted. But whilst this designation may suit the needs of the UN, in practice almost every country applies its own definition.

France, for example, has no legal distinction between a town, city, or other populous conurbation. There is no separate word in the French language for town and city, the word *ville* is applied to both. Towns cannot become cities, as these things are one and the same. In contrast, the USA has some 19,500 or so incorporated communities, legally defined entities, many of which call themselves cities. As Robert Bevan, the journalist and heritage writer, indelicately put it in an article in *The Guardian* in 2014, 'the word "city" has been appended with abandon to any one-brothel main street that once offered relief to travellers across the prairies'[8]. America's veritable trove of cities includes the wonderfully named Granite City in Illinois, Silver City in New Mexico, Oil City in Pennsylvania, and Crystal City in Texas. The specific rules of incorporation vary on a state-by-state basis, which is not without controversy. The 2020 Census showed, for example, that the population of Nelsonville in Ohio had dropped below 5,000, meaning it would be downgraded from a city to a village under Ohio law. A fierce local campaign followed to re-count the population, with a few extra residents somehow coming to light, leading to Nelsonville's city status being preserved.

Further afield, countries like the Czechia and Japan follow a similar model to Kenya, elevating localities to become cities through defined legislation and criteria. China has around 700 cities, but with six different formal city classifications, largely relating to how each type of city is administered. The smallest "county-level cities" make up more than half of all the cities in China, each governed by a parent "prefecture-level city". This does, however, lead to commonplace confusion when it comes to residential addresses, which often include the names of both cities (don't be surprised if your parcel or takeaway delivery goes astray). Belgium's approach is perhaps the most like that of the UK, elevating cities by royal decree. That said, despite being roughly the same size as Wales, Belgium incredibly still

---

8   https://www.theguardian.com/cities/2014/may/08/what-makes-city-tech-garden-smart-redefine

has over 100 cities, around 20 of which have populations of less than 10,000 people. Literally everywhere is a city. Every little Flemish backwater with a solitary pub and a field full of pigs who are destined to become Frikandel sausages has a very good chance of becoming Belgium's next city. This diversity of nationalistic practices is as weird as it is wonderful. If Doncaster were transplanted lock, stock, and barrel to the USA, it would very likely have become a city decades ago. If it were transplanted to Kenya, it may not become a city for many more decades to come. If it were in France, it might never be officially recognised as a city at all.

In Britain the landscape is further confused by having several cities which aren't, in fact, cities. For example, in response to the overcrowding and industrial pollution of Victorian England in the 1890s, parliamentary stenographer Ebenezer Howard set out a vision for a series of seemingly ideal towns, blending city living within proximity to the green belt of the countryside. This led to the establishment of the "garden city" concept and the creation of Welwyn Garden City and Letchworth Garden City in Hertfordshire. Despite their names though, neither is officially recognised as a city. Similarly, in England and Wales, there was a historic tradition that city status was granted to towns with diocesan cathedrals, but this practice was never applied in Scotland. If it had been, Elgin in Moray, a Royal Burgh and cathedral town which dates to the 12th century, would be Scotland's ninth city. Elgin instead self describes itself as a historical cathedral city, wording you will see freely used on the local road signs, and which is most famously reflected through the name of the football team, Elgin City FC. But Elgin is not a city, at least not officially, not that the locals may necessarily be too worried about that formality. Even the politicians sometimes get confused. City Deals, for example, were a policy of the Conservative / Lib Dem coalition government between 2010 and 2015, devolving certain economic powers from Whitehall to England's cities. City Deals that were duly struck covered the likes of Ipswich, Middlesbrough, Swindon, Reading, and Southend, all without any of these places being recognised as cities at that time.

Whilst most countries set specific criteria to elevate cities, or perhaps apply some form of local referendum, the whole notion of a city status competition is something that is uniquely and deliciously British. It draws immediate comparisons with the eccentricity of the traditional best kept village competition, where local do-gooders battle it out with their blooming hanging baskets, immaculately trimmed hedgerows, and fastidiously tidied churchyards. The prize for the winning village is typically a plaque or road sign proclaiming that you have, indeed, arrived in the best kept village hereabouts, along with the associated bragging rights over neighbouring villages, whose second-rate inhabitants must now duly hang their heads in disgrace for a whole year. It is all glorious fun and yet preposterously pointless in the same breath. The narrative of a city status competition though is not all that different from this. There is undoubted pomposity and unbridled snootiness in debating which town has the greater civic pride, or the more deserving heritage, or the least tenuous association with the Royal Family.

You could just as well test each town to see whose mayor can grow the biggest turnip, bake the fluffiest Victoria sandwich cake, or win a school sports day egg and spoon race. I don't say this to unduly belittle the city status competition (well, not too much), but I think it is important to have this perspective firmly sighted. Whilst city status may well be worth aspiring to, the fact that you must "win it" through a convoluted duel with other towns is, in more than one respect, a delightful nonsense.

And when I say, "win it", we should be clear that, apart from the title of city status and the accompanying Letters Patent, there is no actual prize. My son, George, was studying for a degree in economics at Leeds University whilst I was writing the bid, and, having been oddly inspired by the subject, focused his dissertation on city status. A pillar of his study was to compare Wokingham, a town in Berkshire, with Chelmsford, a city (since 2012) in Essex. Both are similar in terms of population and proximity to London, but, according to George's research, Wokingham has consistently outperformed Chelmsford economically despite being just a town. A slight floor in that, as I put it to my boy, is that you will probably always be able to find an example of a town that is outperforming a similar sized city if you look hard enough. At the same time, it is equally incontrovertible that Wokingham hasn't needed city status to maximise its potential. It underlines the fact that city status isn't a guarantee of faster economic growth, but it is the allure of economic growth that invariably drives entrants. It's a bit like a kid winning the Most Promising Student Award at their school or college. They should go on to do great things, but that greatness will inevitably be driven by their own future life choices. They may well still end up stagnating in a dead-end job, struggling to make ends meet.

So, what are the rules of the game for a Civic Honours competition? Well let's firstly dispel a popular urban myth. Many people wrongly believe that a locality needs a cathedral to become a city, and some believe that anywhere that has a cathedral is, by default, already a city. These people are typically not from Nottingham, or Cambridge, or any of Britain's other cities which don't have cathedrals, or from towns like Blackburn or Guildford which do. In Medieval times, bishops held considerable power. A typical day involved consulting with the king about affairs of state, levying taxes on the peasants, and discipling wayward priests who had engaged in drinking, fornication, or gambling (playing dice in public was a definite no-no). Their cathedrals were essentially the head office of their diocese, the focal point spiritually and politically of the surrounding area, giving these places heightened reach and importance. This is why places like Wells, Ely, Lichfield, and Salisbury emerged as important cathedral cities in their heyday but have a much-reduced significance now. With city status granted to most places with a diocese cathedral, and with Britain then being largely devoid of any other significant or noteworthy towns, city making was put on hold.

There was a gap of over 300 years between Oxford and Bristol becoming cities in 1542, and the next English town to receive city status; Manchester in 1853. The industrial revolution was turning Britain on its head. In 1772 Manchester had a population of just 25,000 (not enough to fill even half of the seats at Old Trafford). Boosted by cotton, coal, and canals, and an influx of migrant labour from Ireland and Scotland, that number swelled to 186,000 by 1851; a bacterially prolific increase of over 700% in less than 80 years. Too big to now be ignored, Manchester successfully petitioned to become a city. With similar growth, Birmingham followed in 1889, becoming Britain's first cathedral-less city, albeit St Philip's Church duly became the cathedral of the newly formed Diocese of Birmingham in 1905. Other emerging industrial giants like Liverpool, Leeds, Sheffield, and Newcastle became cities around that time too. Population size and economic significance have been unofficial city status criteria ever since, whilst the presence or otherwise of a cathedral has been significantly downgraded.

In keeping with the recent contests which had come before it, the rules of the Platinum Jubilee competition gave no set definition of what a city had to be. The competition was, at least in theory, open to any elected local authority (or Crown Dependency or Overseas Territory), with proposed cities mapped to the borders of that authority, or to a defined area within that authority. You didn't need a cathedral, or a minimum population size, or a castle, or a university, or a need to meet any other arbitrary requirement. The largest urban sprawl was as welcome to enter as much as the most sparsely inhabited and rurally remote hamlet. This felt like a very 21st century attitude, in not attempting to prescribe what a city should or shouldn't be, but rather letting places decide for themselves as to how they should identify. Having said all this, and whilst it wasn't part of the formal criteria, it is worth noting that no Civic Honours contest has ever awarded city status to an English town with a population smaller than 100,000. Smaller entrants should take heed!

Entrants had to submit proposals following a defined application template. This involved drafting a summary (maximum of 1 page); an introduction covering issues such as civic pride, cultural infrastructure, and associations with royalty (maximum of 8 pages); and a local profile covering issues such as the resident population, economic activity, and public green spaces (maximum of 10 pages). The submission also had to include up to 50 photos of local permanent features, and a map showing the main tourist, leisure, and entertainment sites, as well as the main transport routes. As proposals go this was a relatively modest task in terms of the volume of required content. I would say it was a similar length, in terms of required written content, to a typical local authority tender.

Accompanying the application template was a brief document setting out the entry guidelines, which amounted to just ten bulleted points and six further questions and answers. From a proposal writer's perspective there are clear pros and cons here. On the upside, the light touch guidelines gave us a lot of autonomy and flexibility in terms of the proposal content. On the downside, there was no clear steer in terms of how the application may be won or lost. In public sector tendering it is commonplace to see some form of scoring matrix. This would inform bidders of the range of scores available, and the characteristics that an answer must demonstrate to be awarded a specific score. So, for example, every answer may be worth a maximum of ten points each. To be awarded two points out of a possible ten, the answer must meet some basic criteria. To be awarded four points, it must meet some additional criteria, and so-on-and-so-forth, all the way up to the maximum score award of ten. If you understand what the required characteristics of a ten-point answer are, you can then explicitly work these into your answer to help you achieve that maximum score. This adds some objectivity to the process and requires evaluators to provide a level of justification for the score awarded. If you don't have a scoring matrix, then it's hard to argue whether the evaluators got it right.

The Civic Honours competition had no such detailed evaluation criteria though. Ordinarily this would be a worry, as it leaves the contest open to the subjective whims of evaluators. You may think you have covered all the bases, but there is no way of knowing this for certain. If you happen to be the pet favourite of the evaluators, that may be all you need. This tactic of not giving explicit evaluation criteria was, however, undoubtedly deliberate. If you give out scores, then someone must come first, but equally someone must also come in last place, as opposed to simply having a group of winners and a group of losers. It would be something of a slap in the face to enter a Civic Honours competition and be officially last – the least deserving place to become a city - and that's the type of negative story that The Cabinet Office would no doubt have wanted to avoid. So, whilst the absence of a scoring criteria was a little frustrating, it was arguably an understandable omission.

Beyond this, we enter slightly hazier territory. For example, there is no requirement, formal or otherwise, for a candidate town to have the public support and backing of its local community. There is no requirement to have a highly visible and well marketed campaign. There is no requirement to achieve buy-in with, and endorsement from, key stakeholders, influencers, and decision makers. There is no requirement to generate press coverage, and to get your bid featured in newspapers, or on the radio, or on TV. There is no indication that any of these things are part of the formal decision-making process, or that they are taken account of in any respect when the final decisions are made. Of course, with no published evaluation criteria, it's hard to say for certain what difference things such as these make.

We can find inspiration here from an unusual source, Dr Paddi Lund, an eccentric dentist from Australia. By the late 1980s Lund's dental practice in Brisbane was grossing over a million Australian dollars annually, while he was working around a third of the hours of a typical dentist. But how did he do it? Well, he'd began by repurposing his waiting room, replacing it with an area that more closely resembled a coffee shop, and he introduced private waiting rooms for those who preferred to sit quietly alone. He installed a TV in the ceiling above his dentist's chair, which patients could watch whilst being treated, and he had a big button which they could press if they wanted him to stop drilling. His patients knew the nurse who would be looking after them; he or she would be a single point of contact for booking appointments, greeting them on arrival and looking after their welfare on each visit. He introduced many other small touches that differentiated his business from other neighbouring dentists. The result was to create strong loyalty between patients and the practice. Lund used the term Critical Non-Essentials to describe these differentiators. None were essential things that were expected of a dental practice, but they were all critical to the customer experience (yes, customers, not patients). As a result, 8 out of 10 of his new customers took out treatment plans, with 90% of them starting that treatment at the very first visit. The practice is so exclusive today that it only accepts customers by invitation and does no paid for marketing whatsoever. Lund's concept of Critical Non-Essentials has since been adopted by wider businesses and sports teams alike. Sir Clive Woodward, who engineered England's victory in the 2003 Rugby Union World Cup, integrated it as a key element of his own winning strategy.

The concept of Critical Non-Essentials is equally relevant in the world of proposal writing. Case in point, it's not essential to hire a professional proposal writer to produce a city status bid, but it could make a critical difference! And that's just the tip of the iceberg in the proposal world. These days there are all sorts of bid library software products and, increasingly, artificial intelligence writing tools to help give your proposals an edge. Equally, it can be just as critical to build a brand for your bid, creating a buzz, building anticipation. Perth in Scotland, for example, developed, wrote, and published a full "mock" city status bid in 2009, three years before their real bid won them city status in 2012. If your campaign is being talked about by the people that matter even before your bid is submitted, you are almost certainly giving yourself a foot-up. You can't readily measure the value of this influence or quantify its impact on the result. Nevertheless, the lobbying and marketing machines of many of the city candidates were about to get cranked up into overdrive. Social media hashtags, press releases, celebrity endorsements, photo opportunities, vox pop videos, community competitions, opinion polls, media interviews, jazzy logos, and political back-channelling, all the tools of the trade would be used, all to win that all important critical advantage. How much influence any of it would have on the result was anyone's guess!

Despite everything I have just said, the rules of the game when it comes to city status contests are manifestly vague and hazy. At the end of the day, it's ultimately a highly subjective beauty pageant, where any one of several attributes might turn the judge's heads and prove to be the decisive factor. We can second guess things to an extent, but to second guess too much can be precarious. Indicatively, I believe you are more likely to win if you take the competition seriously, maximise your best efforts in all sections of your bid, and ensure that your campaign gets noticed in all the right circles. That may sound easy, but I assure you it isn't. From an English perspective, I believe these were traits that the winning campaigns from Doncaster, Milton Keynes, and Colchester all had in common. They were all proactive and well executed campaigns. Why they triumphed above the likes of other strong bidders like Reading, Middlesbrough, and Blackburn, well that is a little harder to say with certainty, but there was a clear leading pack;

those who might win, and then those who almost certainly wouldn't. I would go as far too as saying that I believe the campaign is as important, if not more so, than the locality. Doncaster didn't need to be the most deserving candidate, and it probably wasn't. It needed instead to build a campaign that would convince the evaluators that it was the most deserving. That's the sweet spot and the very essence of winning proposal writing.

Doncaster & Me

Many city status bids are written by volunteer historians, local councillors, local authority civil servants, or sometimes perhaps a combination of all of these. In many cases, these are long term residents, people who would proudly claim to be born and bred in the locality. Against that norm I was perhaps an unusual choice to be the author of Doncaster's bid. After all, I am not a Yorkshireman. I was not born in Yorkshire, and I have never actually lived in Yorkshire. My mother was born in Skipton, North Yorkshire, in 1946, so when I was born I must in turn have had at least a teaspoonful of Yorkshire blood somewhere inside me. But Doncaster was, ironically, almost the cause for me to never have existed at all. By the late 1950s my mother was living near Stowmarket in Suffolk. Her father, my grandfather, worked for Suffolk Iron Foundries, a company famous for manufacturing the Suffolk Punch Lawnmower. If your family owned a petrol cylinder lawnmower in the 1950s or 1960s, and most families with a lawned garden did, the chances are it was a Suffolk Punch. In 1960 my grandfather was offered the opportunity to manage a sales territory for Suffolk Iron Foundries in South Yorkshire and, according to my mother, he had even looked at buying a potential family home somewhere very near to Doncaster racecourse. But fate had other plans. Rather than uprooting to Doncaster, my grandfather was instead offered a different sales patch in Kent at the last minute, and the family instead moved to Chartham, just outside of Canterbury. A few years later, when my mum was working on the tea bar counter at Woolworths, she served a young bricklayer who came in and ordered a ham and tomato sandwich for his lunch. He plucked up the courage to ask her if she wanted to watch him play football at the weekend; not really the most imaginative of first dates, but there you go. That bricklayer, and goalkeeping lothario, was, of course, my dad.

I was born in Ashford in Kent in 1973, and grew up in a tiny hamlet called Lenham Heath, nestled at the foot of the North Downs. I lived with my mum, my dad, my older sister, and my grandparents (my dad's parents). It was rare even then to have three generations living under the same roof. There was no discernible centre to Lenham Heath, just a scattered ensemble of farms, fields, lanes, and cottages. You could drive straight through it in a matter of minutes and be blissfully unaware that you had both arrived and then left. It was, in a very literal sense, the middle of nowhere. The small lane we lived on didn't even have a name of its own, and only had around half a dozen houses scattered along it. They call Kent the Garden of England, with its gentle hills, distinctive oast houses, fruit filled orchards, grassy meadows, and fields brimming with canary yellow rapeseed. Lenham Heath was lost amid it all.

Growing up I didn't think of Lenham Heath as really being either rich or poor, perhaps because I didn't really have anywhere else to compare it to. We lived well, but I would also say modestly. We didn't want for anything, but we didn't want too much either. Meals were home cooked, with a stock of vegetables grown in our own garden by my grandfather.

My grandmother helped to keep us fed by baking an endless supply of current buns and jam tarts. As a bricklayer by trade, my dad took care of the house, building an extension to fit us all in. There are hundreds of houses across the home counties today with bricks laid by my father's hand. Mum started out as a nurse at St Augustine's Psychiatric Hospital, formerly known less graciously as the Kent County Lunatic Asylum, supporting patients with mental health needs. When my sister and I were born she stepped away from that and worked part time for a while in the village picking strawberries in the fields or over in the apple coring shed across the road from our house. It's the type of work that many in Britain now bizarrely regard as being beneath them. When we were a little older she went back to the NHS as a physiotherapist for people with conditions such as cerebral palsy. She was working then at Lenham Hospital, a grand institution, and former tuberculosis sanatorium, which looked out over the village from its hillside perch on the downs. People were less kind towards people with disabilities in the 1980s, with the term "spastic" used stingingly by kids on the playground to belittle anyone perceived to be stupid, but people affected by spasticity were the very type of people my mum was helping. It goes without saying that I'm super proud of my mum and dad. I can't say for sure how my childhood compared to that of the kids of Doncaster growing up at that time, but I'm not so sure we were all that different. I suspect we all spent a lot of our time playing out with friends, riding our bikes, getting up to no-good, and only going home when our parents called us in for dinner (or perhaps I should say tea).

Back then Doncaster was just one of those many anonymous towns from somewhere up north whose exact locations all seemed to blur into one. As the crow flies our house was marginally closer to Paris than it was to Doncaster, and Paris may just as well have been on the other side of the world. I couldn't tell you where Doncaster was, how to get there, or what you would find once you'd arrived. My aunts and uncles on both sides of the family all lived in Kent at that time, so family gatherings were all comparatively local. Except for summer camping holidays to the likes of Wales or Scotland, and occasional school day trips by coach to London, the borders of Kent were effectively the boundaries of my own personal universe. My only sense that Doncaster even existed at all was when Des Lynam, the silky voiced anchor-man of BBC's *Grandstand,* reported the Saturday afternoon football scores. Doncaster Rovers' league fortunes flitted between the old Divisions 3 and 4, as they were back then, and they have sadly changed little since. But if it had a football team, then Doncaster surely had to be a real place, somewhere or other.

It wasn't love at first sight for Doncaster and me, but much more of a long-term courtship. We were introduced, we gradually became friends, and over the years it turned into something a little more serious. We first briefly touched hands in 1984, when I was just 11, on a walking holiday to the North Yorkshire Moors with the scouts. Our small group travelled up by train along the East Coast Mainline, which means we must have surely stopped at Doncaster station on the way. I have an engrained memory of being at York station on the way home. I had flitted away all my pocket money by buying up a stack of sew-on badges of the various places we had visited for my mum to stitch on to my camp-fire blanket when I got home. The other lads had some money left to buy ice creams at the station, and I was making a nuisance of myself by pestering my friend Ben to give me some of his money so I could get one too. Rather than share his cash though, and no doubt weary of my relentless badgering, Ben instead chose to smash his own ice cream cone straight in my face, which in fairness I probably deserved. That peculiar memory from York has always stayed with me, but I have no recollection of passing through Doncaster, which I surely did again later the same day.

Doncaster and I didn't cross paths again for many years. By the late 1990s I was living with Anne, my girlfriend and future wife, in a two-bedroom flat in Hounslow in West London. The flat was pretty much right under the flight path of Heathrow, meaning that there was a deafening boom overhead every time that Concorde was flying in or out. Anne was originally from the village of Standish near Wigan (not only am I not a Yorkshireman, but, of all people, I ended up married to a Lancastrian). We had met as students at Middlesex University in North London; she was studying graphic design whilst I was doing a mix of environmental studies and politics. Having both grown up in comparatively rural areas, neither of us wanted to settle down and start a family in the capital. With her parents living in Standish, and mine by then living in Crawley in Sussex, there was an inevitability that one or other of us would end up living a distance away from our families. As it turns out, we both did.

After graduating I had initially worked for a few weeks for the London Borough of Enfield, and then spent a couple of years in the transport sector, doing a brief stint at London Transport and another with the trade association for the bus and coach industry. A career focused on public transport looked like it was going to be "my thing". But then, in 1998, I got a job as a Business Development Manager with a company called Action for Employment, or A4E as they were better known. A4E specialised in delivering employability contracts, helping those who were unemployed and claiming benefits to get jobs. This typically involved services such as guidance in preparing job applications and developing skills through work placements. Tony Blair's Labour Government had just achieved a landslide win at the 1997 General Election and he was rolling out his New Deal programme; a flagship scheme to tackle unemployment, with around two million Brits out of work at that time. A4E had already won contracts to deliver the New Deal initiative before I arrived and had just opened a network of centres in London. My new job was to help them win even more business by writing responses to competitive tenders, setting me on the path to become a professional bid writer. I wasn't attracted by the work alone though. A4E's Head Office was in Sheffield, which importantly provided the basis of a career pathway through which Anne and I could leave London.

Over the next couple of years or so I visited pretty much every A4E centre, with many of these being clustered around Yorkshire and northern Lincolnshire. I found myself dropping in on Leeds, Pontefract, Rotherham, Goole, Grimsby, Scunthorpe, Barnsley, Wakefield and, yes, you've guessed it, Doncaster! Even that visit though, didn't leave an indelible memory. A4E centres were typically leased office floors or shop fronted units, all refurbished in a slightly garish primary colour scheme of custard yellow and a deep navy blue, typically with a couple of training rooms where the jobseekers congregated. The centres all essentially looked and felt the same, which was kind of the point. They were often located close to the jobcentre, in as smart yet affordable building as possible, and where the landlord and other tenants were generally happy to have unemployed jobseekers hanging around, making the centres easy to find on one hand, but not always in the most appealing parts of town on the other. Suffice to say, a lot of my visits all blurred into one.

When I said that I had never lived in Yorkshire that was true, but my career with A4E gave me the opportunity to move to its very cusp. In 2000, the year after we got married, we made the move. I was working at A4E's Head Office, based in part of a converted steel works in Attercliffe, an industrial suburb in northeast Sheffield. Anne was doing freelance graphic design work which she could do from home, so was unconstrained by geography. We packed up our belongings, which back then fitted in a small hire van, and headed up the M1. We didn't know Sheffield at all, so we rented a house in Killamarsh on the outskirts of the city, about ten miles or so from my office, but officially sitting just over the border in neighbouring Derbyshire. We then spent a year exploring and viewing houses right across Sheffield and its wider commuter belt. We visited everywhere from the foothills of the Peak District on the west side of the city, all the way over to the Rother Valley in the east. We didn't want much. It had to be an old house – not a new build, with bags of character, within our budget, big enough for a family, away from busy roads, with a nice garden, close to the local amenities, and commutable to work. It turns out that was a slightly trickier ask than we first thought! We ended up looking at dozens and dozens of houses, so much so that house hunting seemed to exhaustingly fill up every weekend. Then, after a painstaking year of searching, ruling houses in and then ruling them out, we finally found somewhere which seemed to tick all the necessary boxes, a town house in the small enclave of Retford, in north Nottinghamshire and on the edge of the Sherwood Forrest. In March 2001 Anne, who was by then heavily pregnant with our son George, and I moved in, and we have lived there ever since.

Doncaster was the nearest "big town" to Retford, a mere 20 miles away, so it was inevitable then that we would start to spend more and more time going there. Before our daughter Alice was born, Anne used to visit Brockholes Farm Riding School with George, on the site which has since been transformed into the Yorkshire Wildlife Park. Anne got to have a riding lesson which was a welcome respite from being a new mum, the clincher being that the price of the lesson included childcare for George, so he got to explore the farm, watching owls in the barn, sheep being sheared and, notably once, a cow giving birth. Lakeside Village and the Frenchgate Centre, Doncaster's two primary retail hubs, offered us a healthy mix of established

High Street brands for a weekend shopping trip. The Clarks store at Lakeside was a particular favourite to which we made an inevitable beeline every time the kids needed new school shoes, usually accompanied by a browse around the old warehouse sized Toys-R-Us store. The Vue multiplex in Doncaster was our nearest cinema, and both children saw their first big screen movies there. For George it was *The Incredibles* in 2004, which he sat through mesmerised and open mouthed in complete awe. For Alice it was *Shrek the Third* in 2007, throughout which she fidgeted, acted up, and had to be taken out to the corridor more than once to be told to behave herself. I can't remember what Alice's second movie was, but suffice to say she didn't get to go back to the cinema for a little while after that.

Over the years I have become increasingly interconnected with Doncaster. I started Carley Consult, my own bid writing business, in our back bedroom at home in 2007. Having initially had an office in Retford, I relocated it to a new office in Doncaster in 2016 and, for the first time, I was commuting into Doncaster every day. The move also opened a variety of new connections and opportunities. The company joined Doncaster Chamber and we entered their business awards in 2017. Whilst we (unbelievably) didn't win, this still led to my first in-person introduction with Dan Fell, the Chief Executive. He was judging one of the categories we had entered and visited our office as part of the judging process. This introduction was a steppingstone towards me being invited to join the Chamber Board at the end of 2019. My involvement with the Chamber progressed to running some training sessions and webinars for other members, introducing them to the essential aspects of bid writing. It is perhaps then not so far-fetched of a jump from me to go from here to being the author of the city status bid.

It wasn't a disadvantage to the campaign that I wasn't born and bred in Doncaster. To the contrary, I believe that my disassociation from Doncaster was a strength. The late Colin Wedd was leader of Doncaster Council at the time of the application for city status in 2000. He is reported to have lambasted a leaked Home Office report providing commentary on the applicants in that year, and which was more than a little disparaging about Doncaster. 'I dare say that whoever may have written this has not set foot in Doncaster,'[9] he protested. Whilst he was clearly infuriated by the process, paradoxically his misplaced frustration demonstrated a really important point about Civic Honours competitions. With multiple entrants from across Britain there is an inevitability that the decision makers won't have necessarily visited every locality in person. My primary job was therefore not to convince the people of Doncaster that their borough deserved city status, but rather it was to convince a group of people who, despite the past rhetoric and expectations of Colin Wedd, may have quite legitimately never previously set foot in the borough.

As an outsider of sorts, I had never looked at Doncaster through rose tinted glasses. It's not my hometown, or a place that I had previously thought about with an undue sense of sentimental nostalgia. It didn't provoke memories of funny

9   John Beckett, City Status in the British Isles 1830-2002, Routledge 2005, Page 151

things that happened to me "back in the day". I could see all of Doncaster's perfect imperfections without bias or denial. Whilst that may have meant that I have less in common with many people from Doncaster, it conversely also meant that I have more in common with another key group, the people who would be reading and evaluating our city status bid. The ministers, civil servants and expert panellists who were my audience didn't have humorous personal anecdotes about Doncaster that they recounted at dinner parties. They didn't get upset if Doncaster Rovers got relegated, nor celebrate if the team won promotion. They probably wouldn't be able to find their way from the racecourse to the train station without asking for directions more than once. Their attachment to Doncaster had no more substance to that of my own as a child.

Whether for work or leisure, I have previously visited more than a hundred different cities (and it took a fair bit of scribbling and reminiscing for me to work that out). I've been to more than forty British cities, across all four of the home nations, including having lived, studied, and worked in London. I have also been to more than sixty different cities outside of the UK, including some of the most famous places in the world, such as Beijing, Jerusalem, Bangkok, Rome, Sydney, Barcelona, and Las Vegas, to list but a handful. I have stood in front of the White House in Washington DC, as well as the Kremlin in Moscow. I have shopped in the souks of Marrakesh, watched the Blue Jays play baseball in Toronto, taken a gondola ride in Venice, admired *The Last Supper* by Da Vinci in Milan, run a lap of the Formula 1 circuit in Abu Dhabi, and cycled over

San Francisco's Golden Gate Bridge. I took in the unique view of Manhattan from the roof of the World Trade Centre, years before it was mercilessly levelled to the ground by Al Qaeda, a view that my own children will never get to see. I've also been to many far lesser-known cities, such as Utrecht in Holland, Bathurst in New South Wales, and Fresno in California. I know that I have been both privileged and blessed in having been able to experience all these places. But I don't rattle these names off to bullishly blow my own trumpet (well, not too much), nor to imply that I am some sort of unparalleled cities expert. Far from it. I have, however, seen a lot of different places in my lifetime, and in this respect, I think I have a pretty good yardstick of what a new city needs to measure up against.

I wasn't a font of knowledge of local history, I had never been a member of a local history society, and my only experience as a civil servant were those brief few weeks that I had spent at the London Borough of Enfield almost thirty years beforehand. It didn't matter though. Instead, I was a professional bid writer, still with a very healthy appreciation of Doncaster – albeit with an appropriately critical lens, a passport full of city stamps, and a track record of selling to Whitehall. If I had been born in Doncaster's Royal Infirmary, I couldn't have been more motivated. Even if we didn't win, Doncaster was going to have a bid it could be more than proud of. My reputation was at stake on that.

Getting Organised

L et me take a moment to introduce you to the fantastic team of people who made Doncaster's city status bid happen, as well as give you some context in terms of how we organised ourselves. It was in every respect a team effort, the campaign being managed and delivered through what we call Team Doncaster – not the most imaginative title perhaps, but more than fit for purpose. At its core, Team Doncaster is a partnership that spans the public, private, voluntary and community sectors. Members include the Council, the Chamber of Commerce, the college, NHS Trust, the main housing association, and key employers, amongst others. It's based on a collegiate approach, recognising that partners can achieve more by working together than by themselves. That may sound a bit twee and could easily be accused of being idealistic twaddle - where outwardly partners want to be seen as joined up, but in practice they don't play well together at all. In Doncaster though this isn't the case. There is a genuine buy-in to the Team Doncaster concept. The partnership has regular "Gold Meetings" to discuss the spectrum of issues facing the borough, and how progress for Doncaster can be achieved through collaboration. Team Doncaster was the bedrock upon which the city status bid was built; a ready-made forum which already rounded up the essential movers and shakers who would be integral to a winning campaign.

Team Doncaster meetings are ordinarily chaired by Ros Jones, Doncaster's elected Mayor, who was also a paramount backer for the city status application. Put simply, if Ros hadn't been behind the bid, then there wasn't going to be a bid. Nobody else held quite the same sway. A Doncaster girl, born and bred, her father was a coal miner who had worked in the Askern pit. Previously a chartered accountant working in local government and the NHS, and then a Labour councillor, Ros first became Doncaster's elected mayor in 2013, the first woman to hold the position. She won a further 4-year term in 2017 and then, at the spritely age of just 71, repeated that feat again with another election win in 2021. Ros, in many respects, is Doncaster's doyenne, with a reach and reputation that has grown over the years far beyond merely being the mayor. She is the public face of the borough. Whilst not everyone will agree with her politics, she has an obsessive energy and enthusiasm for Doncaster which is rarely matched. Whilst Ros was not hands on with the day to day running of the campaign, she still provided a steer and influence when it mattered. I am sure that she felt that attaining city status for Doncaster, if a bid could be a success, would be a fitting swansong to her career, and perhaps the crowning achievement of her own lifelong service to the borough. With the Mayor's firm backing, everything else could and would move ahead.

I first became aware that a city status bid was on the cards when it came up in discussion at the monthly board meeting of the Chamber in June 2021, shortly after our awayday at Castle Park. Dan Fell had reported that he'd already had tentative conversations with the Council about the competition and was working with partners to consider developing a campaign.

Whilst Ros Jones was the necessary figurehead sponsor that the campaign needed; Dan was without doubt the catalyst in making the whole thing happen. He had been socialising the idea of a new Doncaster bid over the preceding couple of years. With the new competition launched, he had lobbied to get the Council firmly on the hook, offering himself up to chair the campaign and, to all intents and purposes, guiding it from under the wing of the Chamber. Dan had worked at the Chamber since 2005, and had become its Chief Executive in 2014, the youngest Chief Executive of any Chamber in Britain at that time. He's a little on the bohemian side, with a fondness for floral patterned shirts and three-piece woollen suits. Don't be fooled by these modest eccentricities though, he's a very smart cookie. Dan is a self-confessed policy wonk, most at home fronting up campaigns, advocating for Doncaster at key events, and generally greasing the political wheel. His accomplishments had already included leading a successful bid to open the new University Technical College in the town, and he served as Chair of the new purpose-built Cast Theatre in the civic quarter. He was a trusted figure amongst political, business, and cultural stakeholders alike, and an ideal front man in every respect.

I'd put an early marker down with Dan on the back of that discussion. I wanted to be involved in the campaign if I could be. The Chamber board meeting led in turn to a virtual roundtable event at the end of June, using the strapline title of "City Status for Doncaster - what does it mean for your business?" to get the business community engaged. Whilst consideration was given during that call to the relative pros and cons of bidding, there was also some very healthy debate around what a strong campaign might look like. Of the twenty-five of us who took part, no-one was expressly against the idea of mounting a city status bid, and some were overtly positive, but there was also a level of moderation in wanting to have more information to ensure that any decision to go ahead was properly informed. We needed to decide to bid with our heads as much as with our hearts. If nothing else though, the meeting served as an initial toe in the water in gauging the local appetite to bid and, in this respect, the temperature was favourable.

Despite the outcome of the roundtable, Dan was still concerned that wider Team Doncaster partners might view a city status campaign as being a little tone deaf in the current hard pressed economic climate. Convincing business was one thing, but convincing the community at large was something else. What really swung him though was a subsequent conversation he had with Glyn Butcher, Director of a local mental health charity called the People Focused Group (PFG). Glyn himself has lived experience of accessing legacy mental health services that left him feeling powerless for many years, until he came across the type of peer support championed by PSG, where those in need advocate for and support each other. Glyn was an active supporter of city status from the outset, helping to convince Dan that Doncaster should go for it, and adding to the weight of arguments at Dan's disposal to ultimately convince Ros and the Council that it was the right strategy too.

Dan and I had a subsequent one-to-one catch up call in mid-July. Nothing had been determined about how a bid might be put together at that point, and I hadn't presumed or even considered that the Council would look to bring in an external Project Director to produce it. My only goal at that point was to reaffirm to Dan that I wanted to be involved and to share some of my own personal views on how a winning strategy might be carved out. I left Dan with no uncertainty not only about my eagerness to contribute, but also in terms of how I hoped my input and experience would add value to any campaign. In this respect, I doubt that any of the other candidate towns had a professional bid writer sat on the board of their respective Chambers. I was an asset that was willing and ready to be exploited, and I knew too that Dan was not the kind of guy to look a gift horse in the mouth.

Nothing happened, at least not in terms of my own involvement, for a goodly few weeks after that. The traditional summer school holiday period was underway and, following a long winter of Covid-19 restrictions, people were keen to have a break, even if for most that meant a British staycation rather than a couple of weeks on the Mediterranean. The deadline for city status bids was still a long way off in December. The pressure was seemingly off. It was not until September that things started to gather momentum once again. The decision that Doncaster would bid had been firmed up over the summer. Dan's lobbying had paid off, albeit even with Ros on side, any decision was still subject to the Council's governance procedures. On 21st of September the first formal Project Board for the city status bid was convened in the format of a video call, organised by the Chamber on behalf of Team Doncaster.

Around thirty or so people from across the Team Doncaster network were invited. It was a broad and diverse group, with some notably influential local personalities. Amongst its numbers were Carl Hall, the New Zealander who had made over 150 rugby league appearances for Doncaster; Lindsy James, local charity leader and Guinness World Record holder for being the fastest woman to push a pram (and a 9-month-old baby) over a half marathon (in 1 hour and 27 minutes); and Suzy Brain England OBE, Chair of both the Doncaster & Bassetlaw NHS Teaching Hospitals Foundation Trust as well as the Keep Britain Tidy charity, to list but a few. I was still only participating as a member of the Chamber board at this stage, albeit a very enthusiastic one. Culture, business, sports, tourism, healthcare, and the community sector were all represented. This Project Board would meet fortnightly from there on in through to the bid submission in December, acting as a key sounding board for the campaign.

Several city status bidders had a similar Project Board, acting as a sounding board for their campaigns, and providing a means through which different constituents within the locality could play a part. On balance, the size and reach of our own Project Board was just about right, albeit there were some suggestions to seek out additional recruits. James Coppinger was one such name, a freeman of the borough and local legend who had racked up 600 appearances playing for Doncaster Rovers. He was muted as a potential public figurehead of the campaign, but I don't know if that idea ever got followed up. A splash of local celebrity never goes amiss in these types of projects. In hindsight, I think too that we were probably also lacking at least one seasoned local historian to enrich our numbers, perhaps someone from the Doncaster Archives or the Doncaster Civic Trust who could help us more readily showcase some of Doncaster's lesser-known historical gems. It wasn't a deal-breaker, but if we had to do it all again, having somebody with that rich depth of local historical understanding would have been a beneficial asset.

One of the first, and perhaps the easiest, decisions which the Project Board took at that first gathering was to agree that the proposed city would incorporate the whole borough. Both the borough and the principal town are both called Doncaster, albeit the former is the whole egg, whilst the latter is more specifically the yolk in the centre. We had the choice of either, albeit if we went solely for the yolk, then we would have needed to define the city limits more specifically. Opting for the whole borough was more inclusive, treating the borough as one distinct place, as well as enabling the bid to leverage the wider history, heritage, and assets of the wider geography. It would also be far more straightforward and remove any nitpicking arguments over the potential inclusion or exclusion of the town's borderline suburbs. It may sound a little strange to include the borough's rural peripheries within the city, but many British cities are coterminous with their local authority boundaries, so it wasn't all that big a deal. If only all the other challenges that we would face would be that straightforward.

My own involvement as Project Director wasn't handed to me on a plate. To ensure transparency and objectivity, the

Chamber organised a mini-tender to select a partner to fulfil the brief. So, to write the proposal for city status, I first had to write a proposal for the right to write the proposal for city status! The exercise was executed at pace at the back end of September, with only just over a week for us to put a proposal in. I hastily threw a four-sider together against the brief that the Chamber had put out, covering off the criteria they had set. This primarily addressed who would be involved, how we would go about delivering the Project Director brief, and how we would ensure pace of production and deal with any unforeseen circumstances, being mindful of the time then remaining to meet the more important deadline of the city status bid itself. As it transpired the Chamber only received one application, ours! That said, I like to think that we weren't simply handed the assignment by default. I hope that our proposal would have prevailed, even if some other individual or agency had put their name in the hat. But that was now by the by. The gig was ours, and my business and I were installed in the Project Director seat.

Working alongside us at the heart of the campaign were Dan Fell from the Chamber and Lee Tillman, Assistant Director of Strategy & Performance at Doncaster Council. Dan acted as the Project Chairman, which may have sounded unusual given that the bid itself had to be submitted by the Council. The willingness of Ros Jones and the Council to delegate leadership of the bid campaign to Dan was, however, in my opinion, a master-stroke. With Dan as Chair the focus on a partnership driven approach was cemented, and the campaign was unshackled from being solely at the whim of local politics. The result was a culture of greater inclusivity, creativity, and objective challenge. Alongside Dan, Lee was the project sponsor for the Council, and the go-between with the Mayor and the Council's Chief Executive, Damian Allen. Lee's job was to ensure safe passage of the bid through the internal machinery of the Council, gaining necessary approvals and signoffs, keeping elected members on-side, and making sure that any specific must have asks from the Council were factored into the bid. Dan, Lee, and I formed part of what we called the Core Group, the inner players who met each week to navigate the key milestones and decisions faced by the campaign.

The Core Group also included Steph Cunningham, Head of Communications & Engagement at the Council, who did more than her share of heavy lifting. Steph and her team led on creating the visual identity and artwork for the campaign, shrewdly advocating platinum purple as our signature colour. She created the wrap around on the *Doncaster Free Press* for the campaign launch, as well as drafting press releases, stakeholder communication, and social media threads, and running the resident's survey which accompanied the campaign. Lorna Reeve, Destination Marketing Manager for Doncaster, played a key role in helping to co-ordinate the photo images which went into the bid document, as well as being an insightful and considered contributor to all the discussions. Alison Jordan, a Project Manager within the Council, was seconded to the project to utilise her skills in helping to keep the rest of us on track, scheduling meetings, capturing actions, and following up on tasks. Alison was perhaps the most important cog in the wheel, and perhaps the unsung hero of the campaign.

Alongside myself, I then also co-opted a couple of my own staff into the Core Group. Ginny Lindle, my Director of Bid Services, was there to act as a deputy to me, providing a critical eye on the drafting, and standing-in for me when needed. I also bought in Scott MacFarlane, my Digital Marketing & Communications Manager. Scott didn't ordinarily get involved in delivering assignments, but his skill set was particularly apt for this project. He filmed, edited, and produced pretty much all the social media video content used in the campaign. The Core Group was completed by Emma Norton and Yvette Ireland, both from within the communications team at the Chamber of Commerce. This eclectic little group would drive the campaign forward, carrying the burden of ensuring that Doncaster would have the most competitive application, and the best chance of winning.

The confirmation of my tenure as Project Director coincided with another longstanding diary commitment. On Sunday 10th of October 2021, I ran the Manchester Marathon with my son, George. This would be my fourth marathon, having run London in 1993, 1995, and 2016. I had never planned on running a fourth, but the attraction of running together as father and son was too much of a draw to resist. We were entered to run in 2020, but Covid-19 meant that the race got shelved and our entries were pushed back twice into 2021, which played havoc with my attempts to train. Anne's uncle Eddie has recently been diagnosed with prostate cancer, so it was fitting that we decided to raise funds for Prostate Cancer UK, securing over £2,000 in sponsorship. Tragically Anne's dad and George's grandad, Julian, had passed away from pancreatic cancer in the Spring of 2021. It may have been a different brand of cancer, but it added to our resolve to both raise funds and train as hard as we could. I bloody hate cancer! I'd managed sub-4-hour times in my three London marathons, and hoped to repeat that in Manchester, despite the sands of passing time constantly trying to slow down my aging bones. George and I ran together for around 20 miles, but I was flagging towards the end, whilst his younger legs still had plenty more to give. He ran ahead, and I eventually crossed the line behind him in a time of 4 hours and 5 minutes, which still felt respectable. It was a great day, and a wonderful sense of achievement to have taken on the race together.

Running for me is a cathartic pastime. I was only eight when the first London Marathon was held in 1981, but I still remember being inspired by watching those early races on television, and thinking to myself that one day I would run that race too. It was perhaps then no surprise that I had only just turned 20 when I first lined up with starting crowds on Blackheath (ironically, the very same age as George was on the start line in Manchester). The finish back then was on Westminster Bridge, and I can only describe crossing the line that first time as a surreal out of body experience. I was totally exhausted, yet felt humbled, proud, and empowered all in the same breath. The marathon does that to you. For me, running and bid writing are exceptionally well-matched bedfellows. Running is an opportunity for me to let my brain off the leash, letting it tootle off to explore the fields and sniff around the bushes by itself for a bit, while my body is otherwise busy pounding away on the footpath. I play around with ideas and write a lot in my head when I'm running. I scribed a mental first draft of this very paragraph, and lots of the other words in this book, whilst out on a run. Suffice to say, the prospect of writing the impending city status bid had my neurons firing as we ran through Manchester city centre, past Old Trafford, and out through Stretford, Sale, and Altrincham. I may have been a sweat encrusted, middle-aged mess by the time I got to the finish line, but I was a sweat encrusted, middle-aged mess with a head full of ideas.

Whilst Dan chaired the Project Board and Core Group, he pretty much entrusted me with an editorial free hand when it came to the bid itself. His rationale was simple in that, if you are hiring a professional to do a job, then you should trust them to get on with it. That approach suited me just fine. Whilst I wanted to canvass a broad church of opinion and ideas in shaping the bid, I was also keen to avoid what I would refer to as writing by committee. Proposal writing can very readily go off track when you are spending more time appeasing the viewpoints of internal stakeholders, rather than focusing on winning the proposal itself. Fortunately, this wasn't the case here, and I had the comfort of knowing that Dan had my back as and when any differences in editorial opinion may arise.

I instigated two work-stream groups to focus on different aspects of the campaign, working with Alison across both. The first group was focused on marketing and media communications. Its membership included Steph, Lorna, Emma,

Yvette, and Scott from the Core Group. It also included Glyn Butcher and Charlotte Dimond, a local public relations expert. A lot of the attention of the campaign team was focused on this work-stream. This wasn't wholly a surprise, as it is where a lot of the ideas for social media, marketing, and campaign work were nurtured, and this reflected the interest set of most people in the wider group. How the bid would be launched, how the public would be engaged and involved, and how the profile of the campaign would be sustained were all things which would occupy this work-stream. Contrastingly, it was the side of the campaign which I had a slightly lesser personal interest in. I don't say that disparagingly, because this was important work, but my interest was mainly driven by the bid document. To that end, I was happy to let others own, and get hands-on with, the marketing agenda.

The second work-stream group focused on the writing of the bid itself. This workload of this group was nowhere near as glitzy as the marketing group, with far less razzle-dazzle, so, unsurprisingly, fewer volunteers wanted to join. Alongside me, the group consisted of Ginny, Alison, Lorna, and Paul Bareham, the Council's Senior Strategy & Performance Improvement Manager. Paul had been involved in other funding bids for the Council and had a great critical eye for writing. He also had a good mental library of Doncaster related facts, which came in handy more than once. The group focused on content planning, in particular which stories and facts would go into the bid, and where that information would come from. This was particularly helpful, for example, when informing the "green spaces" section, with an informative summary of statistics forthcoming from the Council. Whilst the goal of the writing work-stream on one hand was to capture Doncaster's more enigmatic stories, there was equally a need to build an underpinning social and economic profile, capturing such things as the size of the population, the GDP per worker, the number of public parking spaces and other citycentric indicators. We developed a wider spreadsheet of potentially useful facts to drop into the narrative, with the Nomis, the Office for National Statistics (ONS), and Centre for Cities websites providing fruitful sources in our search. We didn't manage to track down everything (I apologise as I can't tell you how many individual retail units there are in Doncaster), but we captured a lot of the shopping list items, or if not the exact statistic we were looking for then the next best thing.

So that was our line-up. The Core Group set the strategy, the Project Board served as an ideas generator and sounding board, and the two work-stream groups would do the heavy lifting. Dan steered from the bridge. One of our very first Project Board meetings was used as an opportunity to brainstorm and capture points for inclusion in the bid from the collective, and I vociferously spent the session capturing each point and idea on pink post-it notes that were in turn stuck to my office wall. There were dozens of them! It was liberating in turn to pull each post-it back off the wall as the point in question got written up. Alison was on point to keep everyone on task, managing diaries, writing-up agendas, capturing actions, and creating a shared folder in Microsoft Teams as a repository for all the campaign documentation. Many, many more people outside of these semi-formal structures also played a part, and we usually found ourselves pushing on open doors when it came to looking for volunteers.

With structures sorted, and roles and responsibilities agreed, we all put our best foot forward. The game was afoot.

Fourth Time the Charm

Gary Klein is a highly accomplished psychologist from New York. Early in his career, in the 1970s, he worked for the US Air Force, assessing how pilots develop combat expertise at extreme speeds. This fed his interest in understanding how people make life or death decisions under intense time pressure and uncertainty, especially the likes of fighter pilots, firefighters, military generals, and intensive care nurses. His studies led him to pioneer the concept of the "pre-mortem", a term first coined in 1998. A pre-mortem is, in very simple terms, the opposite of a post-mortem. It is based on what psychologists like Klein call prospective hindsight, a process of imagining that a future scenario, and usually something bad, has already occurred. Evaluating this hypothetical scenario increases our ability to correctly identify, and where necessary act upon, the things that led to it occurring. The model can be applied to hypothetical, yet credible, life and death scenarios; a fire that has claimed multiple lives, a failed military assault, a patient who has died on the operating table. By rewinding the likely chain of events, you can assess where the greatest risks manifested, forensically unpicking all the potential wrong turns and pit falls. Better data can in turn lead to better planning and decision making. The fire was controlled, the military exercise succeeded, and the patient's life was saved. No wonder then that, through his psychological insight approach, Klein was part of a team involved in redesigning the Situation Room at the White House to make it easier for the US President to make the right calls during high-pressure incidents.

Since then, pre-mortems have become a more mainstream project management tool, and the model is directly transferable to the world of proposal writing. It's a simple enough idea. Imagine on the first day of your proposal campaign that it is, instead, the day that the result of the competition has just been announced. Bad news, you lost! You're gutted. All the hard work and effort that you put in, all those extra hours, it all came to nothing. Inevitable recriminations and finger pointing follows. If only we had done more of this, or if only we had done more of that! And therein lies the lesson. If we believe that, after the fact, doing more of "this" or more of "that" would likely have improved our proposal's chances of success, why don't we plan for that in advance instead? It was questions like these that pre-occupied my thinking at the outset of the Doncaster campaign. If we were going to lose, why might that happen, and how could we stop it from happening? We needed to adopt some of Klein's philosophy and apply some pre-mortem thinking to our campaign.

Insanity is doing the same thing over and over and expecting different results. That witticism is usually attributed to Albert Einstein, albeit opinion is divided as to whether they were in fact his own words. By the by, it's an observation that holds weight. If you don't learn from the experiences of the past and submit a proposal that does little more than recycle past losing content, then the chances are you will end up losing again. In terms of pre-mortem thinking, the obvious starting point was therefore to firstly reflect upon Doncaster's track record in Civic Honours competitions. With three failed city status bids to its name, Doncaster needed to progress from being also-rans to serious contenders. What I quickly learned, however, is that seemingly little had been done in the form of post-mortems, let alone pre-mortems, on prior bids, and there was little intelligence to build from. I don't think this is unique to Doncaster. The sense I get is that most losing towns prefer to quickly brush the result aside and move-on, rather than challenging themselves more critically as to why they lost.

Doncaster's first attempt to attain city status came in the Millennium Grant competition of 2000, swiftly followed by a second attempt in the Golden Jubilee competition in 2002. Despite these competitions being barely 20 years ago, I have not managed to get hold of a copy of either of Doncaster's bids. Current Council colleagues were unable to locate them during the Platinum Jubilee competition, and I have since reached out to the Doncaster Archives & Local Studies Department, but I drew a blank there too. So, I have no actual idea of how Doncaster originally pitched itself back then, or what might be learnt from those bids. That said, the fortunes of these initial forays were not solely a matter of the written applications submitted. The politics of Doncaster from around 1990 to 2010 followed a series of storylines that might have been just as much at home in episodes of *House of Cards* or *The West Wing*. Corruption, foul play, unscrupulous characters, scandals, ineptitudes, and shady goings on; Doncaster had it all! Even if Doncaster had tabled the most persuasively drafted entries, any expectation of civic recognition at that time was the very personification of optimism.

It begins with the "Donnygate" scandal, described by *The Guardian* as 'the worst local government corruption case since the Poulson scandal of the 1970s'[10], where several councillors were caught out with their proverbial snouts in the trough. Operation Danum, the three-year police investigation into the affair, involved over 2,000 interviews, 74 arrests and, in 2002, the conviction for fraud of 21 Doncaster Councillors. Those convicted included Peter Birks, former Chair of the Council's Planning Committee, who received a four-year sentence for accepting bribes from property developer, Alan Hughes, who himself received a five-year sentence. Hughes had bribed Birks with the gift of a Grade II listed farmhouse, valued at the time as being worth £160,000, in return for planning approvals reported to have netted Hughes over £2 million. You couldn't really get a more clichéd example of political sharp practice. Gordon Armitage, a financial adviser to Hughes, was jailed for a year for aiding and abetting corruption. Most of the other convicted Councillors were found guilty of fiddling their expenses. Former Civic Mayor and Deputy Council Leader, Ray Stockhill, was spared prison because of ill health and instead received a suspended two-year sentence. The scandal stigmatised the town and left a long shadow that would not be quickly lifted.

With Tony Blair's New Labour arriving in Downing Street, and a need for Doncaster to clean up its act, a local referendum

---

10   https://www.theguardian.com/society/2002/mar/13/uknews

was held in 2001 which introduced an elected Mayor for the borough for the first time. Doncaster was one of the first authorities to adopt this new system of governance. The elected Mayor would in turn appoint a cabinet of local Councillors, and that system is still in place today. The Labour candidate, Martin Winter, became the first elected Mayor in 2002, and followed this with a second term win in 2005. Winter's time in office was, however, not without its own controversy. In 2009, following serious case reviews of the deaths of seven local children over the preceding five years, the government ordered an independent inquiry into the Council's Children's Services Department. In each child's case it was found that social workers had missed chances to intervene. The most notorious cases included that of Amy Howson who died in 2007. She was just 16 months old when she was killed in the hands of her own father. Then there is the case of the two young brothers living in care in Edlington, who, in 2009, lured two other young boys, aged just 9 and 11, to a secluded area and tortured them for over an hour. One of the young victims came perilously close to losing his life. I will spare you the specific details, but both cases are as horrendous as they are heartbreaking.

Most Councillors believed that Winter should take responsibility for the Children's Services failures, passing a vote of no confidence in his mayoralty in 2008 to that end. Winter, who was also expelled from the Labour Party just before this, instead determined that he would govern as an independent, and soldiered on to the end of his second term in 2009, keeping just three Councillors on side to form his cabinet. Peter Davies of the English Democrats, the right-wing nationalist party, succeeded him in the 2009 election, but Doncaster's local politics were in freefall by then. The first words of the Audit Commission's Corporate Governance Inspection of April 2010 read that 'Doncaster Metropolitan Borough Council is failing'[11]. It goes on to say that 'the desire to pursue longstanding political antagonisms is being given priority over much-needed improvements to services for the public. The people of Doncaster are not well served by their council.' Jo Miller, then deputy CEO at the Local Government Association (LGA), who was seconded to Doncaster as part of the government intervention in 2010, said the Council was perceived to have 'smallpox – nobody would touch it'[12].

So how does this all circle back to Gary Klein and his pre-mortems? Well, for me, I think it highlights the criticality of choosing the right moment to bid for city status. In March 2000 the Home Office leaked a document to journalists in the House of Commons press gallery entitled *Applicants for the Millennium Grant for City Status*, which was less than complimentary about several of the applicants. In a reference to Donnygate, the document noted Doncaster's 'recent controversy over councillor's expenses'[13]. In other words, Doncaster already had

---

11   Corporate Governance Inspection, Doncaster Metropolitan Borough Council, April 2010, Audit Commission

12   Local Government Chronicle, 12th July 2019

13   John Beckett, City Status in the British Isles 1830-2002, Routledge 2005, Page 151

a significant black mark against its name in Whitehall, and its Millennium bid was almost certainly doomed to fail before it was even written. I can't say with any certainty, but it seems likely that Doncaster's copybook was very likely still blotted in 2002 and 2012. The timing of these campaigns simply wasn't right for Doncaster. Other aspirant cities should take heed. If your local authority is stuck in a quagmire of scandal, mismanagement, financial difficulty, or similar woes, then don't get your hopes up to become a city anytime soon.

Jo Miller, who was a plain speaking, lead-from-the-front, reformer, became the new permanent Chief Executive of the Council in 2012. She had said that 'you have to put a lot of heavy tilling into that infertile ground before you can see a flower bloom,' but she was strongly committed to the task. She was less interested in what Doncaster couldn't do or didn't yet have, the institutionalised mantra that had been holding the borough back, as opposed to it becoming a place that was relentlessly focused on making the best of what it has and what it had the opportunity to go for. When Ros Jones became Mayor in 2013, the two of them became a steadfast and formidable team. The Team Doncaster approach was just one of their brainchild ideas, but they changed the mindset within the Council more broadly and cleared out the dead wood. The Council was reprieved from special measures in 2014 following a now glowing report and clean bill of health from the LGA. Politically speaking, and perhaps for the very first time ever, Doncaster was finally a borough that might be worthy of city status. Whilst it probably wasn't recognised at the time, these were all key foundations for our success.

But even if 2021 was, finally, the right time to bid, we still needed the best possible bid. Doncaster's bid for the Diamond Jubilee competition in 2012 was on hand from the Council, so we did have at least one past proposal to review as a starting point. There were a few sensitivities here as some colleagues involved in producing the 2012 bid were still in post at the council in 2021. Imagine a scenario where the manager of a football team is giving a team talk, telling his players to step-up a level and slay the ghosts of past tournament failures, whilst former managers from those tournaments are stood watching on beside him. It would be more than a little awkward, and there were some days during the campaign when I felt a bit like I was treading on eggshells. I have full respect for the efforts and endeavours of all the people behind the Doncaster bids that came before. To win in a competition such as this is far from easy. There was still a sense in some circles that the previous bids had, indeed, been good enough to win, but Doncaster had instead been stitched up by the politics of the time. There must be some truth in that perception, but I don't think it tells the full story. My own sense was that the 2012 bid wasn't quite good enough, notwithstanding all the political hoo-ha, and you can't really dip that truth in sugar to make it more palatable.

The last bid wasn't all bad per se, and I very much doubt it came in at the bottom of the pile. It's a well presented 43-page document, nicely designed, with plenty of photos, and plenty of information about Doncaster as you would expect, but it also had some clear shortfalls. The opening paragraph, for example, set an immediate yet questionable ambition for Doncaster to become a "tourist destination of international significance". Take a moment to digest that. In my lifetime perhaps a handful of cities have made the breakthrough from being places you may never have previously heard of to becoming tourist destinations of genuine international significance. Cities like Abu Dhabi, Bahrain, Shenzhen, and Baku might stake a claim to be on that list. That is heady company for Doncaster to be mixing with. There is nothing wrong with having ambition, but you also must have a grounded sense of your locality and the type of city it has the potential to be. Most cities are not internationally significant, nor do they need to be, nor will they ever be. This was a key issue with the 2012 bid; the Doncaster it presented didn't really know what it wanted to be, apart from it wanting to be a city.

Doncaster's challenging search for an identity is perhaps best typified by its airport, which was originally named Robin Hood Doncaster Sheffield Airport when it opened in 2005. It is probably the most ridiculous and confusing name ever given to an airport, a textbook example of airport naming by committee. Unsurprisingly the name was changed to simply Doncaster Sheffield Airport in 2016 (albeit that name isn't all that much better). Robin Hood gets a mention in the 2012 city status bid, given his cameo in Walter Scott's *Ivanhoe*, but Doncaster's fixation with the famous outlaw, and its ongoing efforts to appropriate the legend, have constantly troubled me. Yes, David of Doncaster was supposedly one of the merry men, Roger of Doncaster (aka Red Roger) was one of

Robin's adversaries, and there are disputed claims that Robin and Marian married in Doncaster. Robin Hood's Well, dated to 1622, is a local landmark standing in a lay-by on the south bound side of the A1 near Adwick-le-Street. Historical? I guess so. Used by Robin Hood as a watering hole? Very doubtful (not least because he's a fictional character). Let's be candid; the legend of Robin Hood squarely and indisputably belongs to the city of Nottingham, not Doncaster. Everyone knows this. In 1952 the 7ft tall bronze statue of Robin Hood was unveiled by the Duchess of Portland beneath Nottingham Castle, which is still today one of that city's most famous landmarks. Robin is heroically sculpted, handsome, bow stretched, taking deadly aim with his arrow, the stuff of legends. Meanwhile in Doncaster, on a roundabout outside of the Doncaster Dome, there is a bedraggled topiary effigy of Robin which, if you look at it closely, kind of mirrors a similar pose. Truth be told it's a bit of a mess. The contrast between the two figures couldn't more strongly underline Nottingham's true claim to the outlaw. To portray Robin Hood as a Doncastrian legend smacks a little of desperation, and he wasn't going to get a mention in Doncaster's latest city status bid on my watch.

Outlaws aside, the 2012 bid had other limitations. Affirmations, key points, words, and phrases that are repeated, can be a strength in a bid, sinking into the subconscious of readers, and sticking. Balanced affirmation can reinforce your sales message, but if you repeat a particular point too many times, it can read as if you are short on ideas, and overly reliant on the same points. For example, The National Association of British

Market Authorities had named Doncaster as having Britain's Best Market in 2011, an accolade with definite city standard credentials, but this honour was milked more than once in the bid, and perhaps more than was strictly necessary. Doncaster's Roman heritage, international airport, and wildlife park were similar topics that the narrative too keenly looped back around on. This was all interspersed with a highly granular level of detail in places that felt a little redundant. There were tables, for example, breaking down population figures for the borough's outlying towns, the numbers of school pupils by educational setting, and the operating revenues of Doncaster's ten largest employers. But there were no data benchmarks though, nothing to give any of this data a city status context, or to compare it to other established cities. They were all just numbers. They added to a sense that the bid was all a bit random, a compendium of facts and figures, as opposed to being a reasoned, structured, and compelling case for city status. There was clear room for improvement.

The bid had a strong emphasis on past historical events, which was a strength, but with many of these pre-dating the reign of Queen Elizabeth II, as opposed to celebrating local events during her Diamond Jubilee reign. A page was dedicated to the topic of Royal Doncaster, with a dozen bullet pointed facts about Doncaster's associations with Kings and Queens, but little explicitly about Queen Elizabeth II. For example, did you know that King Charles I planted a pear tree in the garden of what is now Doncaster's Tourist Information Centre in 1614? Yes, it's both a royal and historical fact but arguably lacking a little in the "so what?" department. A further claim related to Richard Montagu-Douglas-Scott, the 10th Duke of Buccleuch (pronounced Buck-Loo), and who also holds the inherited title of the Earl of Doncaster (amongst several other titles). Well, his son briefly served as a First Page of Honour to the Queen in the 1990s which, on face value, sounds like a worthy point. The First Page of Honour is a ceremonial role, typically fulfilled by young boys of noble bloodlines, attending occasions such as the State Opening of Parliament to carry the train of the monarch's robes. But, despite his title, the current Earl of Doncaster was born in Edinburgh and lives at Scotland's imposing Drumlanrig Castle, some 200 miles away. As far as I can tell, neither he nor his son have spent much meaningful time in Doncaster (a bit like Prince Harry, the current Duke of Sussex, preferring to live in California). As with King Charles I and his pear tree, the substance of the connection between Doncaster and royalty felt a little tenuous. Most people in Doncaster think of the Earl of Doncaster as the swanky, four-star art-deco hotel of that name on Bennetthorpe near the city centre. In contrast, I doubt many realise that there still is an actual living, breathing Earl of Doncaster, or would necessarily recognise him if they ever met him.

When you add all these little points together, Doncaster's 2012 bid simply didn't quite have it. It was a bit like Cyprus' record of 34 consecutive losing entries in the Eurovision Song Contest; the melodies were pleasant enough, often a toe-tapping blend of Mediterranean folk music and high octane Europop, and the persistence was more than admirable, but the songs were never quite good enough to win. Good enough was not, however, good enough for Doncaster anymore. We needed a rethink. Suffice to say, swathes of content from the 2012 bid were ditched. The strategy was not simply to recycle what had gone before and hope for the best. We literally started the 2022 bid with a clean, blank piece of paper. In doing so we sourced reams of new information which hadn't been included in 2012, with much of that newly included detail predating the earlier bid. If Doncaster wasn't judged to be fit to be a city in 2012, then the new bid had to unequivocally show that it was ready and worthy now. If the identity of Doncaster had been confusing before, now it needed to be clear, coherent, and credible. If the facts in hand didn't firmly underline Doncaster's city status credentials, then better, stronger facts would be researched and presented. No stone would be left unturned.

Nobody wanted to be stood there when the Platinum Jubilee cities were finally announced and not see Doncaster on that list. Nobody wanted to be stood there with regrets, saying if only we had done a little bit more of this, or a little bit more of that. I may not have carried out a perfectly executed pre-mortem, but Gary Klein's principles of prospective hindsight were still firmly front and centre in my thinking from the outset. We had eyes on the pitfalls of the past, and the means and wherewithal to navigate around them with the new bid. Our game faces were on, and we were in it to win it. There had never been a moment when Doncaster was more deserving of the accolade. The fourth time would be the charm.

Peppa Pig and Dr Who

Whilst I take a political viewpoint on many things, I don't, as a rule, air these opinions publicly. Please don't take that to mean that I am politically apathetic, I can get quite animated about any number of causes and issues. I just choose not to lecture anyone from the pulpit and say, hey, I think this, or I think that, and you should too. This reservedness is partly because, as a small business owner, I don't presume to second guess the political convictions of my customers. I am quite certain that some fall on opposing sides of the political spectrum, and I have no desire to offend any of them. The other main reason I don't air my political opinions is because, quite candidly, I don't think anyone else is interested. I am perplexed by the volume of people who use social media as a personal soapbox, putting the world to rights and deluding themselves into thinking that their political standpoints are somehow more valid and more important that anyone else's. They set out their stance, and rebuff anyone with a conflicting viewpoint, branding them simply as idiots. It's ridiculous. I didn't get involved in the city status bid with any desire to make any political party or politician look good or bad. Doncaster has a Labour Mayor and a Labour led Council, and it has been a privilege to serve them. It would have been an equal privilege had Doncaster been led by the Conservatives or Liberal Democrats, and I would not have given any greater or lesser commitment if this were the case.

It's fair to say too that not everyone gets excited about

politics. They simply aren't enthusiastic about green papers, or select committees, or private member's bills. They don't listen to *Today* on Radio 4, read broadsheet newspapers, or get up early on a Sunday morning to tune in to Laura Kuenssberg. Notably in the last century the turnout at a British General Election has only twice topped 80% (in 1950 and 1951, two of three elections fought between Winston Churchill and Clement Atlee). So, if you are that one person out of every five in Britain who is so turned off by politics that you wilfully never exercise your vote, then you may find this chapter a little dry, for which I apologise. But city status is, if nothing else, a political phenomenon and a battleground upon which elected representatives of all party colours have historically jousted. You may not always remember their names, or the political offices that they held, but politicians are invariably central characters in every city status story. The Platinum Jubilee competition was no exception.

It is a customary expectation for Members of Parliament to back a city status bid from their own constituency. That probably sounds blindingly obvious. MPs are, after all, political figureheads, and recognisable spokespersons for their communities. The prospects of a successful city status campaign would be precarious if the local MP wasn't onboard. That said, I am not always sure that such backing for city status is always delivered with 100% conviction. It's arguably a tricky ask for MPs. On the upside, if the bid wins, they stand to gain the kudos of having helped their constituency to achieve a civic honour, adding to their re-election bankability at the polling box. On the downside, they recognise that not every constituent is necessarily a supporter of city status, and they therefore need to avoid alienating these voters. Most importantly though, they also understand that most city status bids are statistically destined to be unsuccessful, regardless of how deserving the local case may be. In this respect, overtly strong and sustained backing for a losing bid carries a degree of political toxicity. It's a more perilous tightrope for politicians to walk than it may first appear.

Doncaster had three relatively formidable MPs at the time of the Platinum Jubilee campaign. The most recognisable and high profile of these was Ed Miliband, the Labour MP for Doncaster North since 2005. Miliband served as a junior minister in the final years of Tony Blair's government and became a cabinet minister when Gordon Brown moved into 10 Downing Street in 2007. Following Brown's defeat in the 2010 General Election, Miliband himself was elected as party leader, notably defeating his brother David to secure the job. He went on in turn to front Labour's ultimately unsuccessful 2015 General Election campaign, losing to David Cameron's Conservatives. Although that resulted in the end of his party leadership, Miliband nevertheless remains as one of the most recognisable faces in British politics. He continues to serve in the shadow cabinet, with a sphere of influence which extends way beyond Doncaster. If Labour wins the next General Election, don't be surprised to see him back in the cabinet and on the government front benches once again.

Alongside Miliband was another big hitter, Dame Rosie

Winterton, Labour MP for Doncaster Central since 1997. Winterton is a longstanding heavyweight herself within parliamentary circles, serving as both a former Minister of State covering health, local government, and regional development, as a Chief Whip in opposition, and then as Deputy Speaker of the House of Commons. Trying to keep a semblance of order over the proceedings in the Commons is perhaps as hard a political job as they come! Finally, there was Nick Fletcher, the first Conservative MP to be elected in the Don Valley seat. Fletcher was elected in 2019, ousting Caroline Flint, another Labour stalwart, with the Don Valley constituency becoming one of the bricks in Prime Minister Boris Johnson's so called "Blue Wall" across the north of England in his landslide General Election win. Fletcher was the new kid on the block, a disruptor to Labour's historical Feng Shui within the borough.

All three MPs supported the city status bid. That said, I think it is fair to say that Miliband and Winterton were perhaps a little more measured, perhaps a reflection that both were in office at the time of Doncaster's previous unsuccessful attempt in 2012. Indeed, Winterton had served through all three of Doncaster's past failures. Perhaps they both had a sense not to set expectations too high this time around? As Shadow Secretary of State for Climate Change, a cause that he is very evidently invested in, Ed Miliband already had a busy diary and full in-tray. He appeared in a short vox pop social media video to support the campaign, filmed with local people planting trees, blending the focus of his front bench responsibility into his city status message. Miliband is also a great supporter of the arts and, in many respects, his biggest contribution to the campaign came long before the competition even began. He had been instrumental in establishing collaborative partnerships between Doncaster's CAST theatre with both the Royal Ballet and the National Theatre; collaborations which would be name dropped within the bid. Whilst the goal of these partnerships was never about helping Doncaster win city status, they were a gift horse that was not to be looked at in the mouth, and Miliband can take a lot of kudos here. Like Miliband, Winterton also appeared in a similar vox pop video for the campaign, in her case filmed outside the football stadium. They both played their part, and I am sure they would have done more had they been asked. Neither though were perhaps as free to pick up the ball and run with it in quite the same way that Nick Fletcher could, as a parliamentary freshman out to earn his political spurs.

Whilst many Conservative MPs were preoccupied with articulating either their avid support or avid condemnation of Boris Johnson's premiership, Fletcher generally avoided getting embroiled in discussing the eccentricities of the Prime Minister, or over-actively backing potential successors when Johnson's days became clearly numbered. As a new MP, he didn't appear to be looking for the fast track to the front benches. Instead, his endeavours were much more constituency focused. After spending a week in the Commons, he would routinely post social media updates showing himself out and about in his constituency at the weekends and championing local causes. If he could do right by Doncaster then perhaps, at the next election, Doncaster would do right by him. Time will tell if he has made the right call on that. Unlike the two Labour MPs, Fletcher was also the only one of the three to have been born in Doncaster, and to have previously established his own business in the borough: Analogue Electrics - installers of electric vehicle charging stations. Maybe it was this that gave him a subtly different outlook, and a little more skin in the city status game.

As with the other MPs, Fletcher also appeared in a supporting video, but he went further still in championing Doncaster's bid in the House of Commons, raising it the chamber with the then Leader of the House, Jacob Rees-Mogg, in November 2021[14]. 'I am sure the Leader of the House knows that there are three Mansion Houses in the country, in Doncaster, York and London' he began. 'He will also be aware that only one of those places is not a city.' To add some clarity here, Fletcher was referring to Doncaster's civic Mansion House, the former official residence of the Mayor of Doncaster, as opposed to mansion houses in a more literal sense, of which of course there are lots across Britain. Fletcher continued; 'Given that Doncaster is home to a Mansion House, a minster, the Yorkshire Wildlife Park, which I am sure is equally as good a day out as Peppa Pig World, and two castles, at Conisbrough and Tickhill, does he agree that Doncaster surely deserves to be granted city status on its fourth attempt, and its only attempt with a Conservative MP?'

There was some obvious political mischief baked into this statement. Whilst it was true that this was Doncaster's first

---

14   Hansard, Business of the House, Volume 704, 25th November 2021

city status bid with a sitting Conservative MP in the borough, the comment was a shameless play to the gallery and blatant political point scoring. Having a Conservative MP was in many senses of neutral significance. Let's not forget that Doncaster's unsuccessful city status bids in 2000 and 2002 had been submitted by a Labour led Council to a then Labour Government, and having local MPs in government colours back then hadn't held much sway. That said, by virtue of being on the same team, Fletcher had a certain level of access to current ministers which his local Labour counterparts didn't have. As a Blue Wall Tory in a marginal constituency, he was also likely to be able to garner some empathetic support on the Government benches more broadly. On balance, this made him an asset to the campaign, albeit one which Doncaster's Mayor and Labour Council still preferred to keep at an appropriate arm's length.

The reference to Peppa Pig World was a poke about a much-ridiculed speech made by the Prime Minister a few days earlier[15]. 'Yesterday I went, as we all must, to Peppa Pig World,' the PM had announced. 'Hands up if you've been to Peppa Pig World!' he proclaimed, albeit I'm not sure that all that many hands in the audience were raised, even by those who may have actually been to Peppa Pig World. Based on the popular children's cartoon character, the theme park in the New Forest offers a variety of rides and attractions aimed at pre-preschoolers. Johnson had visited with his wife and young son and cited it as an unusual exemplar of 'the power of UK

---

15   https://www.gov.uk/government/speeches/pms-speech-at-the-centre-for-policy-studies-22-november-2021

creativity', with the offbeat endorsement that it was 'very much my kind of place'. With infection rates of the Omicrom variant of the Covid-19 virus spiralling across the UK at that time, and dominating the headlines, the Prime Minister's extensive praise of Peppa Pig came across as being more than a little out of touch. The unforgiving front-page headline on the *Metro* the following day referred to the speech as "A Peppa Pig's Ear", whilst the *Daily Star* asserted that the PM was "A Pork Pie Short of a Picnic".

Of course, Nick Fletcher wasn't expecting Jacob Rees-Mogg to openly agree that Doncaster deserved city status, that wasn't the point of the statement. The intent instead was to get the word out there at the highest levels that Doncaster was in the race and a serious contender. 'So deep was my ignorance that I did not know that there were only three Mansion Houses in the country,' Rees-Mogg had replied with a tone of frivolity, 'So I am grateful for that nugget of information'. He went on, predictably, to iterate the competitiveness of the process and the fact as such that he must remain independent but ended by encouragingly adding that 'if my honourable friend keeps on campaigning, he may well find that there is light at the end of the tunnel.' As equally predictable, Rees-Mogg chose to say nothing in his reply about the relative merits of a day out at Peppa Pig World.

As helpful as Nick Fletcher's statement was intended, it was sadly overshadowed by something of a Peppa Pig World moment of his own. Fletcher is Chair of the All Party Parliamentary Working Group for Issues Concerning Men and Boys. In these liberal times where equality, diversity, and inclusion are so central to the national debate, the topic of men's issues might seem slightly toxic for a white, male, Tory MP to champion, but it's a cause which Fletcher has genuine passion for. And so, on the very same day that he waved the flag for Doncaster's bid through his exchange with Jacob Rees-Mogg, Fletcher also spoke at a Westminster Hall debate to mark International Men's Day[16]. His speech was intended to highlight, amongst other things, the importance of male role models for disadvantaged younger men and boys, emphasising that masculinity was 'something that can be celebrated at times rather than being' as Fletcher perceived 'continually vilified'.

The highlight, or low point, of his speech, depending on which way you look at it, was when he said that: 'Everywhere, not least within the cultural sphere, there seems to be a call from a tiny yet very vocal minority that every male character or good role model must have a female replacement. One only needs to consider the discussions about who will next play the James Bond [succeeding the actor Daniel Craig in the role] to see that. And it is not just James Bond. In recent years, we have seen Doctor Who, the Ghostbusters, Luke Skywalker and The Equalizer all replaced by women, and men are left with the Krays and Tommy Shelby [from the BBC drama *Peaky Blinders*]. Is it any wonder that so many young men are committing crimes?'

For the media, Twitterati, and keyboard warriors in general,

---

16   Hansard, International Men's Day, Volume 704, 25th November 2021

this was like chocolate from heaven. Whilst Nick Fletcher's underlying point about male role models had, in fairness, more than a degree of validity, the tantalising suggestion that the casting of Jodie Whittaker, the first woman to play the lead in *Doctor Who*, was a trigger for men to turn to crime was simply too good to resist. A flippant tweet from legal aficionado The Secret Barrister (@BarristerSecret), which garnered over 11,000 likes, read that: 'As somebody who meets their fair share of young men involved in crime, I am glad this brave MP has revealed an uncomfortable truth. Not a day goes by without reading a Pre-Sentence Report in which a robber / drug dealer / murderer attributes their downfall to women playing Dr Who.' And this was just the tip of the iceberg in terms of the relentless roasting that Fletcher received. Indeed, the episode continues to occupy a large chunk of Fletcher's Wikipedia page, hardly the type of legacy story I imagine he would want to be remembered for.

The Dr Who moment triggered what I can only best describe as a collective sigh of resignation within the campaign team. True, it could have been worse, and there were plenty of MPs getting themselves into all sorts of trouble at the time. But having a local MP score a well-publicised own goal was far from ideal. Fortunately, however, the damage only seemed to last for a single news cycle, then the media swiftly turned their attention to pastures new. And to give Fletcher his due, this mishap didn't deter him from continuing to campaign stridently for both Doncaster's bid for city status as well as for men's rights and issues.

Nick Fletcher was not the only politician who championed a bid in the corridors of power during the campaign. Henry Smith, Conservative MP for Crawley, went one better than Fletcher by asking the Prime Minister directly for support of Crawley's bid in the House of Commons[17]. Boris Johnson gave an appropriately diplomatic reply, stating that, in terms of Crawley's application, he was 'sure there is an excellent case in there somewhere.' North of the border, Emma Harper, the Scottish Nationalist MSP for South Scotland, raised the case for Dumfries in a debate at the Scottish Parliament[18]. Meanwhile, Councillor Mohammed Khan, Leader of Blackburn with Darwen Borough Council, took the opportunity of flagging Blackburn's bid with the Duke of Cambridge when he collected his CBE from the Prince at Windsor Castle[19]. According to Cllr Khan, Prince William said that he was 'interested to hear that we [Blackburn] had entered the competition' and that he had 'promised to keep his fingers crossed for the town.' And, finally, no less than former Prime Minister Theresa May, MP for Maidenhead, came out to publicly back Reading's bid, albeit this was only in the form of a brief comment in the *Maidenhead Advertiser*, so I suspect it passed relatively unnoticed[20].

Doncaster's bid also had political support from other quarters.

---

17   Hansard, Engagements, Volume 703, 17th November 2021

18   https://www.dailyrecord.co.uk/news/local-news/dumfries-city-status-bid-discussed-25815552

19   https://www.bbc.co.uk/news/uk-england-lancashire-59696915

20   https://www.maidenhead-advertiser.co.uk/gallery/maidenhead/173884/city-status-for-reading-can-only-be-a-good-thing-for-windsor-and-maidenhead.html

Notably, there was the support of Dan Jarvis MBE, the Labour MP for Barnsley Central but who was also, and perhaps more importantly, the first elected Metro Mayor for South Yorkshire. Jarvis had held shadow minister positions for the arts and justice and was mooted as a party leadership contender after Ed Miliband lost the 2015 General Election. He is well known as a veteran who served in Northern Ireland, Sierra Leone, Kosovo, Iraq, and Afghanistan. He had also endured the death of his first wife, Caroline, to bowel cancer at the age of just 43. This challenging blend of life experiences had made him a formidable politician and a name to be reckoned with. As with the local Doncaster MPs, he too recorded a video in support of the campaign and was an important advocate. Perhaps most important, however, was the backing of the Yorkshire Leader's Board, from whom Doncaster received an open letter of support. The Yorkshire Leader's Board is, as it sounds, a forum of the civic leadership of all the local authorities making up the Yorkshire & Humberside region. To have the political backing of the whole region as the only candidate authority from Yorkshire & Humberside (or at least so we thought), was something of a coup. It elevated Doncaster above some of the local derbies playing out between other candidates and showed that the weight of a significant swathe of the country was behind us. It only later transpired that our local neighbours Goole were in the race too, and that there had been a bleed of political support from some quarters of North Yorkshire towards the bid from Middlesbrough. This didn't, however, unduly detract from the significance and the gravitas of the backing for Doncaster from the Yorkshire Leader's Board.

Alongside this support, Team Doncaster also wrote letters to several relevant Secretaries of State, covering business, education, health, culture, and levelling-up, following on from our bid submission, to add further momentum to the campaign. Each letter was signed by several Team Doncaster partners, typically both the Chamber and the Council, as well as key employers, NHS partners, charities, and education institutes, as most applicable to each Minister's remit. Each letter, likewise, highlighted aspects of the bid that resonated most closely with their Department's remit. This was one of our many Critical Non-Essentials. I can't tell you what influence these letters had, but even if one was successful in raising an eyebrow of interest from at least one Minister, then it was worthwhile sending.

Middlesbrough claimed its bid had the support of the other local authorities in the North East, and I have no reason to doubt that. Only one other bidder appeared, however, to explicitly secure regional political support, and that was notably one of other winners. Will Quince, the Conservative MP for Colchester, brought together seventeen MPs from across Essex to co-sign a letter of support for Colchester's bid to The Cabinet Office. Signatories included Sir Bernard Jenkin, former Deputy Chair of the Conservatives; Priti Patel, the serving Home Secretary; James Cleverly, Minister of State and former Tory Party Chairman; and Vicky Ford, another Minister of State. This was a weighty endorsement, and every inch as purposeful, if not more so, than the backing that Doncaster had mustered. For me, I felt it was a little awry for the likes of the Home Secretary to be endorsing a constituency other than their own (not that Patel's constituency town of Witham was in the race). You do have to wonder though how such backing might impact on the overall impartiality of the contest (and let's be mindful here that Jacob Rees-Mogg and the Prime Minister himself had publicly emphasised their own impartiality). We may never know quite how any of these political game-plays may have influenced the outcome of the competition, but I think they were important. In the case of Colchester, the letter from the Essex MPs may well have been the extra ingredient that tipped the scales in their favour.

I've banded around the names of a lot of politicians and dignitaries over these past few pages. Nick Fletcher, Ed Miliband, Rosie Winterton, and Dan Jarvis can all take pride in how they contributed to Doncaster's success, and let's not forget Ros Jones too. There is probably, however, only one MP whose name will forever be inseparably linked to city status in the Platinum Jubilee year and who is cemented firmly in the public memory, and he wasn't playing for Team Doncaster. He was without doubt the greatest city status campaigner of them all, albeit his name would dominate the front pages in the saddest of circumstances. This story would be incomplete without remembering him, and the tragedy that would ultimately result in his beloved Southend-on-Sea becoming a city. Please raise your glasses, ladies and gentlemen, and join me in a toast for the legend who is Sir David Amess.

Sir David Amess

On the evening of the 19th of December, the final day of business in the House of Commons before the Christmas recess, David Amess, the MP for Southend West, was speaking at the adjournment debate[21]. Such adjournment debates, a sort of end of term summing up of political business, had become something of a party piece for Amess. He would typically give a set piece speech to the House covering important, but somehow equally trivial, political matters from Southend. On this occasion he used his time to share concerns about, of all things, how irritable and deafening modern-day fireworks had become. 'I cannot recall receiving so many letters about fireworks' he proclaimed. 'On firework night I thought that our house was under siege, as bombs seemed to be exploding everywhere.' He went on to discuss pressing challenges faced by local cocklers in Leigh-on-Sea owing to a new type of algae building up in the Thames estuary, and his uneasiness about a historic church having to be potentially relocated to accommodate developments at Southend's airport. He ended his statement though on a much more festive note, suggesting that 'the best Christmas present for Southend would be the according of city status.' This was not, however, Christmas 2021. This statement was made all the way back in December 2001, fourteen years before his knighthood, and twenty years before his tragic and untimely

---

21   Hansard, Adjournment (Christmas), Vol 377, 19 December 2001

death. It was, I believe, the earliest shout-out in parliament for Southend's campaign for city status attributed to Sir David.

Notwithstanding the sustained enthusiasm of Sir David, I think it would be fair to say that Southend had never at any point been a frontrunner to achieve city status. Don't get me wrong, it's a nice enough place, a seaside resort town in Essex on the cusp of the Thames estuary. There are plenty of sandy beaches, fish and chip shops, and amusement parks which you'd expect from such a destination. With over 180,000 residents, it surprisingly has a bigger population than either of Chelmsford or Colchester, its other two city neighbours, a population which swells even further in the summer months. Southend is also home to London's sixth international airport, which connects to a handful of European destinations, and which briefly appeared in the 1964 movie *Goldfinger*. James Bond, played by Sean Connery, suavely pulls up in his Aston Martin DB5 to chase down the titular villain Auric Goldfinger on to a plane. Most famously, Southend has the longest pleasure pier in the world, stretching for an impressive 1.33 miles into the sea. I briefly visited the pier some years ago, when I was in Southend for a business meeting. I caught the little train that runs the length of the pier, and then walked back, buffeted all the way by the strong sea breeze. You can barely make out the seafront buildings from the end of the pier because you're so far out to sea. It's a long, straight, flat walk back, but pleasantly remarkable in its own unique way. There are some definite city status credentials in the mix of all this, but Southend was nevertheless never talked about in the same circles as Reading or Middlesbrough when it came to picking favourites. In many respects Sir David's personal quest for city status had the hallmarks of one of Southend's fairground sideshows; all good fun, but perhaps never likely to be treated all that seriously.

I didn't really know anything about Sir David Amess at the start of the campaign. As politicians went, he was far from being a household name. He was a tall man, with a fop of wispy greying hair, almost always seen in a smart suit, accompanied by a ready smile. He was a family man with five children, four daughters and a son. Although he attended a private school, he came from a working-class background, and attended the Bournemouth College of Technology (now part of Bournemouth University), a stark contrast to the Harrow, Eton, and Oxbridge path trodden by many of his parliamentary counterparts. He became an MP in 1987, first representing the constituency of Basildon in Essex and then, in 1997, taking the seat of Southend West. His career was mainly spent on the backbenches, sitting on select committees and sponsoring legislation, with a particular passion for animal welfare and environmental issues. He was equally, of course, known within parliament for his relentless pursuit of city status for Southend. His preoccupation with Southend's case, readily dropping it into speeches whenever he could, became an integral aspect of Sir David's political character. Indeed, in December 2019 he even secured an entire adjournment debate in the Commons dedicated exclusively to the subject of Southend's case for city status[22]. No locality had achieved that before or since. 'I know that the House has become tired of hearing me ask for city status for Southend,' he laboured to the benches that day, 'but I am not going to shut up until it happens.' He was true to his word in that respect. Sir David was one of the rarest of things, a politician who was seemingly liked and respected by everyone.

Following Southend's most recent failed bid in 2012, Amess had set a personal target for Southend to achieve success in the Platinum Jubilee competition, way before the competition itself was even confirmed. At the summer adjournment debate in July 2021, Sir David rattled through his usual synopsis of offbeat local issues. He ended that statement to the Commons with six simple words, 'we must make Southend a city'[23]. These were the last words attributed to Sir David in the Hansard, the last recorded words he spoke in an official capacity as an MP in the House of Commons. While he didn't know that at the time, I imagine he may be pleased that those final words were the ones that were perhaps the most important to him.

Friday 15th of October 2021 began with a chilly start in Southend, with a stubborn layer of morning cloud battling to keep the Autumnal sunshine from poking through. Sir David was scheduled to hold a constituency surgery at the hall of Belfairs Methodist Church in Leigh-on-Sea, a fairly innocuous looking building in the leafy residential suburbs of Southend. It was the type of affair that Sir David had undertaken countless

---

22   Hansard, Southend: City Status, Vol 669, 20 December 2019

23   Hansard, Summer Adjournment, Vol 699, 22 July 2021

times before, meeting with local people, listening to their issues and concerns, and taking the temperature of local opinion. Nothing in any way out of the ordinary. All MPs held such surgeries as a matter of course, up and down the country, week-in and week-out. It was possible for residents to book a face-to-face slot with Sir David at his surgery session by emailing his constituency team. One such person who did so for that day was Ali Harbi Ali, who claimed in his correspondence that he was a healthcare worker who was moving to the area. As far as anyone knows, Ali had never met Sir David before. Ali grew up in Croydon with his mother, two sisters and younger brother. His childhood was seemingly a happy one, doing well at school, making friends, and having fun, before his life turned a darker corner. He was not looking to converse with Sir David about local politics that day, despite the pretence of his appointment. He wasn't a healthcare worker. He didn't live in Leigh-on-Sea, or have any plans to move there, but instead had travelled there that morning by train all the way from his actual home in Camden, London. It's a journey that takes well over an hour, and I wonder what was going on inside his head as he sat there amongst the other commuters, knowing what he had set out that day to accomplish. He was wearing a hooded full length khaki coat, black trousers, a patterned shirt, and blue trainers, with a small dark backpack slung over his shoulder. Nothing to make him stand out. Nothing to ring any alarm bells.

Swayed and indoctrinated by Islamic State propaganda since his late teens, Ali only had one true reason to meet Sir David. His visit was the culmination of years of research and planning by a young man with a determination to kill a politician, any politician who had voted in favour of British air strikes in Syria. The Syrian civil war had developed out of the country's Arab Spring protests in 2011 and is estimated to have taken the lives of over half a million people (more than entire population of the borough of Doncaster). Air strikes against the belligerents of the so-called ISIS group (the Islamic State of Iraq and Syria) were approved by the UK government in December 2015. The government motion was passed by 397 votes to 223 after a 10-hour debate. The vote was far from partisan, with a mix of Conservative and Labour MPs voting on both sides. Amess himself had voted against military action in Syria in an earlier vote but had now changed his position. Whilst largely effective, the resultant air strikes in Syria which followed the 2015 vote led to a small, and perhaps inevitable, number of civilian fatalities. The death of any innocent often serves to harden the resolve of one's enemies. By voting in favour of the air strikes, Sir David had effectively signed his own death warrant, and entered a precarious lottery where the odds were 397 to 1 of being selected as Ali's victim. Unluckily and unknowingly for Sir David, his number came up. When Sir David entered the church hall on that fateful day, Ali emerged from the group of constituents who had assembled, brandishing a kitchen knife. He murdered the MP, rapidly inflicting twenty one separate stab wounds. It is hard to imagine a more brutal, violent, and sickening death.

Murders of sitting MPs are thankfully very rare in Britain, albeit there have been six since 1979 which still feels like way too many in a country like Britain. Sir David's death stirred painful memories of the most recent of those murders, that of Jo Cox, the former Labour MP for Batley & Spen in West Yorkshire, who was stabbed and shot in similar circumstances in her constituency in 2016. Her murderer was Thomas Mair, a local man described as a white supremacist. Other extremist attacks have sadly become increasingly commonplace over the past decade. In 2019 former offender Usman Khan attended a conference at Fishmonger's Hall in London, wearing a fake bomb vest. During the event he began indiscriminately stabbing people with knives taped to his wrists, injuring five, killing two. In 2017 a van was driven into pedestrians on London Bridge, with its three occupants then going on a stabbing spree in Borough Market, ultimately killing eight people, and injuring 48 more. In the same year Khalid Masood drove into pedestrians on Westminster Bridge, injuring more than 50, four of them fatally. He crashed the car at the Palace of Westminster, where he then stabbed and killed PC Keith Palmer, an unarmed police officer, before he was himself shot dead. 2017 was also the year that Salman Ramadan Abedi let off his suicide bomb at Ariana Grande's concert in Manchester, leaving 22 dead. Before that, in 2013, Fusilier Lee Rigby was killed near the Royal Artillery Barracks in Woolwich. Rigby's attackers ran him down with a car, and then used knives and, of all things, a cleaver to stab and hack him to death. The murder of Sir David Amess was a grim addition to a sickening list which is already unacceptably too long. It is a list that will, sadly and in all probability, get longer still in the years to come.

On the morning of Sir David's murder, 180 or so miles away, Doncaster's city status Project Board met together online, oblivious to the horrors playing out in Essex. This was the first week proper of the campaign with me as Project Director, so I was keen to make a good impression. Spirits were high and things were moving along nicely. The main order of business was focused on the official public launch of Doncaster's city campaign, to be marked by a special wraparound cover on the *Doncaster Free Press*, due to be published the following Thursday. Steph Cunningham and her team at Doncaster Council had already done the heavy lifting in pulling the design of the four-page wraparound together. The main outstanding task was to circulate, review and firm up the copy, including accompanying press releases to go out to other media channels. All straightforward enough. The meeting went well, and the plan was set. We were all geared for Doncaster to finally go public with its campaign.

By that afternoon the media had started picking up on the story that an MP had been stabbed, but the full details would take a little longer to trickle through. I can remember a few people in our office starting to talk about it during the day, albeit it wasn't initially clear as to whether the MP had died or just been injured. Away from the Civic Honours competition, my business was engaged in drafting some bids to win major employment services contracts for a client in Australia, and the deadline for that was now only a week away. Whilst the news about an attack on an MP was troubling, it wasn't overtly distracting me from all the other things I needed to get done that afternoon. It wasn't until later in the day that the murder of Sir David Amess was publicly confirmed, a suspect was in custody, and police were treating it as a possible terror incident. By the evening it was cemented as the top story of the day, the late news bulletins filled with images of the assemblage of emergency responders and heavily armoured policeman who were keeping watch outside the sleepy little church hall, a line of police tape tethered across the street to cordon off the crime scene. A few bouquets of flowers had already been laid, with close-up footage of the poignant tributes written on their little cards. Library images were shown of Sir David speaking in the Commons, reminding viewers of the jubilant man who had been so callously taken away from them. It was all so terribly sad.

As horrendous though as the events were, their significance to the city status competition hadn't yet fully dawned on anyone. Sir David's lifelong quest for Southend's city status didn't really pick up media traction until the following day. In the rounds of political interviews that followed over that weekend, there was an insatiable momentum building for Southend to now, finally, become a city. Home Secretary Priti Patel described the prospect as being a 'wonderful tribute' to Sir David, whilst Deputy Prime Minister Dominic Raab said there was now a 'certain inevitability' about Southend's campaign[24]. How could anyone argue? If there was ever any politician who had dedicated so much effort and commitment

---

24   https://www.bbc.co.uk/news/uk-england-essex-58957086

to seeing his town achieve city status it was Sir David. The MPs were all correct in their collective stance, there really was no better fitting tribute that could be posthumously awarded in his memory. Southend's credentials as a city didn't matter anymore. It could have been the least deserving candidate in every other respect, but who would deny the town the accolade in the wake of such a barbaric tragedy? Who would even want to bid against them? Had, indeed, fate already deemed that Doncaster's bid was over before it had even started?

I won't deny that I had become increasingly agitated over the weekend. On Friday our city status campaign was ready to launch. By Sunday we didn't know with full certainty if the competition may even now still go ahead. Suffice to say that, by Monday morning, the fallout from the murder of Sir David was now top of all our priorities. Damian Allen, Steph Cunningham, and Lee Tilman at the Council were already discussing whether Doncaster's campaign launch should be delayed. Our original plan to launch that week may now have been interpreted as being somewhat tone death given the circumstances. Dan Fell and I readily backed the decision to delay, but it was hard to judge how long we should delay for. An ill-timed announcement too soon after Sir David's death was one thing, but to launch on the same day as a funeral or memorial service could be just as bad, if not worse. We didn't know exactly how things would play out at this point, and the duration of any delay was always going to be a gamble, but the *Doncaster Free Press* needed some notice and clarity on our plans for the cover wraparound too. As this was a murder inquiry of a high-profile individual, the concluding assumption was that investigative proceedings would take some time, so in the end we delayed the launch of our campaign by a just a week. As it transpired, Sir David's funeral would take place more than a month later at Westminster Cathedral.

On that Monday morning I was equally concerned that, if perceptions mounted that Southend was a done deal for winning city status, we may need to seek further reassurance about the forward process from the Cabinet Office. I shared this concern with both Lee and Dan. Dan initially suggested that we might engage with the other places that had already declared an intent to bid, to collectively endorse Southend for city status as an appropriate tribute. This would effectively be as a "plus one" on the winners' list, but to then let the contest still run as originally intended for everyone else, thereby avoiding lots of people and places tying themselves up in unnecessary knots. It was a good idea. Things though were moving at pace. Just after 3.30 pm that afternoon, just 74 hours after the murder, Boris Johnson confirmed in the Commons that the Queen had already accorded Southend city status as a tribute to Sir David[25]. That addressed one question but left many others unanswered. Was the Civic Honours competition still going ahead? If so, would there be one fewer winner in England now given Southend's recognition? Impatience felt wrong in the circumstances, but these were questions which we could really have done with some answers to. It would take three further long days for the

---

25   Hansard, Tributes to Sir David Amess, Vol 701, 18th October 2001

Cabinet Office to confirm that the award to Southend had been made on an exceptional basis, separate to the Civic Honours competition, which was otherwise unaffected. It was three days during which I felt like I was indefinitely holding my own breath.

The by-election to appoint the MP who would replace the late Sir David Amess was held in February 2022. The Labour Party, Liberal Democrats, Green Party and Reform UK all chose not to field candidates, in a mark of respect. This left a relatively clear path for Conservative candidate Anna Firth to comfortably win the Southend West seat with 12,792 votes in a contest that saw a low turnout of just 24% of voters. There were notably over a thousand spoilt papers, more in number than votes cast for any other candidate, reflecting ongoing disquiet in the wake of the Partygate scandal, which was continuing to rock Downing Street, and gave the Tories a symbolic, if perhaps not all that painful, bloody nose at the ballot box. On the 1st of March, Prince Charles, accompanied by Camilla, presented the Letters Patent of city status to the Mayor of Southend. It was perhaps the most poignant of all the proclamation services. At the same ceremony Sir David was posthumously made the first freeman of the new city of Southend, a bittersweet award accepted on his behalf by his widow, Lady Julia Amess. It was a ceremony that should have been all about hope and happiness for the future, but the absence of Sir David was clearly felt, making it a far more emotive and reflective occasion. In April 2022 Ali Harbi Ali was handed a whole-life sentence at the Old Bailey after being convicted of murdering Sir David Amess and for planning terrorist attacks against other MPs. The jury took just 18 minutes to deliver their guilty verdict. I personally find it hard to feel any emotion aside for pity for him.

Sir David Amess was the epitome of the city status ideal, a man for whom Civic Honours competitions could have been personally invented. I won't deny that he has become something of a personal inspiration. For me this was the hardest chapter of this book to write, in wanting to do appropriate justice to Sir David, his story, and his memory. I've lost count of the sentences that I have written, deleted, and then written again. I hope, in the end, that I got it right. Sir David is the giant of this story upon whose shoulders we are all standing. I am not a religious man, but I genuinely hope that there is a better place that we go to when our lives end, and I hope that Sir David Amess is there. I hope he is at peace with the way his life was cut short, and I hope he is appropriately proud of his achievements and his legacy, not least that his beloved Southend is now a city. I never knew Sir David, but if I could meet him now, I would want to say just one thing. Well done, Sir David. Very well done indeed!

Go For Launch

When Donald Trump launched his bid to become President of the United States in 2015 he did so with all his trademark showmanship and pizazz that we are now all accustomed to. He slowly descended a golden escalator at Trump Tower in New York into a throng of waiting journalists and cameramen, addressing them from a makeshift podium adorned with his now infamous campaign slogan to "Make America Great Again". His launch speech controversially hit out at illegal immigrants crossing the Mexican border, baiting a response from the establishment, and earning him headlines and column inches in the next day's papers. Back then Trump was an outsider, an ego-tripper off the telly with no real political experience. More money than sense, some might say. His odds of winning the presidency were 150/1, with reports that his campaign had hired paid actors to attend the launch to pad out the crowd. But Trump had the people's attention, defying his critics and winning voters over. He saw off stalwart senators Ted Cruz and Marco Rubio to win the Republican nomination, and then infamously defeated Hilary Clinton to win the White House itself. Almost 63 million Americans voted for him. There are all sorts of lessons the world may take away from Trump's campaign, but I'll take just one for now: a strong launch can make a big difference!

Whilst Doncaster's campaign launch had been delayed owing to the murder of Sir David Amess, a lot of hard work and planning had already been done. We wanted to launch

Doncaster's campaign with a fanfare, making a statement to the local community and wider stakeholders, not just that Doncaster's name was officially in the hat, but also that we meant business. We were playing to win! Steph Cunningham and her team at the Council determined a brief for visual identity of the campaign. Her goal was to have a dramatic eye-catching design with instant impact, but one that was equally easy for people to 'get'. It needed a strong strapline, one that was active and not the kind of empty vanilla statement often associated with city status bids. The visual identity needed to be rooted in Doncaster, with vibrant colours, further underlining our worth of the status. The design that rose to the top was a silhouetted skyline of Doncaster landmarks, including the Minster, Frenchgate Shopping Centre, and Consibrough Castle. There was a pit wheel, representing our mining heritage; an airplane, for the airport; a lion, for the wildlife park; and a train, for our history of railway engineering. The signature colour was platinum purple, connecting directly with the jubilee theme. A circular logo version of the skyline motif was also developed.

Our underpinning campaign theme was that Doncaster was already 'a city in all but name' – that was the strapline. To ram that home, Steph's designs included a list of tick boxes which appeared underneath the silhouetted skyline. Vibrant communities – tick; World class sports – tick; Award winning green spaces – tick; History, heritage, and culture – tick. The only box that wasn't ticked was the one that was labelled city status for Doncaster. It was a simple but effective idea. The message to the government, which would be underlined in the bid document itself, was that city status should be little more than a simple formality. We've got all the other stuff, now please put a tick in that last, final box.

Unlike in previous jubilee years, by 2021 social media is now a mainstay of everyday life, and the foundation upon which almost every modern marketing campaign is built. Everyone was on Facebook, Twitter, Instagram, Tik Tok, or LinkedIn, and in many cases all of them. So, we needed a hashtag which supporters could adopt, and which would enable us to track the impact of our communications reach. A campaign slogan of "Going for City Doncaster", which was also a play on "Going for It", was popular with the Project Board, which gave birth to the associated hashtag of #goingforitdn, DN being the postcode prefix for Doncaster. There was a downside that the hashtag didn't include the word Doncaster, as opposed to our rivals who came up with the likes of #BackingBlackburn and #CrawleyCity, albeit the effectiveness of any hashtag stems from core partners getting on board and using it, which we were all committed to. Team Doncaster also commonly uses the hashtag #doncasterisgreat, which generally worked in unison with #goingforitdn for the campaign. Doncaster was perhaps a little more social media savvy than some of the competitors, several of which didn't have much by way of a social media campaign at all. Indeed, a few of our competitors were seemingly flying very low under the radar. I suspect that, in the cases of some of the smaller town council led bids, this was probably down in part to lack of both resources and general digital wherewithal.

Central to the social media strategy was the production

of a series of short vox pop videos featuring local people endorsing the campaign. The goal was to release a new video every weekday from the point of launch to the day that the bid was submitted. Scott McFarlane would film and edit most of these, with the videos then posted and shared by the core Team Doncaster partners across Twitter and Facebook. Dan Fell had advocated that the videos should be spearheaded by ordinary Doncastrians; young people, nurses, teachers, shopworkers, charity volunteers, and such like. This would help position the bid as being driven by the people of Doncaster for the people of Doncaster. Video messages from the mayor and local politicians would then feature at the tail end of the campaign, offering support for the people of Doncaster's bid. That advice wasn't heeded though, and Ros Jones opted to lead on the announcement, featuring in the first video to be released. The mayor's video, as well as one featuring Dan, were followed by others featuring Doncaster Rovers' Chief Executive Gavin Baldwin, Doncaster Belles' player Charlotte Dinsdale, Yorkshire Wildlife Park Chief Executive John Minion, local market trader Matthew Davis, fishmonger Martin Peppard, Director of the CAST theatre Deborah Rees, and St Leger Homes Chief Executive Dave Richmond, to name but a few. We did ultimately capture people from all walks of life, with Scott going out on location around the marketplace, town centre, railway station, and lakeside area. Some interviewees were lined up in advance, whilst others were approached on the street and invited to participate there and then. The result was a healthy library of footage which Scott edited into each short, social media ready video. If we could release a new video every day it would help keep the campaign in the public eye and sustain the campaign's momentum.

Doncaster has quite an impressive diaspora of celebrities who were either born or who have lived here, and many of them were name checked in our bid. The list includes the esteemed soprano singer Lesley Garrett; the alternative indie popstar Yungblud; and *The Way to Amarillo* singer Tony Christie, to name but a few. There was a real hope that we might coax some of these household names to publicly support the bid, adding a splash of razzmatazz, and capturing some headlines. Blackburn's campaign was the real leader here. They managed to collect endorsing soundbite quotes from a host of locally connected celebrities. This included the motorcycle champion Carl Fogarty, the *Doctor Who* actor Matt Smith, England and Blackburn Rovers football legend Alan Shearer, and the former Foreign Secretary Jack Straw. Elsewhere, the actress and national treasure Dame Joanna Lumley had given her public backing to Dumfries, where she has a nearby home. 'Dumfries stole my heart from the first time I wandered in its once-grand, proud streets, and leaned on the bridge and watched the Nith shimmer by,' she said[26]. 'Queen of the South in every way but, maybe now, in need of a new ennoblement. If she became a city, it would be like crowning her again.' Actors can be so maddeningly poetic! Of course, it's not like I've got any celebrities on speed dial on my own phone, from Doncaster or

---

26   https://www.bbc.co.uk/news/uk-scotland-south-scotland-60512419

from anywhere else. We were therefore reliant on the Council's little black book of contacts in reaching out to the great and the good. For whatever reason though, we couldn't replicate the Joanna Lumley effect. I don't know who specifically the Council tried to contact, or whether their earnest attempts to engage were idly batted away by gatekeeping agents and PAs, or maybe Doncaster's celebrities simply weren't as nostalgic about Doncaster as we had hoped. Whatever the reason, Doncaster's luminaries were sadly not as forthcoming as Blackburn's. It was all a bit frustrating. There was, however, one local celebrity who bucked the trend and stepped up to the plate and appeared in one of our videos.

John Parr was born in nearby Worksop in 1952. He plied his trade as a young musician playing northern working men's clubs, moving to Doncaster in the 1970s. He is most famous for his enduring 1985 hit, *St. Elmo's Fire (Man in Motion)*, an uplifting pop rock anthem that reached number 6 in the UK charts, and number 1 on the US Billboard Hot 100. Back in the day, a twelve-and-three-quarters-year-old me bought that song as a 7-inch, 45rpm vinyl single to play on my hand-me-down portable turntable. I can't remember exactly where I bought the record, but it was very probably either Woolworths or Our Price, both located on Week Street in Maidstone. Those shops accounted for most of my modest collection of singles. Older readers will hopefully be thinking that I'm rather cool at this point, whereas younger readers will probably think the last couple of incomprehensible sentences were written in Swahili. For your benefit, I can add that the song recently achieved its

150 millionth stream on Spotify, giving you a sense of its reach and popularity. In 2023 it was used in a Virgin Media television advert, featuring, of all things, hang-gliding goats, exposing it to a whole new audience.

The song, which also earned Parr a Grammy nomination, was originally taken from the film of the same name. *St. Elmo's Fire* was a "Brat Pack" movie, a nickname given to a series of teen-oriented coming-of-age eighties films featuring several common young stars. Regular Brat Packers Emilio Estevez, Rob Lowe, Demi Moore, and Andrew McCarthy all appeared. The term St Elmo's fire relates to a rare, plasma generating weather phenomenon, which looks a little like fork lightning and is named after St. Elmo, the patron saint of sailors. In the film, however, St. Elmo's is the name of the bar at the centre of the story, and the "fire" is the sizzling interplay between the central characters (you can see what they did there). Those expecting more of a meteorological storyline, or a catastrophic inferno, will be sadly disappointed. Having explained all of this, it turns out that the lyrics were not inspired by the film, but they were influenced instead by the story of Rick Hansen, a paraplegic Canadian athlete, who at the time was going around the world in his wheelchair raising awareness for spinal cord injuries. The young, soon-to-be-teenage me, happily singing along to his new record up in his bedroom, was blissfully unaware that the song's backstory was quite so complicated. Today Parr still lives in the village of Sykehouse, to the north of Doncaster. The song became a bit of a city status anthem for me personally. I won't deny that I played it at full blast on the drive into work more than once during the campaign. I could feel *St. Elmo's Fire* burning in me!

Doncaster's city status campaign was officially launched on the 28th of October 2021, with the special wrap around cover for that week's edition of the *Doncaster Free Press* being the focal point. "Back the Bid" was the bold print headline, with a cover photo of St. George's Minster, and Steph's purple city silhouette design filling the lower half of the page. The back cover included a montage of photos including the stadium, railway station, and racecourse. The inside cover carried a personal message from Ros Jones, mirrored on the inside back cover by messages from Dan Fell and Courtney Helsby, one of the council's Youth Advisors. Courtney's inclusion played to the priority for ensuring a prominent youth voice. In the main body of the paper, on pages 10 and 11, there were editorials by Kev Rogers and Liam Hoden, the paper's editor. The piece by Rogers included supportive soundbite quotes from several members of the Project Board, including Cheryl Williams from the Yorkshire Wildlife Park, Karen Staniforth of the Frenchgate Centre, and Suzy Brain-England from the NHS. Rogers was assigned to cover the city status story as we moved ahead. Hoden's piece gave a firm and clear backing from the paper to the campaign. I bought my copy that day from a shop in the town centre, but I got an old round pound coin in my change, the type that is no longer legal tender. I'm not sure if that was deliberate on the shopkeeper's part, but it felt like the kind of swifty that Arkwright from *Open All Hours* might pull, which felt almost fitting.

The launch was also cascaded through the council's email database of residents, alongside the press and social media launch. Further press releases were pushed out to the media at large, and the story was picked up by the BBC and ITV. On the following day, a piece penned by Dan Fell setting out Doncaster's case for city status was published in *The Yorkshire Post*, the main regional newspaper. Alongside the mainstream media, letters to garner support were sent by the Chamber and the Council to local businesses, schools and colleges, charities, and local councillors. The aim was to get the word out, and build support, through all available channels. Ros Jones came up with the idea of having bespoke lapel pin badges that could be worn by key stakeholders to promote the campaign. The production lead time meant that the badges wouldn't be ready for launch day, and it wasn't fully clear whose budget would pay for them but, as the idea had come from Ros, it was always going to happen. The design was based on the circular campaign logo and was surprisingly large; bigger than a fifty pence piece. I grew quite attached to mine, wearing it on every relevant occasion.

All seemed to be going well at first, but by the afternoon of the launch day, problems were already surfacing. A little after 3.00 pm, Steph Cunningham alerted the rest of the Project Board that the launch had 'landed a little awkwardly on social media' and that there had already been around 300 non-supportive public comments. And this was just Day 1! In truth it wasn't all negative. One gracious commentator on Twitter said that 'I'm not taking my new uni lanyard off until Doncaster becomes a city – no town more deserving'. Selective positive statements such as this were, however, drowned out by a far greater wall of dissent. 300 people is way less than one percent of Doncaster's population, but a stack of 300 comments still felt heavy. Personally, I wasn't wholly surprised. In my experience Twitter and Facebook have become little more than petri dishes where negativity exponentially reproduces itself like bacteria, and where too many users typically adopt a pack mentality to ridicule, deride, and frankly slag off anything and everything they see, without care or forethought. I think all the city status candidates experienced a level of social media push-back like this. I would have been far more surprised if most comments had instead shown unflinching support for our campaign.

The campaign team was somewhat wrongfooted by the response and was genuinely expecting a much warmer reception. The Council momentarily pulled back on the handbrake and there was a flurry of discussion as to what to do next. To appease the Facebook faultfinders, it felt to me as if dropping the bid altogether was a potential likelihood. The release of the vox-pop videos was suspended in case they should add any more fuel to the flames. Why needlessly antagonise the community by persevering with a bid which is seemingly so unpopular? Councillors all count on votes to keep their seats, and if public opinion is seemingly blowing one way, it's probably best not to walk against the headwind. No sooner had we overcome the threat of the bid being scuppered by the murder of Sir David Amess, the future of the campaign was on the ropes once again. I wasn't party to all the ins and outs of those conversations; it was ultimately the Council's call. I had to wait impatiently instead, drumming my fingers on my desk. Eventually, however, cool heads prevailed, and we all got back in the saddle.

In the aftermath there was an acceptance that we had got the launch a little wrong. Even though we had anticipated some resistance, we didn't really give enough thought to how we would manage and disarm it. We were distracted by the upside, perceiving that Doncaster would largely be banging the drum and waving the flag behind the campaign. We realised though that we hadn't pre-empted the objections and consider our messaging in response. Some comments posted on social media were from inherent naysayers, being largely petty and needlessly antagonistic, being difficult for the sake of being difficult. Others though had far more substance and posed legitimate questions. Our response was to pull together and publish a list of these most asked questions, alongside our answers; a document referred to as the Q&A Myth Buster. This would be accompanied by a short online survey giving residents an opportunity to share their views; not a referendum per se, but an opportunity for community consultation. This still may not satisfy everyone, but at least everyone would have a reasoned and rationale reply. Having launched on a Thursday, we had the weekend to step back and take a little heat out of the situation. The wave of negative remarks had peaked during those first couple of days. By the time the Q&A Myth Buster was released the following week, and the video releases resumed, things were calmer. There were still occasional negative sideswipes, but the hostility had ebbed, and the hardcore naysayers had turned their attention to other things to gripe about.

The launch communications were seen 167,000 times on social media, and 59,000 people opened the campaign launch e-mail from the Council. Despite the levels of hostility in some quarters, the launch received well over 1,000 "likes" across Twitter and Facebook, and 1,600 hits on the Council's website. Many, many more would have read about it in the papers or on the news apps or would have heard about it on the radio. It may not have been a perfectly smooth launch, but at least we were out on the field of play and in the game. A new vox-pop was released each day, and there was a sustained flurry of social media posting from across our partnership. The objections rumbled on, but with far less volume. The incoming survey feedback suggested a fine balance between those in support of city status and those who were against it, but we always assumed, rightly or wrongly, that the greater silent majority was broadly on side. Just getting this far had felt like something of a monumental task, sapping our energy, and beating us down. And this was only the beginning. Our campaign was live, but we still had an awfully long way to go.

The Necessity of Doing Something

Bidding for city status can be surprisingly divisive. The strength of feeling in Wrexham was so strong that a group of around 100 or so placard waving protesters gathered for a rally at Llwyn Isaf, a small park directly in front of the council's offices, on a crisp Saturday morning in early December 2021. Whilst it was a comparatively small group, it takes a certain depth of feeling to give up a Saturday to rally against city status in person. Passionate speeches, led by Carrie Harper, a local Plaid Cymru councillor, were made from the bandstand. In reply, and perhaps as something of a provocative taunt, the council there went on to include a photo of Llwyn Isaf in their eventual bid submission, albeit without a protester in sight! The rally was accompanied by a local petition against Wrexham's bid, which attracted well over 500 signatures[27]. And before you ask, no, I didn't sign it. Despite being a winning city, Wrexham arguably faced the most publicly visible level of opposition to its bid. Fortunately, Doncaster didn't experience anything like the same; there were no protests or petitions. That said, I can confidently say that there was no entrant who had 100% of the local population behind their bid. Whilst the people of Doncaster hadn't taken to the streets, there was nevertheless still a groundswell of objections and derogative comments tabled via social media.

'So many objections may be made to everything, that nothing

---

27   https://www.change.org/p/wrexham-council-say-no-to-city-status

can overcome them but the necessity of doing something'. That's a quote from Samuel Johnson, the 18th century scholar who is most famous for collating his *Dictionary of the English Language*. Channelling that mantra, I am going to take the liberty of using this chapter to share some of the most common objections that the city status campaign faced. The same were faced by most if not all the bidders. I'll also give you a personal, and primarily Doncaster-centric, reflection on each of these. If you agree with my arguments, then that's great. If you don't, and you have a different view, then that is great too. We don't have to agree on everything or share the exact same perspectives. I hope you will nevertheless feel that I have dealt with each of the most common objections our campaign faced with a fair hand, even if you ultimately disagree with my reasoning and verdicts.

Objection #1: Doncaster's character will change if it becomes a city.

A common objection was the fear that city status may irretrievably and detrimentally change the character of a town. A place described as having small-town charm implies that it is perhaps more traditional and more unassuming than a big city, with a slower pace of life, and a certain old-fashioned quaintness about itself. If you had put down roots in such a place, then suddenly woke up to find yourself living in the hubbub of a big city, that could be more than a tad disorientating. Could the serenity of small-town life suddenly be violated by towering new high rises, congested roads, and a disagreeable influx or metrosexual urbanites all sipping on flat whites with soya milk? Perish the thought! But this was a concern from some quarters of Doncaster, who identify strongly with it being a traditional market town, and who perceived that city status would put this traditional identity in jeopardy.

Perhaps the most well-known example of this effect is the city of Dubai in the United Arab Emirates. Prior to the discovery of its oil reserves in 1966, Dubai was an otherwise small and unremarkable Arabian port, its creek congested by the small wooden fishing dhows which drove its modest economy. It had bustling souks where spices and textiles were enthusiastically traded by the local merchants, and dusty gravel roads, traversed mainly by donkeys and the occasional beaten-up truck, leading out into the expanse of the dessert. Western influences were very few and far between. In the 50 years or so since though, Dubai has undergone an unrecognisable transformation into a modern 21st century megacity, fuelled by its reservoirs of black gold. Its population has spiralled from around 45,000 in 1966 to well over 3 million today, pushing its boundaries out along the coastline of the Persian Gulf to make room. Its glassed wall skyline of imposing skyscrapers is capped by the Burj Khalifa, currently the tallest building in the world, and it has become a sun-soaked playground for the wealthy, full of theme parks, 5 Star hotels, Michelin star restaurants, super yachts, and designer shopping malls. The remnants of the old town are still there, but even that has been reengineered as a heritage district for the tourists, full of authentic modern eateries and boutique art galleries. The old Dubai has perhaps been lost forever, swept away by this glistening, bold new metropolis.

But Dubai's story is far from typical. Most cities don't experience anything like that sort of transformation. Take, by comparison, the picturesque cathedral city of Ely on the banks of the River Ouse in Cambridgeshire. Ely became a city way back in 1109, when King Henry I was on the throne. A little over 900 years later it still only has a limited population of around just 20,000 people. The oldy-world persona of this enchanting little fenland outcrop, with its cobbled lanes and cottages, has gone largely unchanged for almost a millennium. Perhaps the only notable change has come in the city's annual eel throwing competition, the centrepiece of the annual Eel Day celebration, a contest where residents line up to physically sling these snake-like fish as far as they can. The tradition of throwing a living, breathing eel has, however, long been outlawed, and replaced by throwing toy eels instead. But beyond gains in the welfare rights of freshwater marine life, little else has changed. Unlike Dubai, of course, Ely is not sat on a reserve of around four billion barrels of oil. If it had been, it too would probably now be a heavily swollen megacity, but therein lies the important point.

Will Doncaster change as we move ahead? Of course, it will. Britain's population and urban centres are steadily growing, and Doncaster is not immune from that. But it is hard to predict exactly what these changes will look like, and how they will be triggered. Whilst the granting of city status may have a bearing on a place, the character of a city is ultimately driven and shaped by much broader influences. In Dubai's case this was oil. For Doncaster, it was coal. Coal undoubtedly had a far greater impact on the character, composition, and infrastructure of Doncaster than the award of city status is ever likely to. The industrial revolution has been and gone, and Doncaster has had to adapt to the 21st century, and it will have to adapt again and again as our economic and social norms progress into the future.

Objection #2: Doncaster is not worthy of city status!

This objection came up a lot, suggesting that Doncaster was somehow too inferior to deserve city status. As one commentator on Facebook put it, 'the Doncaster Mayor needs to put the whole of the borough in order before trying to make a silk purse out of a sow's ear', whilst another wrote 'I love my hometown, but it needs social uplifting not social status.' A variety of Doncaster's imperfections were underscored by such commentators. They aired perceived concerns about the number of vacant and boarded-up shops as well as local problems with crime, homelessness, begging, and substance misuse, most notably the upsurge of the Class B street drug known as Spice, a synthetic cannabis substitute and formerly a "legal high", which leaves those who smoke it in a paralytic, zombie-like trance. As recently as 2018, *The Daily Mirror* had published striking photos of Doncaster's so called "Spice Heads", troubling images of addicts literally slumped motionless in the street in broad daylight[28]. More than one

---

28   www.mirror.co.uk/news/uk-news/zombie-nation-britain-grip-
       spice-13229735 - 11th September 2018

Facebook commentator claimed that they no longer felt safe when out and about in the town.

Let's not beat around the bush, these are real, current, and difficult issues for Doncaster. These are not things that you can simply ignore in the hope that they will go away by themselves. They cannot simply be swept under the carpet. It would be remiss though to suggest that Doncaster Council has done nothing to try and tackle these problems, both in terms of its town centre investments as well as providing support services for those affected by crime, homelessness, and substance misuse. But these are complicated and time immemorial problems for which there are no quick and easy fixes. It is equally true that problems such as these are not unique to Doncaster. Nearly every big city, and indeed every big town, has similar difficult and complex social challenges. Cities are seldom if ever perfect entities. I'm not saying this to duck the issue. It's not okay for Doncaster to accept these problems as being somehow unsolvable, just because they are also an issue elsewhere. The fact, though, that Doncaster isn't perfect should not be a reason for it not to be a city. If you applied that argument verbatim you would need to strip city status away from Birmingham, Manchester, Glasgow and a host of other places, whose social challenges are no less acute. That would clearly be a nonsense.

There is also a chicken and egg factor here too. Some Facebook objectors took a view that the council needed to sort out these social problems first, and only then consider putting the borough forward for city status after everything had been "fixed". There was little recognition though of the possibility that city status itself might be part of the solution; that by seeking city status the council were working to solve the very same issues that the people wanted them to solve. I don't suggest this flippantly, I'm not so naïve to suggest that city status is a wholesale panacea for curing social deprivation and disadvantage. But, if city status has the potential to accelerate inward investment, economic regeneration, and urban renewal, it may also be able to make a dent in overcoming some of these wider challenges too. It is certainly hard to imagine how, by itself, the granting of city status could explicitly make such problems worse. If every town had to solve these problems before they became a city, we may never have any new British cities ever again!

Objection #3: The whole thing is a waste of public money!

According to a Freedom of Information Act request made in 2012, Doncaster Council spent just £652 (about £800 in 2022 prices) on its previously unsuccessful city status bid, which was, according to that disclosure, fully delivered and resourced by internal council staff[29]. Full marks for austerity, but this really was a limited war chest for a competition of this stature. By comparison, the figure disclosed by the Council for

---

29 www.doncasterfreepress.co.uk/news/this-is-how-much-doncasters-last-bid-for-city-status-cost-in-2012-as-queen-set-to-create-more-cities-next-year-3270584 - 11th June 2021

the 2022 bid was £28,000[30]. In the interests of disclosure, this included the fee paid to my company for our role in producing the bid. £28,000 is, to most people, a lot of money – close to the average annual salary for a full-time worker in the UK in 2021. Some may feel like spending that kind of money on a city status bid was a waste, but let's put it in context. In 2019/20 Doncaster Council managed an annual gross revenue budget of around £500m. In other words, the city status bid accounted for around 0.005% of the Council's typical annual spend. If then, for example, city status results in average house prices increasing by just £1 per property, this alone would increase the net worth of Doncaster by over £100,000. When you take all the potential economic investment and regeneration benefits into account, I would conservatively estimate that Doncaster should receive a substantive return on its investment. That's not based on anything scientific, and I'm not going to speculate on specific figures, but if anyone just happens to be reading this in 2033, I invite you to carry out your own research, and I wager it will prove me right!

But what if Doncaster hadn't won? Losing authorities will point to the civic pride and community participation that their bids delivered despite the outcome, a benefit you can't really put a value on, but clearly modest by comparison to the potential upside of winning. But entering any competition such as this, where there is a cost to play, is a gamble. By comparison, punters bet a total of around £300m on the Grand National

---

30   https://www.doncasterfreepress.co.uk/news/politics/doncaster-council-reveals-cost-of-latest-bid-for-city-status-3521630 - 10th January 2022

each year, and a minimum of around 15 million tickets for the National Lottery Lotto draw are sold each week (with odds of winning the jackpot of around 45 million to one). I suspect that everyone who suggested that the city status bid was a waste of money have played the lottery at least once! Most people, of course, lose. Doncaster Council spent, what is in local authority terms, the price of a lottery ticket, with significantly better odds, and they won. Whilst there may, debatably, have been "better" things that they might have spent £28,000 on, there are plenty of worse things too. A BBC report in May 2022 revealed, for example, that Slough Council, declared bankrupt the year before, had spent £28,000 on 200 indoor plants at its offices which had then been uncared for and left to simply die[31]. Personally, I would rather see local authorities show some aspiration in bidding for accolades such as city status, rather than ill-considered vanity projects such as Slough's.

Objection #4: Cities don't get any more public money than towns.

This is true, and an objection I can't argue with. Winning city status doesn't come with a cash prize or open the door to any direct additional extra funding from Whitehall. There are, of course, a variety of other government regeneration pots that local authorities can bid into, and one is not explicitly dependent on the other. The exception though is Scotland. When a town becomes a city in Scotland it can also join the highly exclusive

---

31   https://www.bbc.co.uk/news/uk-england-berkshire-61617295

Scottish Cities Alliance (SCA). SCA members have access to the £7 million Cities Investment Fund, designed to accelerate cities' access to inward investment by providing foundations to access other funding. A part share of £7 million is arguably small potatoes in terms of public funding, but it is a cash prize, and it more than offsets the price of bidding. A similar fund in England, Wales, and Northern Ireland may stimulate several more bids, and would arguably be, plainly and simply, a good idea. As I've argued above, city status creates the potential of extra investment, but this isn't currently handed over on a plate. There's not much I can really add to that!

Objection #5: This is just an excuse to put Council Tax up!

Doncaster's city status bid was never, at any point, driven by some surreptitious desire for the council to raise Council Tax, the tax levied by local authorities on residents for the services that they provide. The suggestion is somewhat ridiculous as you don't need to be a city to put Council Tax up. In 2022 the highest reported percentage increase in Council Tax, at 9.1%, ironically came in my own birth town of Ashford in Kent[32]. True, there were some notable Council Tax increases in parts of Greater Manchester and Greater London in the same year, but there were also plenty of smaller authorities who significantly increased their Council Tax charges by an average of over

---

32   https://www.cityam.com/revealed-the-uks-biggest-council-tax-increases-with-some-councils-adding-145-this-year-alone/

£100 per household too, including Hyndburn in Lancashire and Broxbourne in Hertfordshire. In other words, if Doncaster wanted to hike up its Council Taxes, it didn't need the excuse of winning city status to do so. Doncaster's Council approved a 3.99% increase in Council Tax in February 2023, a few months after its city status was officially conferred. This was below the 5% rise recommended nationally and left Doncaster's rate still amongst the lowest in Britain. Challenges in local authority spending alongside the UK's ongoing cost of living crisis mean that Council Tax rates will likely creep up for everyone in the coming years. It really does, however, have nothing to do with city status.

But could city status affect other cost living costs? Surprisingly there is little hard data available on this. One exception is a study that showed that residential property gains value faster in cities. That's great news for current homeowners but, of course, probably less welcome for first time buyers. In 2021 GetAgent, a house price comparison site, researched price growth across six localities which had all gained city status since the turn of the millennium: Brighton & Hove, Wolverhampton, Newport, Preston, Chelmsford, and St. Asaph[33]. The study showed that, on average, house price growth across these localities rose by 14.2% in the first year after becoming a city, versus a comparable average house price growth of 11.6% across England and Wales as a whole. The study may have had some limitations in making these comparisons, but there is a valid hypothesis in that city

---

33   https://www.propertyinvestortoday.co.uk/breaking-news/2021/11/city-status-could-bring-about-a-house-price-boost-for-southend?

status can, and probably does, lift property prices more swiftly. Following that logic, other living costs may experience a city upturn effect too, but there are swings and roundabouts here. Say, for example, average taxi fares go up. The downside is that it costs the passenger more, but that increased fare means too that the local taxi driver should be earning more, putting more money back into the local economy.

Objection #6: We should only go ahead if we have a referendum to decide.

The Scottish independence referendum in 2014 and the Brexit referendum in 2016 have a lot to answer for. I don't mean in terms of their impact on Scotland's relationship with the UK, or the UK's relationship with the rest of Europe. I'm talking more specifically about our attitudes towards the principle of democracy. Britain's democracy involves electing officials, our politicians, mayors, and councillors, to make decisions on our behalf. The recent referendums have challenged that principle though, with more and more people believing now that they should have a direct say on more and more things. That might be a purer brand of democracy, but if we are all making decisions on everything, and everything is put to a public vote, then there is a very good chance that our entire decision-making process will grind to a halt. Any fully democratic local referendum on a city status bid would incur a far higher cost to the public than the cost of bidding itself. In the case of Doncaster, we are comfortably talking about a seven-digit figure, maybe even eight. It is totally disproportionate. Some localities have tried to side-step this with polls run over social media or via local newspapers. Such polls are typically not devised by experienced pollsters, they are not democratic, and they are most readily embraced by the most hardened objectors. I am not aware of any such poll that has ever returned a result in favour of city status. Not even close.

A-ha, I hear you say. Isn't that the point? There has never been such a poll result because the people just don't want it! If you paid the money, and had a proper referendum, a democratic consensus would say the same thing! Well, maybe you are right. What I will, however, say is this; in all the places that have become cities, there has never then been a petition or a call for a local referendum to ask for that city status to then be revoked. There are no marches, protests, or riots. Political candidates don't cite it as a campaign issue on the doorstep. Now, you may say that the people are just grinning and bearing it and, again, maybe you are right. But, honestly, I think the more logical reality is that most people who live in big towns are at worst indifferent to them becoming cities, and at best they are enthusiastic, albeit sometimes silent, supporters. Whilst we should rightly respect the views of those who most passionately object, the reality in most cases is that they are probably quite a small, albeit disproportionately loud, minority. I don't think you really need a referendum to work that out.

Objection #7: It's not the right time to be distracted by this.

Almost 900 people died in the borough of Doncaster between

January 2020 and June 2021 owing to Covid-19 related reasons. This is a brutally sobering statistic. Some of these people were very elderly, some had underlying health conditions, and more than 1 in 5 died in care homes, but none of that is important. They were all someone's mother or father, husband or wife, brother or sister, or their grandmother or grandfather. They were all people like you and I, and they were, I am sure, all loved by someone. Doncaster was still deeply grieving the loss of these people. Of all the objections to a potential city status bid, the suggestion that it was the right priority at the wrong time was perhaps the hardest to grapple with. Whilst the vaccination programme was turning the tide on the disease, a public health emergency remained. Alongside the hundreds who passed away, there were hundreds more whose health and wellbeing had been, and continued to be, affected by Covid-19. If the Council had any additional bandwidth to spare, then surely it should be focused on this?

If you believe that Doncaster shouldn't have bid for this reason, there is nothing I will say that will convince you otherwise. If the Council had decided not to bid, but to instead maintain an undistracted focus on Covid-19, I don't think anyone would have held it against them. Some towns who might otherwise have bid, but who decided not to, put this at the forefront of their own reasoning. If you lost someone you love to Covid-19, then you have my genuine and sincere sympathy. I would like to believe that most of the local victims of Covid-19 would have wanted the bid to go ahead, but of course I really don't know if that is true. I hope nevertheless that they, and their loved ones, would be proud of what we achieved.

Sensitivity around Covid-19 was never far from the campaign team's thoughts. At the same time, we recognised that the Platinum Jubilee was intended as a much-needed reprieve from the stranglehold that Covid-19 had inflicted on the country, as much as it would be a celebration of the Queen's reign. It was an important steppingstone in helping the country to get "back to normal". The Government, rightly or wrongly, embraced this by instigating the competition in the first place. The competition would go ahead whether Doncaster entered it or not. As I've already discussed, the comparative cost of bidding was modest. The upside of generating some much-needed good news for community was great. The 38 other localities who entered the race recognised this too. As a winning city, it's easier to look back and justify the decision. Had we lost, would people have been less forgiving? Maybe so. But we won, and I think we helped, even if only a little, to put the smile back on Doncaster's face.

The Duck Test

So, this is the fun part, at least for me. This is the chapter where I will share some insight into bid writing as a discipline and the importance of the power of words. To the untrained eye, the differences between how Doncaster's bid was written compared to its rivals may not immediately jump out, but that is the essence of our tradecraft. Proposal writing is ultimately about the art of selling and persuasion. The job of the proposal writer is to convince a buyer to purchase their organisation's goods or services, or in this case, to award their locality city status. Sometimes the messaging may be overt in trying to persuade you ('our city has a bigger and better thingamajig than your city') but often the subtlety of writing and presentation is just as important, if not more so. We don't just want you to agree that Doncaster deserves to be a city, we want you to have a fuzzy warm glow about the whole idea.

Let's start with the essentials. It is a common misperception that proposals must be convoluted, using lots of big fancy words and complex language. In fact, the opposite is true. The average reading age of the UK population is nine years; that is, the average person has achieved the reading ability normally expected of an educated nine-year-old. That may sound terrible, so let me firstly stress that the average educated nine-year-old is a good reader. By the age of three most children already know around 1,000 different words, and they continue to acquire up to 5,000 more words per year during their school years. By age nine, the average child knows approximately 30,000 to 50,000 different words. This is a more than an adequate depth of vocabulary for the typical adult to navigate their way through life. Still, levels of education and socialisation ultimately influence the level of reading we individually achieve, and the types of things we like to read about. *The Guardian*, for example, has a target reading age of approximately fourteen, whilst *The Sun* has a target reading age of approximately eight. This reflects the sociodemographic readership that each paper respectively targets and goes some way to explain why the print edition of *The Sun* outsells *The Guardian* by a ratio of around 10:1. Now, to be clear, I'm not suggesting that proposal evaluators have the reading age of a 9-year-old (well, not all of them), but as a rule most people prefer to read things that are easier rather than harder to digest. In the world of proposal writing the ideal sentence is short, clear, and specific in the point that it is making.

Proposal evaluators are also typically time poor, adding to the importance of keeping the writing simple and easy. There were 39 city status contenders, submitting a combined total of around 700 pages of proposal content. If a single evaluator had to read every bid it would be a hell of a lot of written content to process. The average response was around 8,000 words, which would, generously, take a typical person around at least half an hour to read, line by line, in full, without any breaks. Just to read mind, that excludes any time spent reflecting on, writing notes about, or scoring the answers given. So, it would take in the ballpark of 20 hours, without any breaks, give or take, to read all 38 bids back-to-back, working through them all at a reasonable trot. You could easily double that estimate, and then some, when time for scoring and moderating is added back in. And did I mention the photos? With up to 50 photos per bid, that's a potential 1,950 photographs to look through. An awful lot of churches, castles, stately homes, and public artworks, which must surely all start to blur into one after a while. It would be like your most annoying relative popping around to show you their holiday photos, album after album after album. To digest it all would translate to well over a full working week of someone's time, and that is being very conservative. How might the evaluator's attention hold up? Most bids presented a cycle of similar content; we have a historic building here, or we had a visit from a royal over there. It would be almost forgiveable if a reader was several pages into a proposal, only to forget which specific town or locality he or she was reading about. Strong coffee or, better still, a descent bottle of red wine, might be justifiably called into service.

We applied several presentational features to help readers navigate their way through our proposal. We used platinum purple as the signature colour of Doncaster's campaign for headings, bullet points, and to emphasise key words and phrases in bold font. We used bullet points quite liberally, in setting out each fact and feature covered. With just two exceptions, every paragraph in the proposal was no longer than seven lines, most being shorter still. Key subheadings were set at font size of 14, with the main copy at a font size of 11. We integrated boxes into the draft, where copy appeared on a backdrop fully shaded in purple, to help these sections further stand out, and break up the formatting. One box detailed key dates in the history of Doncaster, another highlighting local celebratory events for the Platinum Jubilee that were already planned, and another covering off details of Doncaster's governance. We added a similarly formatted table detailing Doncaster's main sporting venues and their capacity. For the annex of photos, we added the corresponding map reference to the caption of each shot. Evaluators not only saw a photo of each asset, but they also knew exactly where in the borough that asset was located, and where the photo was taken. We were the only bidder to do this (another Critical Non-Essential). Spacing between paragraphs was minimised, to help maximise the copy, whilst still ensuring clear white space between each point. Critically, all these style points were workable within the constraints of the official template format. We could have done something much more visually glossier, abandoning the template, and painting outside of the lines as some of our competitors did, but striking the balance between visual impact and keeping to the rules was key.

Now let's turn to some more nuanced considerations. The proposal writing community is split in terms of whether the first person or the third person narrative is the best approach for winning bids. It is a topic that is rarely addressed in proposal writing texts, perhaps because the jury is out in terms of what constitutes best practice. Third person advocates (i.e., 'this author writes in the third person') would point to this being a more formal and business-like approach to writing, which minimises ambiguity. The first person, which I personally subscribe to (i.e., 'I write in the first person'), is generally considered to be more conversational and, dare I say, more salesy. I can't say empirically that one approach is right and the other is wrong, but I can say that writing bids in the first person has always served me well and there was never a doubt that I would apply it for the city status bid. But I went further than that though, by writing the bid from the perspective of Doncaster itself, or at very least the people of Doncaster. So, we had phrase like: "we are the gateway to Yorkshire and the North" and "we are a city of interconnected places and communities". Third person purists would challenge this, disputing who exactly is the "we" in these statements, and they would be justified grammatically in doing so. The people of Doncaster are not a gateway in any literal sense. But I would counter that the meaning is not only clear but is baked into the fabric of the language of the entire bid. This was a bid by Doncaster, for Doncaster, from the people of Doncaster. We used the word "we" 72 times and the word "our" 118 times, collectively far more than any of our rivals. It gave the bid a highly personalised tone, leveraging the voice of the people as much as that of the place.

Several rivals wrote their bids firmly in the third person voice, including Coleraine in Northern Ireland and Newport on the Isle of Wight. For me this created a detachment between the writer and the locality, almost as if these bids were written as a report or a dissertation, with the town in question positioned somewhere at arm's length, a thing to be commented upon. This takes nothing away from the factual content, or the underlying case for city status being presented. It just made the narratives slightly dry and procedural. Whilst the difference in words is very subtle, the impact of saying "we deserve this" compared to "the town deserves this" is marked. It builds a deeper, intimate relationship with the reader. Interestingly, most of the Civic Honours bid were written as hybrids between the first and third person, with paragraphs written in both voices. Many leaned towards the formality of the third person but had a splattering of first-person highlights. This included most of the other winners. Others such as Crawley and Blackburn, both more overtly first-person, were unsuccessful. This underlines the point that perceptions on this topic remain highly subjective.

This brings us to The Duck Test. There is a saying in popular culture that goes like this: if it looks like a duck, swims like a duck, and quacks like a duck, then it probably is a duck. In other words, where something is so obvious in its identity, it doesn't need a label to describe itself. It's a simple principle. The Duck Test was something that we applied and adapted to our writing of the city status bid. Put simply, if something looks like a city, sounds like a city, and has the attributes of a city, then it probably is a city. In terms of our bid, there needed to be no doubt for anyone in that they were reading about a city and not a town or any lesser conurbation. This reflected the campaign mantra, in that Doncaster was already a city in all but name, and that the Civic Honours competition presented the opportunity to ratify this status. To achieve this desired effect, we needed to position and affirm Doncaster as a city from the very first page of the bid, all the way through to the very last page.

The Duck Test may have sounded like an obvious bid strategy, but surprisingly it's one that many of our rivals didn't adopt. Whereas we were painting a portrait of Doncaster as a city in waiting, several rivals were painting portraits of towns that were modestly hoping to be raised up to become cities. Again, it's a subtle but critical nuance. This can be most easily illustrated in terms of the frequency of the words "city" and "town" as they appeared in the respective bids. In Doncaster's bid the word "city" appeared 84 times, whereas the word "town" only appeared 19 times. Not only did we use the word "city" more than our rivals, but we were also one of a very small number of bidders who used the word "city" more than we used the word "town", and way out in front in terms of the ratio between the two. Milton Keynes, another winner, was also in that select group who notably used the word "city" more. By comparison, at the other end of the scale, both Dorchester and Ballymena used the word "town" more than 100 times, but the word "city" barely appeared in either bid. Suffice to say, if it looks like a town, sounds like a town, and describes itself as a town, then it probably is just a town.

I must give proper credit here to Paul Bareham from Doncaster Council who, through our sub-group conversations, first latched on to the idea of applying a "city standard" within the narrative. It became a key strategy in developing the content. The idea draws on the successful Marks & Spencer "food porn" TV marketing campaign of 2007. Viewers were presented with images of the most succulent, mouth-watering, gourmet dishes on screen, which left us physically salivating on our sofas, whilst the sultry voice of Irish actress Dervla Kirwan told us 'This is not just food, this is Marks & Spencer food'. Whilst there is no formal definition of what a city is, the concept of a city standard asset was easy enough to grasp, just as easily as a Marks & Spencer signature dish. Such an asset, that you might reasonably expect to find in an established city, should be more scalable, more abundant, and more impressive. The biggest landmarks, biggest museums, biggest cathedrals, and biggest stadiums are all found in cities. Cities typically have more of everything; bigger, higher, busier, and better! In considering which assets and attributes would make the cut for inclusion in the bid, they had to measure up against the principle of this standard. For example, not just a shopping centre, but a city standard shopping centre; not just a sports venue, but a city standard sports venue; not just a public space, but a city standard public space. So on and so forth.

To truly capitalise on the city standard concept, our proposal needed breadth and diversity. For example, where the template asked us to demonstrate Doncaster's record of innovation, we gave more than a dozen varied examples. There were historic examples, such Thomas Crapper, the Doncaster born sanitation engineer, who, in the 19th century, developed the first floating ballcock which are found today in literally every toilet cistern in the world. There were also current examples, such as local engineering firm AgemaSpark, who designed and built parts for the International Space Station, as well as high-precision engine casing components used on a 33-million-mile space mission to Mars. The contrasts of old and new were equally important. We weren't relying solely on bygone events, our claim to cityhood was pertinent, relevant, and sustained over the centuries.

The second tactic was to apply data to quantify our claims wherever we could. For example, we didn't merely say that Doncaster Station is a busy railway interchange on the East Coast Mainline and Trans Pennine Express routes. We added that it had 3,022 scheduled services per week (2019-20), making it Britain's 59th busiest railway station nationally. We referenced that, in 2019-20, the station had 3.94 million passenger entries and exits, 1.7 million passenger interchanges, and 10,812 daily average passenger start/end journey points. We pointed out that Doncaster has direct rail connections with London, Birmingham, Newcastle, Edinburgh, Manchester, Sheffield, Leeds, Bradford, and Hull. We also mentioned that Doncaster has the highest number of train operating companies serving a single station (seven) equalled only by Crewe and Liverpool Lime Street. In other words, we didn't just have a railway station, we had a city standard railway station. We applied this same tactic throughout the bid, quantifying everything that we could, quoting big numbers and, wherever possible, comparing them to like-for-like data from established cities. So, we didn't just have a cinema; we had a city standard multiplex with 11 screens and 1,386 seats. We had more than 30 full size public football pitches, 20 public bowling greens, 16 cricket fields, 12 golf courses, and 3 tennis clubs. We had 5,000 hectares of publicly accessible green spaces, with over 100 public parks and playing fields, as well as 65 woodlands, and 76 allotment sites. We had over 200 play areas, 19 skate parks, 56 multi-use games areas, and 17 outdoor gym areas. Every sentence had to make Doncaster look, feel, and sound like a city. With every number cited we layered in scale and significance across all our assets, but this was a level of detail that barely any of our competitors attempted to offer or consider.

There is an element of gamesmanship here too. For example, part of the bid criteria was to demonstrate the inward volume of commuting to your locality. That's a sensible test; you would expect a city to provide a level of employment to the surrounding communities. Doncaster has a wide labour market catchment area, with around 1.6 million people living within 30 miles of the borough. Before the pandemic, 26,494 people were commuting into Doncaster every day. Notwithstanding the traffic congestion which that generates, it's an impressive number. Of course, what we deliberately omitted from our bid was the number of people commuting out of Doncaster every day. I can't remember the specific number, but if I recall correctly, it was about twice as many, all heading off to Sheffield, Leeds, and similar places. As every good bid writer knows, you can generally pick and choose statistics to endorse the point you want to make. As the 19th century political theorist Henry David Thoreau put it: 'It's not what you look at that matters, it's what you see.'

To further achieve this desired effect, we also left a lot of details out, uncluttering the messaging. It would, for example, be possible to write a whole book about Conisbrough Castle or Brodsworth Hall, but in the bid they were only awarded just a few lines each. The headline details were key, not the minutiae of the backstory. Brodsworth, for example, had many eminent owners and occupants over the centuries, but there was very limited value in attempting to list them all. Many of our rivals fell down rabbit holes here, where they detailed minor historical facts and figures that arguably added little oomph to their cause. The detail is not always necessary and, dare I say, is not always that interesting unless you are a hardcore local history nut. I've not analysed this, but I am confident that Doncaster covered a broader range of stories and examples than most if not all our rivals. We demonstrated breadth and diversity across our history, assets, landmarks, and infrastructure, rapid firing point, after point, after point. With so much collateral to choose from, how could we not be a city?

Good proposal writing is also about tonality, tailoring sentences to demonstrate assertiveness and confidence, as well as aspiring to be engaging and, dare I say, even a little entertaining. Good writing is a hard skill to bottle, but for me it often comes down to choosing a word or a turn of phrase that your reader isn't expecting. For example, Tickhill Castle is owned by the Crown Estate; it was ultimately the property of the Queen. That's kind of interesting, but equally a slightly vanilla point that doesn't unduly stand out (monarch owns castle). To mix things up, we described Queen Elizabeth II as being a Doncaster homeowner, by virtue of her castle, and you can't get a better royal association than that. In my book it can be the little twists like this that can make a bid more conversational and stick a little more firmly in the evaluator's memory. This is the very essence of writing creatively.

From a content perspective, we also aimed to add 21st century relevance and diversity. Whilst, for example, there are no official statistics to record the size of the LGBTQ community, we nevertheless attempted to estimate this for Doncaster (around 4,200 people across the borough). We were the only bidder to do this. Indeed, only 1 in 6 of bidders mentioned the LGBTQ community at all. Fairing a little better, around 1 in 3 bids talked about their disabled communities. Again, Doncaster aimed to go the extra mile by showcasing its disability sports teams and participation initiatives, such as the Club Doncaster Titans. Similarly, only around 1 in 3 bids, including Doncaster, spoke about their apprenticeship community, and students taking non-traditional education pathways. We celebrated our faith groups, our mix of nationalities, and the diversity of languages spoken. At one end of the spectrum, Doncaster has a significant community of around 4,500 Poles, who mostly arrived after Poland joined the EU in 2004, and at the other end it has a small community of around 200 Gurkha families, established since 2000 by ex-servicemen of the Royal Gurkha Rifles Regiment settling locally. We didn't just brag about our diversity; we offered tangible examples of it.

Stories about global warming and the climate emergency have never been too far away from the headlines in recent years. It seemed likely to me that other towns would want to promote themselves as environmental leaders in this context (albeit, once again, hardly any did). There was a delicate line here, as we didn't want to be accused of so called 'greenwashing' our bid, making Doncaster out to be a more environmentally conscious place than it really is. That said, I was surprised to find out that there was a lot more happening on this front than I first thought. Doncaster is, for instance, a leading local authority when it comes to installing solar panelling on its social housing. Doncaster Rovers was the first league club to install solar panels on its stadium and, before it closed, 25% of the energy used at Doncaster Sheffield Airport came from an on-site solar farm. Doncaster's wind-farms collectively have 30 turbines and generate a combined output to power around 40,000 homes every year. Many of the new distribution centres and engineering facilities opening in Doncaster are being built to high standards when it comes to minimising energy wastage and integrating renewables. The borough has even secured net zero funding from the government to manage and restore peatlands to maximise their potential to cleanse greenhouse gases from the atmosphere. This doesn't make Doncaster the greenest place in the UK, but it's not a bad résumé as a start point. More importantly, we ensured that we included all this stuff in our bid.

Much of what I have covered in this chapter is the real sweet spot of bid writing; the subtle nuancing of language that elevates one proposal above another. Billions of pounds of public money is awarded to suppliers every year, based on the comparative strength of written proposals. It is a massive marketplace. Success is obviously linked in part to how good your organisation is at producing the specified gizmo or widget that the government wants to buy. But that's just the half of it.

Much of this spend is decided on how a few pages of writing hang together, and how they sway the civil servants holding the purse strings. With the stakes this high, every word, every statistic, and every articulation counts. Bid writing is sometimes described as a "dark art" and it's easy to understand why. If we are doing our job well, we will have persuaded you that our offer is the best of the bunch, and you will very likely not even realise that we've done that.

Paddington Meets the Queen

Queen Elizabeth II and Paddington Bear, two indisputable national treasures, became enduringly bonded through the Platinum Jubilee when they appeared together in a short sketch broadcast as the opener of *The Party at The Palace*, the showpiece concert staged in front of Buckingham Palace, in June 2022. Paddington is the affable and hapless young bear from darkest Peru, created in 1958 by the children's author Michael Bond, whose adventures bring him to London where he is taken in by the Brown family. I grew up with the Paddington of the 1970s, the original animated BBC children's series immaculately narrated by Michael Hordern, who also provided the voices for all the characters. A much more dynamic, digitally animated version of Paddington, voiced by the actor Ben Whishaw, first came to our cinemas in 2014, and it was this iteration of the loveable character who appeared alongside the Queen. In the sketch the Queen reveals that, like Paddington, she keeps a spare marmalade sandwich close at hand, pulling one from her handbag, whilst Paddington movingly thanks the Queen for 'everything'. It was without doubt a stirring highlight of the Platinum Jubilee celebrations, but this wasn't the first time that Paddington and the Queen had met!

You may be surprised to learn that the very first Paddington Bear soft toys were designed in Doncaster. Shirley Clarkson made them as Christmas presents in 1971 for Joanna and Jeremy, her two children. And before you ask, yes, this is the same

Jeremy Clarkson who would go on to find fame as a presenter of *Top Gear*. Shirley's original Paddington was admired to the extent that she started to make more of them, with Michael Bond himself becoming aware of their growing popularity. Gabrielle Designs, Shirley's business, began at their family home, before relocating to small factory in Adwick-le-Street which became fondly known as The Bear Factory. The business was granted the first ever official Paddington product licence to manufacture and sell the toys in 1972. That's no mean feat when you think these days you can get all manner of Paddington branded goods (lunch boxes, back packs, mugs, pyjamas, etc.,) and there is now even a shop at Paddington Station in London which solely stocks such merchandise. All the Gabrielle bears were made by hand in Doncaster. The company sadly ceased trading in the 1990s, and the factory closed, but there is still a healthy antique market for these original bears. One recently featured on an edition of the BBC's *Antiques Roadshow*. The Victoria & Albert Museum in London lists two Gabrielle bears amongst its own collection; a Paddington Bear, made in 1980, and Paddington's Aunt Lucy, made in 1978. When Queen Elizabeth visited Doncaster's civic Mansion House in 1991, she was presented with two Gabrielle Paddington Bears, one each for Prince William and Prince Harry (then aged 9 and 7). I have no idea where those bears are today, but I am sure that they would be worth an absolute mint! As a 50th birthday present from my wife, I am now also the proud owner of a Gabrielle Paddington as well. You can still buy a Paddington Bear in Doncaster's Tourist Information Centre today, although most likely he would have been made somewhere overseas. But as Paddington himself said in the very first of Michael Bond's books, 'It's nice having a bear about the house.'

I love Doncaster's Paddington Bear story, and I love the fact that Jeremy Clarkson's mum is its central character. It's a story that has relatability on so many levels; you don't need to come from Doncaster to connect with it. Bizarrely, however, it's a story I knew nothing about prior to the city status campaign. This was a personal epiphany for me. Here was this town that I drove in and out of every day, and within it was this amazing story of Queens and bears and television personalities which I had simply never previously come across. And if I didn't know about this story, what other stories didn't I know about? What else was Doncaster keeping a secret from me? These questions evolved into something of an unhealthy personal quest, to amass as many of these quirky stories as I could and play them into the city status bid. The more I looked, the more and more of these stories I found.

Storytelling is important in proposal writing. Every proposal must obey the qualities of good writing: focus, development, unity, coherence, and correctness. Storytelling provides a structure and a flow, handholding the reader through the critical pitch points in a logical, progressive, and navigable order. We don't want our reader to get lost, confused, or simply lose interest. But storytelling is more than that. The sweet spot is when your reader gets fully invested, connecting on a more personal level with the writing. I'm not saying that they need to take your proposal on holiday, and avidly read it on a sun lounger by the pool as if it were the latest bestseller by Richard Osman or Colleen Hoover. If, however, the content is engaging, entertaining, and relatable, then reading it should be, for the lack of a better word, fun. Writing that is enjoyable to read sticks in the memory; we remember our favourite books, not our least favourite. A bad proposition can still therefore win if the proposal is well written, and, vice versa, a good proposition can fail. Good storytelling helps by leaving a memorable trail of little breadcrumbs in the evaluators head, cajoling their mental taste buds, and flattering them to circle back to award us the highest score. This is why evidence, examples, and case studies, all just other ways to describe stories, are so important. And Doncaster has lots of good stories.

So, let me take you to the early nineteenth century, when a Doncaster confectioner named Samuel Parkinson invented a new boiled sweet made from butter, treacle, and brown sugar and decided to call it butterscotch. Initially the sweet was little more than a local treat but then, in 1851, Parkinson shrewdly presented some to Queen Victoria when she visited to open the St Leger festival. The Queen was quite taken by it, and it reportedly became a personal favourite. This led in turn to Parkinson marketing his product as Royal Doncaster Butterscotch. The rest, as they say, is history. Butterscotch is now both an internationally loved boiled sweet, and a widely adapted flavouring used in all manner of foods. Today you can readily buy butterscotch flavoured liqueurs, biscuits, cakes, sauces, and popcorns. Butterscotch flavoured ice cream has become a national desert in India, whilst butterscotch pie has become a popular classic in the midwestern and southern states of the USA. The Americans celebrate both National Butterscotch Brownie Day in May, as well as National Butterscotch Pudding Day in September. Parkinson's business survived in different guises in Doncaster before it eventually closed in the 1970s, but the original recipe is still produced today by another local business in Bawtry, and the legacy of Doncaster's butterscotch is truly global. As well as Paddington Bears, you can also pick up a box of butterscotch at Doncaster's Tourist Information Centre.

If butterscotch isn't your thing, then how about budgerigars? The Budgerigar Society World Show, affectionately known by members as the Club Show, has been held in Doncaster since 1984. In simple terms, it's the equivalent of Crufts, with anywhere between 2,000 and 5,000 of these wonderful, small, colourful chirruping birds competing each year for the coveted prize of Best in Show, or one of the other 90 or so category prizes up for grabs. The Doncaster Dome is transformed for a couple of days each September, with endless rows of shelves and uniform display cages, each hosting a single bird, invariably the result of years, if not decades, of careful breeding. Twice crowned as the world's strongest man, former Olympic shot putter Geoff Capes is a leading budgie breeder and has been a regular celebrity entrant at the show. It's serious stuff, with judges having to pass tests, follow a handbook, and develop a keen eye for comparing the relative merits of each bird. It's an expensive hobby too; keeping, exhibiting, breeding, and maintaining the blood line of these birds is not for the faint hearted. In the cut and thrust world of budgerigar breeding, thefts and, dare I say, assassinations of rival birds are also not unheard of. At the same time there are some concerns for the future of the craft, with the numbers of budgie loving bird fanciers in Britain sadly in steady decline, but I love that this show exists, and I love that it has found a home in Doncaster.

I've mentioned *Open All Hours* already, but it rightly deserves a more detailed mention here. Roy Clarke OBE was born in Austerfield in Doncaster in 1930 (Goole's city status bids have wrongly claimed he was born there; he wasn't, albeit he did live there). Clarke created some of Britain's best loved sitcoms, including *Last of the Summer Wine* and *Keeping Up Appearances*, but it is *Open All Hours* which is most firmly anchored in Doncaster, and a show I remember watching fondly as a child. It is a little slice of pure Yorkshire. The sitcom follows the day-to-day lives of Arkwright, a tight-fisted stuttering shopkeeper, played by Ronnie Barker, and his much belittled and put-upon errand boy Granville, played by David Jason. All the exterior shots of Arkwright's grocer shop were filmed on Lister Avenue in the Doncaster suburb of Balby. In real life the shop is a hair salon. The sitcoms' storylines centred around Arkwright's miserly efforts to make a quick pound, whilst avoiding spending his hard-earned savings, alongside his ill-fated romantic pursuit of Nurse Gladys Emmanuel, played by Linda Baron. Each episode ended with Arkwright stood outside the shop, putting-away and closing-up, accompanied by an inner monologue voice over, usually beginning with him saying 'It's been a funny day...' as he reflected on the latest comings and goings. The show originally ran for 26 episodes in four series between 1976 and 1985, attracting around 17 million viewers per week. Six series of *Still Open All Hours*, a sequel created by Clarke, and with Jason reprising his role as Granville, who has now inherited the little shop, have been made since 2014, all filmed in Doncaster. The original show is a national institution, part of Britain's golden era of sitcoms, not least in its pairing of Barker and Jason, two comedic giants.

RAF Finningley, with its exceptional runway, which is almost two miles long, was known as the home of the 'V' Bomber during the Cold War. Avro Vulcans, Handley Page Victors, and Vickers Valiant squadrons, all with a distinctive V shape, were all stationed there. The Avro Vulcan XH558 Spirit of Great Britain was the first Vulcan B.2 to enter RAF service in 1960 and is today one of the last of these jet-powered delta-winged bombers to still survive. It weighs 37 tonnes and has a wingspan of 30 meters. Let's not dwell too much on the fact that it was originally designed to dispatch weapons of mass destruction (I know, I know), originally nuclear bombs, then latterly adapted to carry a payload of up to 21 high-explosive bombs, each weighing 1,000lbs. From the mid-1960s, the Vulcan's white paint-scheme was replaced by its trademark green and grey camouflage signature, a visible change in tactics from high-level to low-level attack. Whilst the Vulcan was intended primarily as a deterrent, it saw active service during the Falklands War in 1982. Operation Black Buck involved bombing runs made all the way from Ascension Island in the mid-Atlantic, a non-stop flight of 6,600 nautical miles, and

16 hours, to hit targets in the Falklands and then return. They were the longest-ranged bombing raids in history at that time. It must have been terrifying to hear the low whistling roar of their engines, steadily building to a deafening crescendo, as they approached through the clouds over the horizon.

The Vulcan to the Sky Trust, the brainchild of former RAF serviceman Dr Robert Pleming, pioneered a major fundraising and restoration initiative which saw the Spirit of Great Britain return to flight in 2007 after having been grounded for fifteen years. It returned to Doncaster Sheffield Airport, the former site of RAF Finningley, in 2011, and enjoyed a renewed purpose in air displays at home and abroad before being retired again in 2015. I saw it a few times flying over Doncaster. You couldn't really miss it if it was in the sky nearby, it was a head turner, the type of plane you just naturally need to look-up at. With recent uncertainty over the future of the airport, there are question marks as to how long the Vulcan might stay in Doncaster. Having already lost its best-known steam giants, The Flying Scotsman and The Mallard, it would be a huge shame if Doncaster couldn't hold onto this final engineering wonder. I hope we can find a way to keep it here.

Not into airplanes? That's fine, let me flip back then to where this chapter started, and the subject of bears. Not Peruvian bears like Paddington though, but polar bears, for which Doncaster has equally become well known for. The Yorkshire Wildlife Park is the largest centre for polar bears anywhere in the world outside of Canada and is the only place in England where you can see these majestic beasts. There are currently eight polar bears living at the park: mum Flocke (the eldest of the group, born in 2007) and her triplets Indiana, Yuma, and Tala, as well as a further four strapping lads, Nobby, Hamish, Luka, and Sisu. They share a 10-acre reserve, carefully landscaped to reflect the tundra of their native habitat. The park is at the forefront of international conservation, rehabilitation and research efforts working to preserve polar bears, the largest of the land carnivores, weighing in as much as up to 1,500 lbs (you could, in theory, get 14 of them inside a Vulcan's bomb bay), as their habitat in the Artic Circle faces increasing threat from global warming. Indeed, there were suggestions in the city status campaign to refer to Doncaster as the Polar Bear City. I'm not sure that the bears have been here quite long enough yet for that title to be fully deserved, but perhaps one day, who knows? And if you don't happen to like polar bears, the Yorkshire Wildlife Park is home to over 460 other animals across more than 60 different species.

Ten miles or so from the Yorkshire Wildlife Park, on the other side of Doncaster, you come to Conisbrough Castle. The castle is cited as being an inspiration for Sir Walter Scott's classic novel *Ivanhoe,* first published in 1819, which is based in part in and around Doncaster. Scott reportedly wrote the novel whilst staying at the Boat Inn, an oldy-worldly establishment in nearby Sprotbrough, on the bank of the river Don and just a stone's throw from Conisbrough, and where you can still drop in for a pint and a bite to eat today. Ivanhoe, the titular character, is a charismatic twelfth century Saxon knight who falls for childhood sweetheart Rowena, a spirited Norman lady.

The novel is set against a backdrop of feuding and antagonism between the Norman and Saxon circles of nobility at that time, requiring our hero to navigate a series of entanglements with various opponents, including the evil Prince John. After a lot of protracted swordsmanship and skulduggery, Ivanhoe gets the girl, and the bad guys get their comeuppance. It's a weighty affair, spread over three volumes, which includes a cameo appearance by Robin Hood (why can't he just stay put in Nottinghamshire?), as well as a stop off at Conisbrough Castle itself for good measure. The novel has been reprinted and translated countless times, and sold thousands, if not hundreds of thousands of copies. It's been made into a film no less than eight times to date, the most famous of which came in 1952, starring screen legend Elizabeth Taylor and picking up an Oscar nomination for Best Film. It's also been the subject of a long line of television adaptations, with a young Roger Moore playing Ivanhoe in the first of these in 1958, as well as being adapted into half a dozen different operas.

Not all of Doncaster's stories are as upbeat as those which I've described so far, and the borough has seen its fair share of tragedies, many arising from its mines. Between 1912 and 1978 over 190 men lost their lives in pit explosions, earth tremors, shaft falls, and underground derailments. The biggest loss of life was the death of 91 men at the Cadeby Main pit in 1912. That's a tragedy comparable to the 72 who were killed in the Grenfell Tower fire of 2017, or the 97 who died in the Hillsborough Stadium crush of 1989, but Cadeby Main is a disaster that few today may be familiar with. I, for one, was not aware of it. Perhaps that's because it has slipped from living memory into the annals of history, or perhaps it's because it was overshadowed by the story of the Titanic, which had sunk just three months beforehand, with a staggering loss of 1,500 lives. Cadeby Main should, however, be rightly remembered. Early in the morning of 9th of July 2012 a methane and coal dust explosion engulfed the south district of the pit, asphyxiating 35 men, and leaving their scorched bodies in its wake. Three more would die later from their injuries. In the cruellest twist of fate, later that morning, a second explosion killed 53 more men who had been sent below ground as a rescue party. King George V and Queen Mary had visited nearby Conisbrough Castle the day before, witnessed by hundreds of the Cadeby Main miners and their families. Many had taken an unofficial holiday for the royal visit, which meant hundreds fewer than normal would clock on for the fateful night shift that evening. Bizarrely, the royal visit had saved the lives of scores of miners who would have otherwise been in the pit at the time of the first explosion. The death toll could easily have been doubled if not trebled, perhaps giving Cadeby Main greater historical provenance, but for all the wrong reasons! The King and Queen movingly stayed on and paid their respects to the victims at the pit on the evening of the disaster. Perhaps the most surprising aspect of the story is that a permanent local memorial to the victims was only unveiled at the centenary of the disaster, in 2012.

A more recent, but thankfully far less devastating disaster in terms of any loss of life, were the Doncaster floods of 2019. South Yorkshire was hit by severe flooding that November, with a month's worth of rain falling in a single day. The River Don burst its banks, flooding over 700 homes, and requiring the evacuation of over 1000 residents. It's a story that had a stranglehold on the national headlines for several days, not just terms of how the victims were affected, but also in terms of fitness of Britain's flood defences, and the extent to which climate change was driving tragedies such as these. The Environment Agency deployed a legion of pumps in a bid to reduce the floodwater, and an RAF Chinook helicopter was used to carry aggregate to shore-up the banks of local drainage channels. The Prime Minister declared the floods as a national emergency to bolster the financial help available to displaced families. But as distressing as the floods were, they also showcased the spirit and resilience of Doncaster's communities. In just a few days over £300,000 was raised for the relief appeal, with much more donated in terms of food, clothes, and essential items. To thank the people and agencies who helped, the people of Fishlake, one of the villages worst affected, documented their experiences in a special fundraising book (*Flood: The story of a village underwater*). It would take weeks for the water to abate, and the clean-up to be completed. Even Prince Charles, in his final visit to Doncaster before becoming King, came to Fishlake to see the damage first hand and meet those families who had been affected.

There were many other stories and titbits of trivia that found there way into Doncaster's bid. There was the fact that the Duke of Wellington (aka the Iron Duke), victor of the Battle of Waterloo and British Prime Minister, was given the Freedom of the Borough in 1829. Doncaster had also been the birthplace or sometime home of various celebrities and people of historical importance. These included Ted Hughes, Poet Laureate from 1984 to 1998; William Bradford, Mayflower Pilgrim Father and Governor of Plymouth Colony; Dame Diana Rigg, the BAFTA and Emmy Award winning actress, best known for her roles in *The Avengers* and *Game of Thrones*; Donald Pleasance OBE, another BAFTA Award winning actor and seminal Bond villain, with four Tony Award nominations; Donald Watson, founder of The Vegan Society and first to coin the term vegan; and Sir Douglas Bader CBE, the double leg amputee Battle of Britain pilot and disability champion, to list but a few. Doncaster has hosted international fixtures in rugby league, women's six nations rugby union, world title boxing bouts, World Matchplay Snooker, and the Union Cycliste Internationale (UCI) Road World Championships. At one end of the spectrum, Doncaster has produced Chelsea Flower Show Gold Medal Winners and, at the other, it has hosted British Museum Touring Exhibitions featuring works by Picasso and Matisse. The list goes on, and on, and on, and on.

These stories are not just fascinating in themselves, but they were all critical for our bid. Stories make places, they are part of any locality's identity. These were not the only stories that Doncaster had to offer, we also had our share of historic battles, births, and buildings as much as anywhere else, but these stories were amongst the quirkiest and more unusual. I think that's important, as it draws out more of a "I didn't know that before" reaction and a sense that there was perhaps a bit more to Doncaster than many may have realised. We had stories of confectionery, of endangered bears, of budgerigars, of sitcoms, of classic literature, of cuddly toys, of heartbreaking tragedies, and of famous airplanes. These stories were noteworthy for both their variety and their individuality. They caught both the eye and the imagination. A good city status bid needs to stand apart from the crowd and offer something that other places can't. Through our stories we did that, and I think this was central to our success. All these stories contributed to one larger story, Doncaster's story, and that is a story definitely worth telling.

Say Cheese!

Think of a famous photograph. Maybe something like *Lunch atop a Skyscraper,* taken in 1932, the iconic black and white photo featuring eleven ironworkers sitting on a steel beam 850 feet above the ground, on the sixty-ninth floor of the RCA Building in New York. Or perhaps the cover photo of the Beatles' *Abbey Road* album, taken in 1969, featuring the fab four walking single file over a zebra crossing outside of the famous recording studio in West London. Or how about that photo taken on Victory over Japan Day in Times Square in 1945, showing a U.S. Navy sailor in his full-dress uniform and white doughboy hat, passionately kissing a girl, laid back in his embrace, surrounded by jubilant onlookers. Yes, a great photo can stir our emotions, leave a lasting connection, and trigger both the happiest and saddest of emotions. It's easy in many respects to see why they say that a picture can paint a thousand words. That said, as a bid writer, it's not a saying that I personally subscribe to.

Nothing really says a thousand words more so than, well, a thousand actual words. A photograph, a graph, or a chart ordinarily illustrates a singular thing. Take my opening paragraph here. I described three world famous photos, each in a single sentence, and I wager that each time the exact image popped straight into your head. In a similar vein, imagine too if I showed you a photograph of Buckingham Palace as viewed from The Mall. The photo would tell you that Buckingham

Palace is an old house of impressive scale, with lots of windows, decorative columns, a central balcony (well suited for family photoshoots on special occasions), and a flagpole on the roof. But, as extraordinary a building as it is, you can still more or less sum up a photograph of it in a single sentence. It's a very big, old house. If, however, I had a thousand words to tell you about it, roughly around a couple of typed sides of writing, I could provide you with so much more context and detail. I could tell you, for starters, who designed it, what type of stone it is made from, exactly how big its dimensions are, and when it was built. I could tell you the names and functions of some of the rooms behind each window. I could tell you a bit about the Victoria Memorial which stands in front of the Palace, or perhaps something about the King's Guards with their scarlet tunics and bearskin hats who ceremoniously defend it. (Note: I can't actually tell you any of these things, but I could if I were bothered to research them). Sure, I accept that a photograph would give you a far more immediate sense of what Buckingham Palace looks like, but there is so much more to what you are looking at that it doesn't tell you.

In bid writing, and especially for public sector tenders, the specified format which bidders must follow typically includes a mandatory page limit for the answer to each question. With some bids, the inclusion of photographs or other types of graphics is prohibited, full stop. This is becoming increasingly common where bidders are being asked to submit text directly into an online portal or a text box on a templated proposal form. Where they are permitted though, bid writers invariably face a difficult dilemma as to whether to include graphics. A graph, chart or photo will typically take-up several lines of space. Even a small photo may perhaps use up a quarter of a page which might otherwise be used for around, say, 100 to 200 words of copy. The key data contained in a basic, yet space consuming, chart could still instead be described in a short sentence, taking up a fraction of the same space. A chart may be more eye-catching, but a well worded sentence could still do the same job.

Readers of a more kinaesthetic disposition, who might think of themselves as visual literates, may well be silently screaming at the page by now. Yes, I accept that some people, including some bid evaluators, prefer to digest pictorially presented information. They will always prefer colour, shape, form, and design. Brochures for new cars, typically one of the most expensive things that most people ever buy, are ladened with sleek imagery and eye-catching graphics all designed to cajole our visual taste buds. You want me, you deserve me, you would look great driving me, you should buy me! For certain types of selling, visual influence is absolutely the right way to go. But this visual emphasis doesn't always translate in the world of bid writing. To demonstrate my point, the city status bids from Boston, Dudley, Crawley, Middlesbrough, and South Ayrshire were arguably the slickest designed and most visually engaging in the competition, yet they were all unsuccessful. For a diagram or chart to be included in a bid, it really does therefore have to justify the space that it takes up, and ideally add detail and context on multiple levels. In my experience this is rarely the case, which is why I generally avoid including images, charts, and graphs in the bids that I write. To those who may disagree, all I can say in response is that my light-touch philosophy on graphics has historically served me well. In my experience, most bid evaluators prefer depth and detail.

The city status bid was a little different though. Whilst over engineered layouts and graphics weren't called for, the bid format for applications still asked for photos to be included. Specifically, the guidelines asked for: *Up to 50 photographs of permanent features of the area (rather than events or people), with brief captions describing what is shown. The emphasis should be on giving a representative and reasonably comprehensive impression of the area - especially the part that constitutes or would constitute 'the city centre' - rather than photographic artistry.* It seemed at face value like a clear ask, but it still generated a level of debate within our core group in terms of an exact interpretation. Firstly, there were some suggestions that we should incorporate photos into the main body of our response, punctuating the narrative, as well as including the stipulated 50 photographs alongside that. Given my own bid writing philosophy I was against that, as this would steal from the available copy space for our written answers. It might also be perceived as breaking the rules, gaming the format to include more photos than our competitors. Besides, the ability to submit 50 standalone photographs already gave us more than generous scope to present a comprehensive portfolio of imagery of the borough. Some of our rivals nevertheless adopted this strategy. By having a mixture of photos in the main body of the response as well as in the designated photo annex,

Northampton's bid included over 100 photographs, including a montage of images by way of a cover page. Dudley was not too far behind, with 70 distinct photographic images, and South Ayrshire had over 60. Most bidders however played ball and kept to the stipulated limit of 50 photographs in a designated annex. Doncaster followed that line.

Secondly there was a real desire to present photographs of people and events even though the guidance was seemingly steering us away from that. The idea of presenting an image bank of buildings and landmarks, devoid of people, felt wrong. What was a city without its people? Doncaster's people would ultimately be the benefactors of city status. Market traders, shoppers, carers, teachers, football fans, children - they were all central to the identity of Doncaster. Surely their faces should count! Whilst I always felt that the guidance was clear on this point, the Council nevertheless sought clarity from the Cabinet Office. The e-mailed reply received left us in no doubt[34]. 'There is nothing to prevent you from including photographs with people in them, however we would advise the emphasis should be on permanent features as described in the entry guidelines and application form.' That was that then, there would be no people shots in the Doncaster bid.

Again though, several rivals threw caution to the wind. Crawley, for example, included photographs of the Queen herself visiting their town. That seemed like a logical play in many respects, given that the competition was ultimately

---

34   Email from the Cabinet Office to Doncaster Council, 22nd November 2021.

celebrating the jubilee, and Doncaster could have quite easily done the same. In particular, there are various strong images of the Queen visiting Doncaster in 1977, during her Silver Jubilee year. Bangor, the winning city from Northern Ireland, mirrored Crawley by including a photo of a visit from the Queen in their bid. In one respect this showed that the rule not to focus on photos of people wasn't hard and fast, it certainly didn't derail Bangor's prospects, but then again this may have equally depended on the people in question in the photo. It's hard to imagine how the inclusion of an image of Her Majesty herself visiting your town could really count against you.

Some of the photos selected for inclusion by some bidders were strange to say the least. Alcester's bid, for example, included a photo of their local Waitrose supermarket - you won't find any of that Aldi or Lidl riffraff in the finer corners of Warwickshire! Not to be outdone, Warrington, Northampton and Crawley all included a photo of their local Cineworlds – who needs a cathedral when you have a photogenic multiplex? Meanwhile, Ballymena in Northern Ireland included a photo of one of Britain's most common and everyday animals, the grey squirrel – an image which surprisingly didn't make the cut for any of the other bids! No doubt anticipating Ballymena's strategy, the bid from Newport on the Isle of Wight trumped this with an image of the much rarer and locally native red squirrel, surely winning hands down the bragging rights for best squirrel photo.

In literally going from chalk to cheese, Crawley also gave us a brooding black and white photo of homegrown gothic pop band *The Cure*, taken, I imagine, sometime around the height of their fame in the 1980s. The equivalent for Doncaster would have been to include a photo of local *One Direction* boy band star Louis Tomlinson, but I can honestly say that the thought of doing so never crossed our minds – so, apologies to Louis and all the 1D fans out there. Crawley were not, however, alone in playing the celebrity photo card. Dudley included a photo of Sir Lenny Henry, proudly holding up the Black Country's flag, whilst Middlesbrough's bid featured photos of comedian Bob Mortimer as well as the late Brian Clough, the legendary and more than outspoken football manager, wearing a Middlesbrough scarf.

This brings me to Goole. Ah, good old Goole, what can I say? I really don't want to be unduly disparaging about the bids of our competitors, and especially not that of Doncaster's nearest Yorkshire rival, but the bid from Goole included such a bizarre collection of photos that it really would be remiss not to acknowledge it. Their selected images included, of all things, a carved pumpkin, fireworks going off in the night sky, a minibus, a toadstool, a frog, a grasshopper, a dragonfly, a woodpecker, and a butterfly with half of one of its wings missing (and which may in all possibility have been dead). In each case it was hard to know with absolute certainty if each photo had really been taken in Goole. There were more photos which were more obviously specific to Goole, but it really was hard to see beyond these more peculiar inclusions, and so many of them! I'm absolutely intrigued by the decision-making process, if indeed there was one, which determined the selection of such an eclectic, off-the-wall mix of images. I'd love to know how the evaluation panel received them too.

Further afield, the bidders from the overseas territories had a chance to show off the uniqueness of their localities. Whilst several captive zoo animals, including one of Doncaster's polar bears, had appeared in the photos of the UK entrants, Stanley in the Falkland Islands was able to go one better and include photos of native wild sea lions and penguins loitering around the town. Elsewhere, the photo submission from George Town in the Cayman Islands felt more like a luxury Caribbean holiday brochure, showcasing its blue skies, sun-drenched sandy beaches, and abundant palm trees. Perhaps not city standard attributes, but so what?

Whilst it was a first for me to have editorial control over a series of photos to be included in a bid, I nevertheless had a clear idea of how to approach the task. The start point was to devise a long list of sites and assets to potentially include in the submission. Our city standard mindset was front and centre, we needed to create an encyclopaedic photo portfolio of a city, including all the assets you would expect to see, including notable landmarks, sports venues, educational institutes, shopping destinations, places of worship, transport infrastructure, and green spaces. There were some obvious assets which were nailed on in terms of making the cut, such as Doncaster Racecourse, the civic Mansion House, Cusworth Hall, and St. George's Minister. Other sites were more debatable. The list was therefore whittled down through a process of collating votes from five key core group colleagues;

Dan Fell, Lee Tilman, Steph Cunningham, Lorna Reeve, and me. For each suggested asset this panel of "voters" were asked to rate each asset on a scale of 100% Yes, 75% Yes, 50/50, and Probably Not in terms of their respective merits for photographic inclusion. These votes were combined to create a ranking, determining our Top 50. This was not an easy task and, such was the pedigree of local options, the process inevitably resulted in some notable casualties. Bentley Pavilion, The South Yorkshire Aircraft Museum, Doncaster Deaf School, and The Boat Inn in Sprotbrough (where Walter Scott reportedly penned *Ivanhoe*) were amongst the notable local assets that missed out on the final list. There were probably also a few more options that should have at least made it onto the long list. We didn't, for example, consider including a photo of Arkwright's shop from *Open All Hours,* an image that people outside of Doncaster might have readily connected with. Still, we had our list of 50 target photos to attain, and it was a very strong list indeed.

We then come to the sourcing of the actual photographs and the criteria that the selected images had to achieve. Dudley in the West Midlands approached this by inviting residents to submit photos, which seemed like a great way to build active participation in the bid whilst creating a large bank of photos to choose from. An impressive haul of 500 photos from around Dudley were submitted. There was a danger here though that artistic licence might distract from the core purpose of the photo submission. Budding amateur photographers often prioritise creative perspectives, dramatic lighting, and artistic merit.

Consider, by comparison, that you are looking to book a hotel room for the night. You've researched a couple of options, with similar ratings and comparable prices, but which one do you choose? The chances are that an online photo may sway your decision. Thumbnail photos of hotels typically fall into one of two categories; a general exterior shot of the hotel itself, or a shot of the interior of an example hotel room, often centred on the bed. Such photos are typically functional in terms of composition – this is what you get for your money, imagine yourself sleeping here! A good photo may give you a sense that the room is spacious, clean, modern, with good natural light, and that it is neutrally yet tastefully decorated. But occasionally, the photo doesn't tell you much of any use at all, perhaps inexplicably focused on the check-in desk (somewhere you really hope to be spending minimal time), or maybe a close-up of a very specific room feature, such as a discerningly arranged cluster of scatter cushions. Nice to look at, but not all that helpful in weighing up the overall standard and desirability of the room.

I wanted to apply this "hotel thumbnail" yardstick to the photos in the Doncaster bid. This was important to me, as I knew that most evaluators would not be familiar with Doncaster's landmarks, so the images had to do them justice. Imagine, for example, that you had never seen the Statue of Liberty before and were then shown a photograph of just her face. Artistically it may be a great photo, but it would leave a lot of unanswered questions as to what, exactly, the Statue of Liberty is. I therefore had a simple set of rules, albeit mainly framed in my head rather than being written down. Firstly, there had to be zero doubt about what the subject of the photo was. Whether it was a church, or a stadium, or a stately home, this had to be immediately and clearly obvious. No abstract angles or perspectives. Nothing overtly arty. The asset had to neatly fill the frame, with no endless swathes of sky in the background, or rolling lawns in the foreground. Not too close though, the totality of the asset had to be captured. Each photo also had to be of a professional standard, high resolution, strong colours, sharply focused. Then there was the city standard test. Things had to look big, selecting the most imposing angle to enforce a sense of scale, including aerial shots where they gave a better perspective. For example, we included an aerial shot of the Keepmoat Stadium (now known as the Eco Power Stadium), emphasising its 15,000-seater capacity. Blackburn, by comparison, included a dimly lit street level shot of the outer façade of Ewood Park, taken at night, giving no sense of the 31,000 seats on the other side of the wall. Our stadium was half the size, but you wouldn't know that based on our respective photos.

The photos of our landmarks were then presented in a rough order of their strategic and cultural importance. Doncaster doesn't really have a singular standout landmark, so we started with the key buildings in the redeveloped civic and cultural quarter and went from there. Again, for contrast, despite it being Warwick's standout landmark, Warwick Castle was bizarrely only positioned as the 17th photo in their bid. Meanwhile, a photo of Gatwick Airport, by far and away the most important economic asset in Crawley, only appeared as the 49th and penultimate photo in their bid. And just one photo. Madness! For some of our key assets, such as the Mansion House, The Frenchgate Centre, and St George's Minister, we included both an interior and exterior shot to provide extra context. Two photos of the same asset were arguably a luxury, but sometimes a second perspective helps to add important clarity. Our photos would also all be formatted to the same size, two images per portrait page, each presented as a landscaped image, one above the other. This resulted in a professional, harmonious album, a definitive pictorial guide to Doncaster.

As a bid writer you get used to haggling with contributors about a specific turn of phrase or choice of words. Would it sound better if we replaced this word with that word? The photo album for the city status bid was an equal if not greater challenge. Agreeing the list of assets to include was one thing, but agreeing the specific photo of each asset that would ultimately be included was something else again. We were limited in part by the range of photos available to us. The Council had a modest portfolio that we could access, and we supplemented that by purchasing some stock photography. I nevertheless found myself bartering with colleagues over the specific images that would be used. This stemmed from basic subjective preferences when it comes to photography, and in quite a few cases, if I am being honest, there wasn't a huge amount of difference between the photos under consideration. Nevertheless, I was sticking to my guns in terms of my hotel thumbnail criteria.

Not every photo could be provided for by the Council or from stock photography, and Scott McFarlane and I had to go out and take original photos ourselves. I don't profess to be a professional photographer, but I have a pretty good sense of composition, and the photo of one of the courtyard cafés in Bawtry, taken on a horrible wet day, was one of mine! I also took the photo of the Guru Kalgidhar Gurdwara, whilst Scott took the photo of the Sultania Masjid. We wanted to highlight Doncaster's multiculturalism, but the pool of existing photos of Doncaster's mosques and Sikh temples at our disposal was surprisingly poor. Nevertheless, one way or the other, we gathered up good photos of all our target landmarks.

Inevitably I didn't get everything my own way, and there had to be a little give and take (humbug!). For example, there was a late push from the Council to include an image of the Thorne and Hatfield Moors, part of the Humberhead Peatlands in the northwest of the borough. This wasn't an asset that was even on our original long list for consideration! We didn't have a great image of it on hand, and it's a hard asset to really do justice to (it's essentially a big, flat, wetland). I don't really like the photo we ended up using, an image of an elevated wooden viewing platform looking out over said big, flat, wetland. It was a bit nondescript for my tastes. To make room, we axed the proposed image of a former pit wheel from one of the collieries. I had been keen on keeping this but, in fairness, a good pit wheel shot was proving stubborn to source, which made it easier to chop. I also fell on my proverbial sword in agreeing to images of the Potteric Carr Nature Reserve and

Conisbrough Castle, neither of which were my own personal first choices. It may all sound pedantic, but I genuinely believe that our choice of photos made a difference, and that this aspect of our submission was far stronger than that of most, if not all, of our rivals.

The requirement to include a set of photos had been applied in earlier Civic Honours competitions, and I have no doubt that the same will be seen in future competitions, and I really hope future bidders take heed. Regardless of how good your written narrative is, a poor photo submission is probably guaranteed to sink your bid. There is no reason to assume that it isn't just as important as the core written answers and needs to be treated just as seriously. I would go as far as suggesting that several bids seriously undersold their localities with substandard photo submissions. A great photo submission should really be in the gift of every candidate city to create. But if you are struggling with photographs, you are probably going to be even more lost with where we are headed next. You will need a good map!

X Marks the Spot

Ilike maps. I can look at a map for hours, just for fun. I'm sure that probably makes me sound very weird, but it's true. I'm not alone in this regard. In developing the storylines for *The Hobbit* and *The Lord of the Rings*, the author J.R.R. Tolkein is quoted as saying 'I wisely started with a map'. I guess my own affection for maps began when I was in the scouts, going out on hikes, and it was further nurtured when I got into orienteering at school and went on Duke of Edinburgh Award expeditions. I started driving before satnav was a thing, so getting anywhere depended on an ability to follow a map. In my early career I drove a lot, literally all over the country, and the AA road atlas that I kept in my car was in constant use. My wife says that I have a pigeon sense, as in homing pigeon, as I have an ability to successfully find my own way to or from pretty much anywhere, which I put down to all those hours poring over maps and road atlases. I still get lost in maps today (to use an intentional oxymoron), planning running and devising holiday itineraries. I like to get my bearings, knowing where I am going, what I might pass along the way. Ordnance Survey's classic 1:50,000 Landranger maps, with their distinctive fuchsia pink covers, are arguably as much of a British cultural icon as a Mini Cooper or a Wellington boot. I still have a box of them in my attic (maps, not boots), acquired from various trips and adventures over the years. Each one is tattered, dog-eared, and awkwardly refolded, but loved and admired in equal measure.

I hadn't originally planned to dedicate a whole chapter to

maps, but as I started writing about them, the content seemed to naturally evolve. The Civic Honours competition required bidders to submit a one-page map of the locality of their proposed city, with a focus on the city centre. A single page, way less to look at than this chapter I have written talking about it. Aside from the executive summary, it was the shortest component of the response. It would be very easy to conclude that the map wasn't all that important. An annex of sorts, a formality. Hardly a deciding factor. It certainly felt that several bidders saw the requirement in this light. In some cases, the maps presented were simply reproductions of existing local tourism maps or town centre guides. For some, like Alcester in Warwickshire and Peel on the Isle of Mann, you could even see a clear fold mark on the map image, presumably where the original had just been taken off a leaflet rack and stuck under a photo scanner. Peel's map was dated 2009, which may also have qualified it as the oldest (and most out of date) map used in the contest. As you might expect, these types of maps tended to highlight key visitor attractions, and main thoroughfares, but typically little else in terms of core city assets. They tended too to focus on town centres, and central visitor attractions, rather than the totality of the town.

Other candidates used direct reproductions of maps originally produced by the likes of Ordnance Survey or Natural England. These invariably focused on boundaries, land use, and topography, but conversely with less emphasis on pinpointing cultural and heritage assets. These types of maps are routinely used by local authorities in dealing with planning applications and economic regeneration initiatives, meaning that they are readily at hand and familiarly used. Crewe, for example, used a standard, off-the-shelf 1:20,000 black and white Ordnance Survey map of the area, and simply added numbers to it to label key buildings. Northampton did effectively the same thing but didn't go quite as far as Crewe in labelling any of their landmarks, rendering it to be slightly pointless. Whilst maps like these met the requirement of the competition, they were somewhat dull and pedestrian things to look at.

The request for bidders to include a map was important though. First and foremost, the ask was geared to help clarify the exact locality which was asking for city status, to which any Letters Patent may apply. This was easier for localities like Doncaster where the proposed city was co-terminus with the boundaries of the local authority. A map of the city and the local authority area were one and the same thing. In contrast, Bournemouth's map delineated its proposed city boundaries, within the wider Bournemouth, Christchurch & Poole (BCP) Council administrative area. Box ticked very neatly on their part. Not every bidder got it though. Oban, for example, is a town that falls under the much broader geography of Argyll & Bute Council, but their bid omitted to define the boundary of their proposed city at all. Their map instead showed a sub-regional perspective of Argyll & Bute, where the whole town of Oban was effectively just a remote dot on the coastline of the Firth of Lorn. This may sound picky, but if you are going to award city status it's a reasonable ask to know where exactly that city officially starts and ends. The City of Manchester, for example, is indeed (and as its name suggests) a city, whilst Greater Manchester is not. Details are important!

Indeed, the whole business of maps seemed to present a much greater challenge to bidders than you may expect and was one of the most inconsistently interpreted requirements of the whole competition. Medway's bid document, for example, didn't include a map at all. In many competitions an omission like that might be judged to be a non-compliant bid, leading to immediate elimination. The level of detail of what to include on a map was another conundrum. Greenock's map only identified one road, the main A78 which runs east to west through the town and along the Clyde estuary towards Glasgow. If you took the map at face value, you might wrongly conclude that there are no other roads in Greenock at all. Meanwhile, Coleraine's map had dot symbols to mark sites of "accommodation", "entertainment", and "leisure", but without naming or identifying any specific buildings or landmarks.

Not all the maps were left wanting though. Whilst Doncaster may or may not have had the best overall bid in the competition, I must concede that the award for the best map had to go to Milton Keynes. They did, however, have a secret weapon when it comes to cartography. Step forward Sheree Murray, an illustrator who designs bespoke maps for a living. Having graduated from the University of Manchester in 2003, she went off travelling, which in turn fuelled her passion for mapmaking. In 2010 she started her own business, Cute Maps, in Manchester's northern quarter, designing her maps for councils, museums, and other clients. As her business name suggests, her maps are indeed very cute. They include quaint miniaturised hand-drawn pictures of specific buildings, and visual symbolism to identify common points of interest (e.g., little stacks of books to denote libraries, artist's palettes to denote galleries, that kind of thing). Murray creates easy-on-the-eye, crowd pleasing maps, which you might readily hang on your living room wall, but whilst still being accurate, scaled, and navigable. She returned to her hometown of Milton Keynes and designed her signature cute map of the town, which was exhibited in 2017 at the MK50 exhibition to celebrate the town's half century. The map has since been incorporated into public artworks in one of the parks in Milton Keynes. Murray's range has grown to include tea towels, fridge magnets, t-shirts, cushion covers, note cards, and a range of other items all featuring her map designs. And whilst she has drawn maps of various towns and villages, Milton Keynes is still front and centre of it all. It was therefore a proverbial no-brainer for the Milton Keynes campaign to invite her to adapt her designs for their city status bid map.

Murray's map of Milton Keynes is clever as it not only fulfils the requirement of the brief (yes, it's a map) but it makes you naturally want to take a closer look at all her little drawings, and dwell on the page for longer. There are more than 40 different buildings and landmarks illustrated in miniature. There are occasional little red buses drawn on the roads, cows and deer in the green belt, and boats on the canal. Arguably all this detail made the map perhaps a little unnecessarily busy. That said, regardless of the city status credentials of Milton

Keynes, it was an original, innovative, and unique take on the map requirement. You can't really say with any certainty how much of a difference the map made for Milton Keynes, but I am certain it's a highlight that the evaluators would have enjoyed.

So, what about Doncaster? Well, we had a secret weapon of our own too. Whilst we may not have had a professional map illustrator like Sheree Murray on hand, we had somebody just as good. I've already introduced you to my wife, Anne. Being married to a graphic designer is more than fortuitous. There are not many bids that I work on that require the skills of a graphic designer; public sector procurement is typically much more preoccupied with the written word. Every now and then, however, I write a bid that requires a more sophisticated graphic or a bespoke cover. That is when my better half steps up and lends a hand. As with the written content of the city status proposal, the Council were relaxed about my team producing the map, so Anne was enlisted. It was nice for me personally to work with Anne to design the map; we don't get opportunities to work together like that very often. I don't know for certain, but I'm guessing that we made a bit of history together too. I doubt many, if any, other married couples have worked together in producing a winning city status bid. I say "worked together" in a liberal sense, as Anne did all the artwork. My role was more advisory, contributing from the sidelines in terms of what needed to go where.

The requirement to include a map was nothing new. Doncaster's 2012 bid had two maps in it. The first was a 1:14000 Ordnance Survey map showing the "town centre boundary", albeit as far as I can tell the boundary line displayed was completely arbitrary in terms of where the town centre began and end. Design files for the second map of the whole borough, and which had presumably been designed specifically for the bid, had been lost, so it couldn't be used as a start point for a new map. That wasn't the end of the world though, as the old map arguably wasn't at the level that we needed. Yes, it was a map of Doncaster, and it was no worse than some of the maps entered by some of our rivals in the Platinum Jubilee competition, but it could have been so much better. The 2012 map used a base colour of mustard yellow to denote the area of the borough. Yellow is a colour that ordinarily triggers positive emotions, but it's a not a colour you often associate with maps or, indeed, cities. In Anne's words, it made Doncaster appear barren, and almost desert like. Several of Doncaster's assets were then shown as icons in primary red, which contrasted poorly with the yellow. These were labelled with red fonts which similarly weren't easy to read on a yellow background. The railway lines, motorways and main roads were shown, but the motorways were illustrated using disproportionately heavy grey lines which were the first things to grab your attention. The inference was that Doncaster was surrounded by a wide and impenetrable moat of tarmac. More than 30 of Doncaster's outlying towns and villages were named, showing the inclusivity of the borough, but adding a high volume of non-essential text. This may all sound like an overly pedantic critique but, added together, the 2012 map of Doncaster was relatively forgettable. If it were on magazine page in a Sunday supplement, readers would readily flip right past it without second a thought. This is where the small details in a competition like this had to count, the Critical Non-Essentials. Every aspect of the bid had to have impact, including the map.

So, Anne and I set about creating a new map of Doncaster from scratch. I dug out my Ordnance Survey Landranger Map Number 111, covering Sheffield & Doncaster, and used masking tape to fix it to the wall of our home office to act as a reference point. There were a few design parameters we set upon early doors. For starters it seemed logical to create a second smaller map to zoom in on the centre of Doncaster, as an inset to the main map of the whole borough, albeit fitting both maps on a single page to keep within the rules. We weren't the only ones to do this. Colchester and Milton Keynes, the other two winning English bids, both did the same. So did Blackburn, who also produced a commendably well-designed map. Their campaign logo utilised the letter "B" and this was used as the shape of their inset map, a clever touch! The inclusion of an inset map was the smart play. South Ayrshire, for example, covers an area of almost 500 square miles, but their bid map only covered the very centre of the town of Ayr, less than 1% of the total area of their proposed "city". South Ayrshire's other substantive towns, such as Prestwick and Troon, were not mapped at all. In contrast, other bidder's maps presented the totality of the proposed city, with the centre insufficiently detailed and lost in the mix. Neither approach really seemed to do justice to the task.

Striking the right level of detail was key. This began for

us by considering what the purpose of the map really was. It wasn't a map to help hapless day tripper's find their way from the Civic Quarter Car Park to the markets, or to let you know where the nearest public toilet was in case you were caught short, or which stop you needed to wait at to catch the Number 203 bus to Hooton Pagnell. Indeed, the primary purpose of any map, in navigating from A to B, was wholly secondary to this map. The map was similarly never going to be used in a planning application or for any other official council purpose. No, this wasn't a regular map at all. Like everything else about this bid, the point of the map was solely to present Doncaster as a city. You needed to look at the map and immediately say 'yes, that looks exactly like a city'. Think about the reaction you have when you see the London Underground map, or the satellite map image in the opening titles of BBC's *Eastenders,* showing the distinctive unfolding curve of the Thames around the Isle of Dogs. In both cases you implicitly know that you are looking at a city. If you have ever visited New York, you will know too that the city grid street maps of Manhattan Island are similarly iconic. That was the desired effect to aim for. Taking that as our brief, we started with a blank piece of paper, and went from there.

Anne, sat at her Apple Mac and applied some graphic-design know-how that I won't profess to have fully followed, using various maps sourced online to build up the detail. Effectively she traced levels of information into the new design, one on top of the other. The boundary of the borough was the start point. This had a shadow effect at the boundary edge, making it look like Doncaster had been dug up from the rest of England, and served up by itself as an individual portion. Rather than yellow, Anne used a pastel green as the base colour, reflecting the fact that the borough is primarily rural. Then the primary main roads, railway lines, railway stations, motorways, and waterways were mapped on. Where the motorways reached the borough boundary, there was an arrow added to show the onward direction (i.e., to Leeds, to London, to Grimsby, to Hull, and to Sheffield). This helped to give context for the less familiar as to where Doncaster is exactly. Alongside the town of Doncaster itself, the core conurbations in the borough were mapped and coloured a pale brown, representing built up areas. This was far more selective than the 2012 map, incorporating only around half as many place names, such as Bawtry, Thorne, Mexborough and Armthorpe. The inset of central Doncaster used grey as the base colour, helping delineate the urbanisation of the centre, with more minor roads added. Country parks and woodlands were mapped in a darker green, and the Trans Pennine Trail was shown as a dotted line. Only one icon symbol was used, the silhouette of a plane to mark the location of the airport.

As I've already mentioned, we were the only bidders to align our map with our photo submission. Each of the photographs had a corresponding, numbered dot added to the map to show the location of the asset on view. Some extra unphotographed landmarks were also added, such as Doncaster's five hospitals, giving us a resultant key of 66 different points of interest. Each category of numbered dots was colour coded. We had purple dots for civic, cultural, and heritage sites; turquoise for main educational sites; yellow for sports venues; brown for visitor and leisure attractions, and so on and so forth. This meant that the map had a lot of detail (again, more than many rivals), but did not look overly cluttered. The colour coded dots also helped to visually illustrate the depth and diversity of Doncaster's assets. Anne and I spent several hours over several days working through all this, making sure we had all the right dots, and that they were positioned more-or-less in the right place. It was less about cartography, and more about creating an informative picture. The numbering system worked sequentially through one colour category at a time, and then in alphabetical order within each category (so, in the purple category, dot one was for Brodsworth Hall, dot two was for the CAST Theatre, and so on). Occasionally I would realise that an extra dot might need to be added. Anne frowned at me and shared some terse words each time this happened, as it invariably meant she would have to spend time renumbering at least half of the other dots too (how we laugh about it now!).

Whilst there was a lot of debate and comments made in terms of the written content of Doncaster's bid, and the selection of the accompanying photographs, I can't remember any specific feedback given in relation to the draft map. That either means we got it bang on at the first attempt or perhaps, even within our own campaign team, people didn't view it as importantly as other aspects of the bid. I suspect perhaps a little of both. The finished product looked modern, clean, and informative; an integral part of the bid, rather than a last-minute bolt-on. I like to think of it as being something of a modern classic (not just because it was created by my wife), and that it had some modicum of influence in the success of the bid. After all, why ask for a map to be included at all if it didn't have some form of bearing? It certainly gives Sheree Murray a run for her money, and perhaps one day, just like her Cute Maps of Milton Keynes, it will also appear on a souvenir tea towel.

Petra & The Lionesses

There is never an ideal time to book a holiday when you are a bid writer. You set out with the best of intentions and second guess when things may be a little quieter, a month when there may be fewer bid projects kicking around, then seize the window of opportunity to sneak away for a week or two of rest and relaxation. Fate, of course, typically has other plans. The last thing you want is to book leave and then have a major bid project spanning your planned break or, worse still, a deadline falling whilst you are due to be away. It goes without saying that it is hard to sit on the beach and relax when you are fretting over a deadline. Of course, you can delegate things and rely on your colleagues to keep things on track in your absence, but when it is a "must win" bid it is hard to completely let it go. The ping of every message on your phone steals your attention away from the ice-cold beer you are trying to enjoy as you stretch out on your sun lounger. You have inevitably tried to cram in all the work before you left, or you are aiming to have a concerted push as soon as you get back, or most likely both. And of course, the ultimate distraction is to take your bid project on holiday with you, for which you need a very understanding family indeed. You end up questioning your whole work-life balance, and whether this is even a holiday at all.

It was then perhaps inevitable destiny then that I had a holiday booked smack bang in the middle of Doncaster's city status campaign. In all my career, if there was ever a "must win" bid to trump all the others, then this bid was it. At the same time though, this was also one of the most important holidays I had ever booked too, a literal perfect storm. You see, in the Autumn of 2021 my wife, Anne, turned fifty. It is one of those all-important milestone birthdays that demands a statement gift from one's husband. But Anne has never been all that bothered about jewellery, or perfume, or designer accessories. In this regard she can be bit of a nightmare to buy presents for. She does, however, love to travel, and preferably somewhere hot. In fairness, we both do. Back in the day, shortly after we had married, we had written a list of places in the world that we wanted to visit together, and that list still lives on the magnetic notice board in our kitchen. Slowly and steadily over the years, we have been ticking the destinations off. For her fortieth birthday we had spent a week in Rome, so for her fiftieth I needed to raise my game once again.

My dilemma had been further complicated by the Covid-19 restrictions, which had already kept us contained in the UK for over a year. Prior to her birthday Anne had not been abroad for over two years, probably the longest gap in all the years we had known each other, so, despite a level of reservation on one hand about travelling in the wake of the pandemic, she was climbing the walls to get away on the other. As we traversed 2021, with official travel rules being constantly revised every few weeks, it was far from certain as to where we might be able to visit, if anywhere at all, and what level of vaccination status or proof of negative Covid-19 tests we may need to produce to do so.

I nevertheless decided to take the gamble. Just before Christmas 2020, when the flights first came on the market, I started planning a trip scheduled to take place the best part of a full year later, in November 2021. This would fall just after Anne's birthday in September, allowing me to do a big reveal on her actual birthday ('ta-dah, you're going on holiday!'). Of course, I had no idea how busy I may be workwise that far ahead. There was bound to be something in my in-box, there were always bids that needed writing, but nothing that I surely could not leave in the capable hands of my team. A city status bid for Doncaster? Well, that was the unlikeliest thing that I could imagine myself being involved in. No, a holiday in November 2021 felt like as safe a bet as any. The destination I had chosen was Jordan, the small middle eastern country which is the home of the ancient Nabataean city of Petra, one of the outstanding destinations still on our list, and a place that I knew Anne really wanted to go to. And even though it would be the winter, the weather in Jordan would still be more than pleasant at that time of year. I set about booking the flights and hotels, as well as a finding a local guide to take us around the sites, a highly recommended and, as it turns out, quite lovely man called Jihad Abu Zahra.

Keeping the holiday secret for that long was painfully difficult, especially on the days that Anne protested about our lack of travel and that she really needed to go somewhere warm. How little did she know. I nearly cracked more than once! It was difficult too in terms of my own anxiety as to whether we may even get to Jordan. Like many countries, Jordan started out on the Government's so-called Amber List when the system was introduced in May 2021. That meant at the time that you needed a pre-departure Polymerase Chain Reaction (PCR) test as well as having to quarantine at home for ten days upon your return. It wasn't an ideal scenario but, assuming we didn't catch Covid-19, it was workable. But during the year some countries were still flipping from the Amber List to the Red List, effectively prohibiting travel altogether. This left me regularly checking the data on Jordan's infection and vaccination rates. As a developing country, the vaccination programme was understandably lagging way behind those of the UK and Western Europe, and the weekly vaccination figures seemed to inch forward hopelessly slowly. Still, I was an optimist. Globally the vaccination drive was working and, as the year went on, restrictions of all types were gradually lifting. By October the Amber List had been scrapped and, whilst we still needed a negative PCR test to enter Jordan, we didn't need one to come home again. We took our tests at a special testing station at Doncaster Sheffield Airport a couple of days before we flew, going through the now familiar motion of swabbing our nostrils. It would be another 24 hours before we got the "all clear" confirmation emails. Jordan was on!

When my business was first engaged to support on the city status bid in early October 2021, I obviously knew that, with my fingers crossed and the wind blowing in the right direction, I would be away in Jordan for a key phase prior to the submission deadline in December. This focused the process as to how to produce the draft. My modus operandi for bid writing is to get to a good full first draft as soon possible, and then mercilessly polish it to make it the best draft possible. To that end, I wanted, or dare I say needed, to have a great first draft of the Doncaster bid before I got on the plane. There were 34 calendar days between the date that we were appointed to support the bid, and the date that my plane was due to take off from Gatwick. If we are splitting hairs, it was only 26 working weekdays. Just 5 weeks to draft 19 pages setting out a fully considered, evidenced and compelling first draft as to why Doncaster should be a city. There was also the matter of the accompanying locality map and the 50 required photographs of Doncaster to be addressed. Not to also mention all the other aspects of my day job in running and managing a small business.

So, I pulled out the stops to produce and circulate a first draft of the bid to the core group by the evening of Friday 12th November, the day before our departure. This had involved eating into my evenings and weekends to get the words down and get them organised on the page. That may sound arduous, but this was a bid that I was really into, and very different from the sort of thing that I usually get to write about. The writing was more of busman's holiday rather than a chore. I would wake up each day thinking about what to write in the bid, and still be thinking about it when my head hit the pillow in the evening. I was fully energised and enthused. I would write, then re-write, painstakingly pushing the draft along. Dovetailing with the writing was an ongoing flow of desk research, unearthing hidden gems of information that had the appropriate wow factor, and literally writing them straight into the bid as I went. If the actual deadline had been the 12th of November, the quality of draft would still, dare I say, have been good enough to see off many of the fully finished drafts of many of our rivals.

But once the draft was shared, I could take my foot off the gas a little and enjoy the holiday. For the first week away our guide, Jihad, would be taking us on a tour around some of Jordan's best sights. This would include a couple of days in the imposing Wadi Rum dessert, a stopover at the Dead Sea to float in its saline rich waters, and a visit to the Roman remnants of the city of Jerash; all of which were awe inspiring experiences. We got to know Jihad too, everything from how his mother and sister had been instrumental in choosing a wife for him (and yes, he is very happily married), to the ins-and-outs of Jordanian family cuisine, which included him impulsively stopping off when we passed roadside traders to buy full crates of fresh aubergines and tomatoes. He was the perfect guide, fluent in English, and just a nice bloke to spend a few days with. Nothing was too much trouble. He was a mine of information on everything we saw, including a few attractions away from the mainstream tourist trail. But the high point was always going to be Petra, the jewel in Jordan's crown.

If you are around my age, a demographic generally referred to as Generation X, you are most likely to recognise Petra from the movie *Indiana Jones and The Last Crusade*, released in 1989. Jones, played by Harrison Ford, is the adventuring archaeologist who, in this instalment, is trying to locate the Holy Grail, the cup which Jesus infamously drank from at the last supper. The Treasury, one of the signature sites at Petra and carved straight from the sandstone rock, doubled as the location of the temple in the Canyon of the Crescent Moon, where Indie and his adventuring counterparts discovered the Grail at the climax of the movie. In real life Petra is the ancient capital of the Nabataeans, a nomadic people native to Northern Arabia, who inhabited the area from as early as 7000 BC. Enclosed by towering rocks and irrigated by a perpetual stream which flows through it, Petra not only possessed the advantages of a fortress, but it was a strategical post which controlled the main passing trading routes. It is sometimes called the "Rose City" because of the colour of the stone. The Nabateans carved living spaces and funeral chambers directly into the rock faces, creating an elaborate warren of structures; there are no freestanding buildings. Many of these structures, such as the Treasury, were crafted in what is known as the Hellenistic style, with elaborate columns, doorways, pediments, architraves, and friezes. Whilst the Treasury, and a similar structure called the Monastery, may perhaps be the most recognisable and most photographed examples, Petra is made up of a wealth of over 500 tombs, mausoleums, and other structures. It's a deceptively large site; we walked a total of 11.5 miles that day, taking us five hours to traverse the length of Petra and back again (I tracked it on Strava, my exercise app).

The irony of the experience was not lost on me. There I was giving my all to help establish a brand-new city, and yet I found myself in one of the oldest cities in the world. On first impression Petra and Doncaster could not be less alike, the epitome of chalk and cheese, but city status, or at that time the ambition of city status, was a point of commonality. As we walked around Petra, in total awe of these magnificent sights,

I reflected further on the whole concept of what it means to be a city. At its peak Petra was home to up to 30,000 people, but today, aside from the daily coachloads of tourists and the small groups of local Bedouin who still sleep in some of the caves, it is empty. Erosion is taking its toll and the intricate carving on many of the sandstone structures is slowly being wiped clean by the rain and the wind. Yet I stood there with a clear sense of being in the presence of greatness, inspired by the ingenuity of the Nabateans and their pioneering civilisation which was, in many respects, centuries ahead of its time. Then it struck me that it wasn't just cityhood that the two places had in common, it was also a spirit of aspiration, the desire of the people to want to better themselves. That lit a small fire in my belly and a call to action to add a splash of Petra's majesty into Doncaster's bid. Our walk took us full circle back to the Treasury, and Anne and I stood there, hand in hand in the late afternoon, taking it in for one final time, neither of us really wanting to turn our back on it and walk away. But Jihad was waiting, and there were other sights still for us to see.

For the second week of the trip, we said a fond farewell to Jihad, and decamped to the Red Sea's Gulf of Aqaba, at a small resort called Tala Bay. From our hotel balcony we could see straight across the Gulf to the shoreline of Egypt, no more than about five miles away. Around two miles to the south of us was the Saudi Arabian border, and just fifteen miles to the north was the border with Israel, and the city of Eilat. I don't think I've ever been so close to so many different countries all at the same time. Our hotel was lovely, with a choice of pools and a short walk to a couple of more than pleasant local restaurants. There was little to do but sit in the sun, read books, splash in the pool, enjoy a cold beer, and play Travel Scrabble (that's not a euphemism, we always take Travel Scrabble on holiday with us). As blissful as it was, this was still November, which meant the sunset each day was around 4.30 pm. Still too early for dinner, and too late for sunbathing, this brief gap in proceedings created a window of opportunity for me to spend a couple of hours each day to edit the Doncaster bid, and work in the feedback that was steadily now trickling in. Anne was content to carry on reading whilst I did a little work, or to simply just chill out. It's worth pausing at this point to acknowledge that Doncaster's winning bid for city status was primarily written in three different locations: at my office in Doncaster, at my house in Retford, and in my hotel room at the Mövenpick Resort & Spa in Tala Bay, Aqaba, Jordan. You really can't make this stuff up!

Back home the annual Team Doncaster Summit was taking place at the Doncaster Dome leisure centre, a well-attended yearly get-together of all the local stakeholders. This was a key opportunity to keep partners up to speed and sustain the momentum of the campaign, so unsurprisingly the city status bid was on the agenda. My holiday meant I couldn't attend, so Ginny Lindle stepped up to deliver a brief presentation on the progress that we had made with the campaign thus far. She was on the billing directly after Ed Miliband, in the final session of the event, just to add a little extra profile! She was joined on stage by Glyn Butcher of the People Focused Group, representing the voluntary sector; Owen Marshall-Dungworth, one of Doncaster's Youth Councillors, representing young people; with Tariq Shah of the Vigo Group and Karen Beardsley of Unipart Rail representing the business sector. All shared a few words and perspectives on what the campaign meant to them, and the mood in the room was unsurprisingly supportive of our ongoing work.

Back in Aqaba, I took a call from Carl Hall at Club Doncaster. The Lionesses, the England women's senior football team, were due to play Latvia in a World Cup Qualifier in Doncaster at the end of November. This was still seven months before the team would go on to historically win the Women's Euro 2022 competition, beating Germany 2-1 in front of almost 90,000 fans at Wembley, and then reach the World Cup final in Sydney a year after that. The Latvia game was a couple of weeks' away when I spoke with Carl, with only around 8,000 tickets, just over half of the stadium's capacity, sold at that point. Club Doncaster were as such open to a tie-in with the city status campaign, with a potential block booking arrangement of 450 seats for Team Doncaster partners on the table. Attending supporters could then be issued with city status flags or banners, creating a photo opportunity, and leveraging the live coverage of the fixture on ITV. The stadium had previously worked a similar strategy for a Doncaster Knights fixture against Bradford, helping in part to secure Doncaster's role as a Rugby League World Cup 2021 host city. It was a great idea in principle, but one which I really couldn't steer or resolve from Jordan, and which I needed to hand-off to the project team back home instead. The main barriers were the cost to the campaign even with a group discount, the availability of enough partners to attend at short notice, and further costs of producing customised flags or banners. Given these barriers it was, regrettably, a straightforward decision to turn the offer down, but it was a decision that still needed to be managed with appropriate sensitivity. A few wires got crossed though, to the extent that the offer wasn't initially discussed at the first opportunity back home, and a clear decision hadn't been relayed back to Carl. Carl chased me up. I chased up the team.

This was not the only issue brewing in my absence. Alongside uncertainty around the Lionesses game, the marketing workstream group had hit some bottlenecks. Much of this focused around preparations for 8th of December, the deadline day for bids to be submitted, and how this occasion would be marked. Too many well-intentioned but ultimately underdeveloped ideas were in play, and concern around this was enough for Dan Fell to ask for an impromptu online meeting of the core group to be convened, which I duly joined online from my hotel balcony in Aqaba. As ever, calm heads and constructive discussion allayed some of the issues, and things were boxed off with Carl. There would be more work to do to finalise a deliverable plan for deadline day, which I will return to shortly, but the new direction of travel involved finding a simpler, less congested path. My time in Jordan was nearly over though and, whilst it had been an amazing holiday, there was a part of me that was keen to get home and see Doncaster's city status submission over the line once and for all.

Fortunately, neither Anne nor I caught Covid-19 during our time in Jordan. The disease, and how Jordan had coped with it, was a subject that we quizzed Jihad on. A combination of warmer climes, a much younger average aged population (the median age in Jordan is 24 compared to 40 in Britain), and a culture of spending more time outside, amongst other things, meant that the Covid-19 death rate in Jordan was far lower than our own. By and large they had just gotten on with it. Aside from navigating some officials decked out with full PPE suits at the airport when we first arrived, the aura of Covid-19 that had reached into every enclave of everyday life back home was far less noticeable here. The Jordanians had missed out on having an equivalent of Chris Witty, Britain's Chief Medical Officer, asking for 'the next slide please' during televised briefings, or newsreaders serving as the harbingers of doom by ending every bulletin with the latest national body count figures. Indeed, there were days we had in Jordan where, for the first time in months, Covid-19 didn't come up in conversation at all.

In the end, over 12,000 spectators went to watch the Lionesses in Doncaster. Not a capacity crowd, but not too far short. It turned out to be a record-breaking night for the Lionesses, a 20-0 win over Latvia (yes, twenty-nil, it's not a typo), the biggest ever England winning margin in a competitive match. Ellen White's hat-trick saw her become England's leading all time female goal-scorer (she finally retired from international football in August 2022 with 52 England goals to her name). Meanwhile Lauren Hemp had scored four, whilst Beth Mead and Alessia Russo also registered hat-tricks. Suffice to say that, even though we didn't have the means to have a visual presence at the game, this internationally record-breaking night in Doncaster was immediately written into our city status bid. I'm not sure if an England football team of any description will ever achieve a bigger winning margin, meaning Doncaster's place in the international footballing history books is assured for quite some time to come. And something tells me that, if the Lionesses were to play in Doncaster again any time soon, there probably wouldn't be too much difficulty in selling all the tickets.

Deadline Day

The deadline to enter the Platinum Jubilee Civic Honours competition for city status was 4.00 pm on Wednesday the 8th of December 2021. All bids had to be submitted by e-mail to The Cabinet Office by that date and time, and not a second later. In most cases a bid deadline doesn't warrant too much attention. Aside from a few deserving thank you emails to all the contributors, there is rarely much of a fanfare or any unnecessary pomp and circumstance. Deadline day is instead more of an opportunity to have a glass of wine, a hot bath, and an early night before you all go again on the next bid. Of course, though, the city status campaign was different. Deadline day this time presented a tantalising public relations opportunity to all the bidders, not just Doncaster, to give their bid an appropriate send off, and raise the profile of each campaign in the process. It was a tailor-made news story there to be reported on. To secure the most airtime and column inches, however, you ideally needed a deadline day concept that would really capture the imagination. This drive for something innovative became something of a pre-occupation for our Project Board in the run up to the deadline.

I will be honest here and say that deadline day was probably the biggest headache of Doncaster's entire city status campaign. There were lots of good ideas of how the day could be marked but mobilising any of these ideas proved to be a near impossibility. The first idea to gain traction (Plan A) was a reception event to be staged on deadline day at the Houses of Parliament.

Such receptions, organised for a variety of lobbying reasons, are not uncommon, and I'd been to a few during my career. The Terrace Pavilion, adjoined to the Palace of Westminster, and perched on the bank of the Thames, essentially exists for this very purpose. Such events typically involve a glass of something sparkly, some trays of assorted canapés, and a few well-meaning speeches. As part of its winning campaign, the city of Perth had hosted a parliamentary dinner in 2012, so there was some precedent here. Our proposed event had a working title of "Taking Doncaster to the Centre". Leveraging the backing of local and regional MPs, it would be a three-pronged campaign to help Doncaster secure a new hospital, the mooted new headquarters of GB Railways, and city status. A long list of esteemed guests was even drawn up. Cracks however started to quickly appear. The three-pronged message was perhaps a bit confusing, with muddled priorities. The cost of the event, although not ridiculous, was still a consideration, especially in shipping a goodly number of people between Doncaster and London and back again. The tone and timing were also a factor. Should Doncaster's leaders really be hobnobbing it down in London on the back of a pandemic and during a cost-of-living crisis? For all these reasons this plan fell over very quickly.

Plan B was what we called the "City for a Day" concept. We were actively discussing this idea within the core group and Project Board as early as mid-October, which made it more frustrating when we didn't manage to pull it off. The idea itself was straightforward enough. It involved getting key partners and stakeholders to rebrand for the day, on deadline day, under the guise of Doncaster being a city for that one day. So, for example, Doncaster Station would become Doncaster City Station, Doncaster Council would become Doncaster City Council, and so on and so forth. The plan was not to physically change any signage, but rather to change headers on social media accounts or selectively photoshop the word "city" into relevant images which could be posted online. This was critical; whilst the initiative would require some manpower, it ultimately shouldn't have been a financial burden for anyone. Scott McFarlane did some concept work on a short social media film, weaving all these threads together. The focal point of the day would be a Team Doncaster gathering at the Yorkshire Wildlife Park (or, just for the day, the Doncaster City Wildlife Park). The staging would be adorned with backdrops and banners, with a showcase video telling the story of our campaign and highlighting the very best of Doncaster. The winning children from our local schools' competition (more on this later) would be invited, with the winning film screened at the event. There would be some rallying speeches and some great photo opportunities for the local and regional media, who would all be invited along, with some lions and polar bears thrown in for good measure. Owen Marshall Dungworth, Project Board member and a budding trainee pilot, had even volunteered to fly a plane towing some form a celebratory banner over the town that day. But the City for a Day event never happened.

It was a great idea, but it also served to highlight a lingering Achilles heel of the Project Board. The Board was a veritable melting pot of great ideas, we had these in spades. What it proved to be less effective at was turning those great ideas into reality. I think is a cautionary tale for any potential city status bidder. If you have limited funds and equally limited manpower dedicated to your campaign, then you need to cut your cloth accordingly. Whilst the Yorkshire Wildlife Park were generously happy to host the City for a Day reception at no cost to the campaign, and the Chamber offered to pay for transport for the school kids, there was no real continuity in terms how different partners might meaningfully rebrand for the day, and no extra money to do anything out of the ordinary. We were reliant on voluntary good will in terms of the time that partners could commit, and where the city status campaign sat against their own wider organisational priorities. We even came up with an easy-to-follow list of suggestions through which partners could support the day and take part, but that didn't help. City for a Day simply wasn't the number one thing in everyone's in tray. Sometimes the right person to make something happen wasn't always a Project Board member, but rather someone else in their organisation, someone perhaps a little less invested in the campaign. The voluntary nature of the whole project was both a strength and a weakness. It was great when somebody put their hand up, but equally a frustration that there was no means to ensure that people made good on their pledges. By mid-November it was becoming clear that City for a Day wasn't going to happen. There was a suggestion that, if we couldn't do it on the 8th of December then perhaps it could take place later, on another day. That suggestion was, however, quickly kicked into the long grass. If we were doing anything it had to be on deadline day, else there simply wasn't a news story. The whole point was that we were marking the deadline and the submission of the bid. That leverage was available for one day only. But the City for a Day idea was rapidly starting to fizzle, and the plug was ultimately pulled.

So, we come to Plan C. This was really something of a convenient compromise given that our more ambitious plans had fallen over. Plan C would, very simply, be a Project Board photocall at the civic Mansion House. It was a far cry from the originally planned Westminster reception, but it was at least something that we confidently knew that we could get done. I questioned myself a little about the downscaling of our plans. After all, I was supposed to be the Project Director. Wasn't it my job to make all this work? The downside, however, of being an external consultant is that you often don't have the proverbial stick to beat people with. If your boss at work tells you to do something, and you don't then do it, the consequences are usually quite different. In any event, I prefer to think of myself as more of a carrot rather than a stick kind of manager. But this exposes what I think is the real challenge with projects like a city status campaign. They are largely reliant on good intentions to make things happen, and that invariably delivers mixed results. Whilst the ambition is to make as bigger splash as possible, there is a lot to be said for keeping things simple.

Despite all the woes of trying to organise a deadline day event, it was beginning to feel a lot like Christmas, and the festive lights were already up around the centre of Doncaster.

The star-studded seasonal romantic comedy *Love Actually* is a staple Christmas favourite in our house. There was a showing of this festive heart warmer, accompanied by a live orchestra, at Sheffield City Hall the night before deadline day, so I duly treated Anne and Alice and took them over to watch it. As Billy Mack, the insufferable, washed-up rock star played by the incomparable Bill Nighy, says in the film, 'I realized that Christmas is the time to be with the people you love.' It was a fitting way not just to begin our own festive season as a family, but also an appropriate send off for the Doncaster bid once and for all. I had spent hours and hours writing this bid, but now I was done. No more tinkering, no more editing. The metaphoric pen had been put down. Doncaster's fate as a potential city was no longer in my hands.

I had arrived in the centre of Doncaster a little early the following morning for the deadline day photo call. Storm Barra was battering the coastline of Wales and Ireland, with gusts of wind of up to 80mph, and the after-effects of that were reaching as far as Doncaster. It was a miserable, wet day; perhaps a sign that abandoning City for a Day was the right call after all. A little bit of rain wasn't going to dampen my spirits though. *God Only Knows* by The Beach Boys was playing on a loop in my head. The iconic track with its classic harmonies features in the closing scene of *Love Actually*, as the ensemble of characters all appear in the arrival lounge at Heathrow Airport. It was something of a metaphor for the key characters in our city status campaign all converging on the Mansion House that morning. As I had a little time to spare, I grabbed a take-out latte on

Baxter Gate. Coffee in hand, I headed back out and up the High Street towards the Mansion House. Doncaster was quiet that morning, with only a handful of people out and about, most probably on their way into work, and haplessly trying to keep themselves dry. I had a spring in my step though, and a smile on my face, knowing that this was, to all intents and purposes, the last day of our campaign.

The High Street in Doncaster can sometimes get a bit of flack, with its banks and cafés interspersed with betting shops, pawnbrokers, and charity stores. It is, however, part of a local conservation area, with many listed buildings, some dating back to the Georgian era. If you take a moment to appreciate the buildings themselves, they really are quite impressive. The Tourist Information Centre is a case in point, sited at Number 1 Priory Place, on the corner of the High Street, butting up against the Mansion House. It's a wonderful, romantic old building, with mock columns and sash windows, built sometime around the end of the 18th Century. As I approached it that morning, supping on my frothy coffee, my eyes were drawn to the Doncaster coat of arms positioned above the pediment over its doorway.

Doncaster's coat of arms depicts two lions, sat upright on their hind legs, and facing towards each other on either side of a shield. The shield itself loosely illustrates Doncaster's original Roman fort, with wavy blue and white lines beneath it to illustrate the River Don. Behind the fort the shield is divided equally down the middle into a black panel on the left, representing Doncaster's former coal industry, and a green panel on the right, representing its history of agriculture. It was, however, the motto of Doncaster that is positioned underneath the arms which most readily caught my attention that morning: Be Steadfast! Only two little words, but such a strong, resolute, and unfaltering phrase. Two little words that neatly summed up the identity of Doncaster and its people, and the way we had approached the whole campaign. Two little words, full of grit and determination. Two little words, that momentarily wiped the smile cleanly off my face. Why? Because they were also two little words that had, frustratingly, never made their way into our bid for city status. There was an inevitability that good things about Doncaster would come to light after the deadline that we hadn't included in the bid, and I'll detail a few more shortly. I hadn't, however, anticipated that the first of these would come up quite so quickly!

No matter though, I didn't let it spoil my day! A dozen of us gathered at the Mansion House that morning. Ros Jones and Damian Allen represented the Council, and Dan was there from the Chamber. Ginny Lindle and Scott McFarlane from my team were there. The ensemble was completed by Akeela Mohammed, Chinwe Russell, Revd. David Stevens, Tariq Shah, Carl Hall, Karen Staniforth, Cath Witherington, and my good self. Whilst we were modest in numbers, between us we represented Doncaster's public services, arts, businesses, faith community, voluntary groups, and sports teams. It was a good mix. Alison Jordan was there too, albeit for some reason she didn't join in the official photographs – in hindsight she probably should have. It many respects it was nice to all be together in person. Most project meetings had been conducted as videocalls, so being in the same physical space at the end of campaign was poignant. Hands were shaken, backs were patted, smiles were exchanged, and there were probably one or two hugs as well. We'd all made it to the finish line. Everybody got to wear the #goingforitDN pin badge. When everybody was there we assembled on the staircase, and a photographer from the *Doncaster Free Press* took some snaps. A small campaign banner had been made up, with Ros and Cath holding either end. We looked a little like a bizarre community choir about to burst into song.

Other members of the Project Board who were not there in person were still able to offer soundbites for the accompanying press release. Community and business venues were encouraged to light up their buildings in Platinum purple, and to share photos on social media using the campaign hashtag. Places that were lit up in purple on that soggy evening included the Mansion House, the Corn Exchange, Cusworth Hall, the Savoy cinema, the Wool Market, Doncaster Royal Infirmary, Silver Street, and the Lakeside shopping complex. Staff at the Frenchgate Shopping Centre all dutifully wore purple for the day, and I did my bit by wearing a purple tie (I don't otherwise have a lot of purple in my wardrobe). We also put an advertorial in one of Doncaster Rovers' December matchday programme ("OUR GOAL is to be a city for Doncastrians to be proud of" – cheesy, but effective).

One of the more interesting bits of information latterly released by The Cabinet Office was not simply the list of localities which had bid for city status, but also the exact day and time that each bid had been received. As a bid writer this was fascinating, as it's a piece of insight I had never seen in any other proposal competition before or since. Doncaster's bid was officially logged as having been received at 16:35 on Tuesday the 7th of December. Dorchester had long since taken the accolade of being the first to submit their bid. They had submitted on the 21st of November, more than a fortnight ahead of the deadline. Whilst any bid writer worth their salt will tell you that it is sensible not to cut it too fine when it comes to submitting, sending your bid in that early is more than a little bizarre. Dorchester had so much more time to improve and polish what they had produced, a competitive opportunity simply wasted. Peel on the Isle of Mann was the second place to declare, and not too far behind Dorchester, curiously submitting their bid at the exact stroke of midnight on the 25th of November; seemingly having a self-imposed late-night finish just for the fun of it. Around half of all the bidders had submitted before the deadline day, with most of these submitting in the days immediately beforehand, but the other half left it to the very final day. George Town in the Cayman Islands was the last to submit, logged at 15:59 on the 8th of December, exactly one minute before the deadline. Talk about leaving it late; I imagine it was a bit of a squeaky bum moment for their team that afternoon! My assumption is that everyone who planned to bid got their bid in on time, but I don't know if there were any late, and therefore disqualified, submissions. I'm guessing not.

Surprisingly, hardly any other bidders made a splash about submitting their bid. This did make me wonder if our original, more ambitious plans had ever really been necessary at all. Indeed, the lack of a sendoff from most bidders seemed strange to me. If an underpinning motive to achieve city status was one of civic pride, then surely the submission of your bid would be something to shout about. In an era where news cycles turn very quickly, the submission of your bid was also a rare opportunity to shine a light on your campaign for both the community and evaluators alike. Of those few that stepped up, most hosted fairly straightforward photo calls not unlike Doncaster's. In Middlesbrough, Mayor Andy Preston was photographed with local children under the town's famous Transporter Bridge, holding copies of their bid. In Dudley, council leader Patrick Harley and Mayor Anne Millward posed with their bid document next to a red pillar box, pretending to post it. Down in Reading, Council Leader Jason Brock also posed with a campaign board. The photos were accompanied by press releases and to make a final plea to anyone reading as to the city credentials of each town. All attracted local news coverage, as you would reasonably expect. In the end Doncaster had held its own, albeit the ultimate accolades on the day really belonged once again to Milton Keynes.

Milton Keynes had arranged a stage-managed photo call outside of the town's gallery where Mohammed Khan, the Mayor, placed their bid document in a Starship Robot to be delivered to the Queen. These ingenious little automated robots have been making local home deliveries for online shoppers across Milton Keynes since 2015. At the forefront of carbon zero technology, they look a little like a large icebox with six wheels. The symbolic bid document had a cover made from vellum manufactured by WG Cowley of Newport Pagnell, the last parchment and vellum works in Britain, who still provide the vellum for declarations of royal births. Attendees at the event included 12-year-old Thea Callaghan, who had won a competition to design a flag for the new city, which was already flying in the town centre. The whole spectacle was of course a showpiece (submissions had to be sent in by e-mail, not by robot), but it was smartly done, and all very well presented. The mayor popped the bid into the robot's compartment, and off it trundled to the applause of the gathered crowd. Unsurprisingly news cameras from BBC's *Look East* were there to live broadcast the send-off. There were, of course, no points awarded for making the flashiest submission, but Milton Keynes were taking nothing for granted when it came to getting noticed. I won't deny that I was a little envious. Milton Keynes was schooling everybody in the art of Critical Non-Essentials.

After the photocall at the Mansion House I went back to my office. I sat there at my desk for a bit, staring at my laptop screen, looking for inspiration. There was a gnawing inside me to find out something new about Doncaster, or to write something new about Doncaster, or to just open our now submitted bid document and just look at it. It was like an overwhelming wave of procrastination. You always get a little bit like this on bid deadline days, but today felt a bit different. It took me a while to figure it out, but then I realised what the problem was. I simply wasn't ready for this bid to be over. I'd enjoyed it a little bit too much. It was a melancholy moment in many respects, a sense of loss, like your best friend at school suddenly announcing he was moving away, and school days would never quite be the same again without him. That school friend was the Doncaster bid, and he'd left me behind, moving on to find some new friends in Whitehall. Who was I going to hang out with now?

Being December, the sun had already set by 4.00 pm. Storm Barra was easing a little, but it was still raining steadily, taking a little shine away from Doncaster's purple illuminations. I closed the office up and headed home in the dark, windscreen wipers at full pelt, with a mixed sense of both achievement and lament. I flicked on the radio to hear Slade smashing out *Merry Christmas Everybody*, and my mood was lifted. Who doesn't enjoy a cheesy Christmas classic? Before I knew it, I had pumped up the volume and was singing along. 'Look to the future now', I warbled, 'it's only just begun!' It may not have been all that tuneful, but it was strangely accurate. The bid may have been submitted, but the journey wasn't over yet.

Things Left Unsaid

With a tight page count there were always going to be things we could have included in the bid, but which we didn't. Some of these were intentional omissions, things deemed not quite potent enough to make the cut, and which were ultimately left on the cutting room floor. Some of these calls were easier to make than others. You will recall, for example, my earlier ramblings about Doncaster's misguided attempts to appropriate the legend of Robin Hood from Nottinghamshire. With no lesser guile and resolve than that of the evil Sheriff of Nottingham himself, there was no way I would be letting that cunning outlaw swindle his way into the pages of our bid. Other calls were a little trickier than that, but with a tight page count something was always going to have to give. In hindsight, I'm not sure that we got all those calls right, but I should perhaps let you, on the merits of this chapter, be the judge of that.

There were also a good number of facts, figures and soundbites that didn't cross my desk until long after the bid was submitted, things that otherwise had the necessary je ne sais quoi, but that simply did not show up on the radar in time to be included. Even now, all this time later, I keep tripping over amazing facts about Doncaster which, if I'd known about them at the time, would very likely have been squeezed into the bid somewhere. Given that the bid was successful, it would be a little harsh to beat ourselves up too much about the things that we missed, but I would doubtlessly feel a little differently if we had been unsuccessful. So, this chapter is a worthy homage to some of the facts, figures, and stories about Doncaster which you won't have seen in our city status bid, the things that were left unsaid.

Let's start with the conscious omissions, things like Robin Hood which we could have included, but deliberately chose not to. For starters, I intentionally excluded references to bygone buildings and structures. In other words, even if it was a city standard asset in its day, but was no longer standing in 2021, then it didn't go in the bid. Take, as a reference point, the city of Hillah in Iraq. You've never heard of it before? Well, that's not a complete surprise to hear. You will, however, be familiar with the name of the former landmark which reputedly once dominated its skyline, The Hanging Gardens of Babylon, one of the Seven Wonders of the Ancient World. The towering gardens were an inspiring amalgamation of horticulture and architecture, with a multitude of exotic plant species housed on tiered stone beds held up by majestic columns, covered with elaborate carvings and colourful façades, and all explored by an intricate maze of stairways, snickets, and waterways. The presumed site of the Hanging Gardens, just to the north of Hillah, is a short walk from Etemenanki, a giant Mesopotamian temple who some believe was in fact the Tower of Babel, the scriptural landmark from the Book of Genesis, described in the Bible as being so large that its very top was in the heavens. If both landmarks existed today, they would be amongst the world's most visited destinations, ranking comfortably alongside The Great Wall of China, Machu Picchu, and The Taj Mahal. Hillah would be as worldly famous as Cairo or Athens, with hundreds of thousands of visitors every year, a literal gateway to the Gods.

The Hanging Gardens are, of course though, a lost wonder, and some believe that they were no more than a poetic creation that never actually existed at all. Etemenanki is likewise now a ruined foundation, and whether it really was the actual Tower of Babel is little more than the stuff of legend. To therefore talk-up Hillah as a city of global significance because it may once have been home to some ancient and theological wonders feels like something of a reach. It would be a bit like showcasing the twin towers of the old Wembley Stadium, The Crystal Palace which housed the Great Exhibition of 1851, or London Bridge (the one built in 1209 which was latterly sold, shipped, and reassembled in Lake Havasu City, Arizona in 1967) as notable landmarks to promote Britain's own modern-day capital. Impressive as these landmarks all were in their time, none of them are sadly there anymore.

This segways me nicely to Doncaster's very own lost wonder. The Sand House, built alongside Doncaster's Hyde Park Cemetery close to the town centre in the 1850s, was the creation of Henry Senior, a Victorian businessman. Victorian entrepreneurs often had a fancy for the eccentric, exotic and unusual, and Senior, who had made his fortune in sand excavation, was no different. His house was uniquely created and impressively engineered by excavating the ground from around a massive block of sandstone and then hollowing out each of the rooms within it, to create a building that was roughly the size of two tennis courts laid end to end. Just pause on that for a second; this guy literally carved a mansion house, with 10 bedrooms, out of a single, massive rock, and then lived in it. The ballroom, the centrepiece of the house, was said to have space for 200 people and was renowned in its day for its spritely tea dances. At first glance, from the outside, the house looked like a regular fine home of its day, nothing out of the ordinary. It had Victorian windows, doors, chimneys, a slate roof, and a blanket of ivy hanging from its walls, all disguising the fact that the house itself was, rather remarkably, a single piece of stone. The tell-tell giveaway of its real identity came from the fact that the house was located at the bottom of a small, landscaped quarry, with its roof being below the street level of its neighbours.

As well as carving the house itself, Senior surrounded it with a network of tunnels, cloisters, and catacombs, again all carved out of the sandstone bedrock as part of the overall structure, and all decorated with the most unusual and exquisite carvings and sculptures. These were perhaps the most remarkable and impactful features of the whole site. The most elaborate and imposing sculpture in the tunnels was that of a life size elephant and its Indian mahout (what we might call a handler), celebrating the colonial ties of the day. There were also likenesses of Henry VII, Elizabeth I, and Inigo Jones, as well as an Irishman and woman in national dress, clowns, cherubs, and all manner of other oddities, all set into the sandstone of the tunnel walls. If you can imagine the lovechild of the Great Pyramid of Giza and a Ripley's Believe It or Not odditorium, then it would probably look a lot like Doncaster's Sand House. Whilst stone carved buildings are not unique, I'm not aware of any creation, anywhere in the world quite like the Sand House. If it was still standing today, it would be a building of national significance, with visitors arriving by the coach load, and would have been front and centre of our city status bid. History though, as it often does, had other plans.

Senior, who lived in the house for 40 years, bequeathed the property to the Council when he died, perhaps perceiving them as the appropriate custodians to protect his legacy for future generations. Sadly, however, culture and heritage were not a high civic priority during the interwar years, and the future significance of the site was overlooked. The house quickly ran into disrepair and, by the 1930s, the site was being used for, of all things, landfill. The tunnels survived into the 1940s and 1950s, where children who were typically up-to-no-good would still adventure and explore. Then, in the 1960s, Silverwood House, a rather less remarkable 17-storey block of flats, was constructed on the site. In 1984, to stabilise the land, the remaining tunnels were closed off and filled in with concrete. Today, the Sand House only survives in memories and photographs, and there is no real prospect of it ever being restored. The story of the Sand House was one of my most favourite things that I learned about during my city status journey, and it pained me greatly to leave it out. To disclose, however, that Doncaster was once home to one of Britain's finest Victorian marvels, but which had since been filled with garbage, tarmacked over, and replaced with a tower block, didn't really strike the desired chord. Clearly not one of Doncaster's finest historical chapters and, alas, the Sand

House would have to make way.

Doncaster has lost many other historical sites over the years. Notably, Doncaster's leaders fully embraced the brutalist architectural trend of the 1960s, embarking on a fruitful frenzy of genocidal town planning. They idolised bland, featureless structures, built dual carriageways, did away with public transport, and poured as much concrete everywhere as they possibly could. Take the imposing Georgian Guild Hall on Frenchgate, built in 1847. The former seat of Doncaster's Town Council had a façade of four imposing columns, each three stories high, supporting an equally majestic pediment. A proud, handsome, and historic building by every measure, which was bulldozed in the 1960s to make way for a new Marks & Spencer, which had all the charisma of soviet era office block. You might have been able to reach this shiny new M&S by using Doncaster's trolleybus network, which replaced the former tram system in the late 1920s and had six different spoke routes servicing the town centre. Sadly though, the trolleybus network was closed in 1963. At the same time, swathes of lovely old buildings were being demolished to make way for the likes of the Arndale Centre (since made over as the Frenchgate Centre), the Doncaster North Bus Station Car Park (since demolished), the ABC Cinema (now derelict), and the Waterdale Centre (also demolished). What a glorious urban legacy the 1960s left us with. Unsurprisingly, Doncaster's golden era of concrete and fabricated steel was a topic that our city status bid readily swerved away from.

Another intentional omission, which may undoubtedly

raise an eyebrow or two, was the Danum Shield, possibly Doncaster's most famous historical artefact. The Roman shield was discovered in 1971 at the site of the fort which is now occupied by St George's Minster. It was found in the remnants of a Roman bonfire, and the theory is that it was intentionally burnt when the garrison abandoned the fort. Whilst in a perilously fragile condition, preventing it from being salvaged and preserved intact, the shield was otherwise remarkably complete. It was rectangular and was approximately 2 ft by 4ft in size, so a substantive, and quite heavy, means of defence. The board was made from three layers of wood; a centre of oak with outer layers of alder joined by glue. It was covered in leather and decorated in bronze sheeting, and was believed to be painted, albeit no one knows for sure what colour it was. Surprisingly hardly any Roman shields have been discovered anywhere by archaeologists, so the Danum Shield is more historically significant than it may first sound. The surviving iron boss and handgrip of the shield are on display at the Doncaster Museum & Art Gallery, alongside a reconstruction of the full shield, made in 1978.

Editorially, the Danum Shield was a conundrum. Yes, it's a historic artefact which is almost 2,000 years old, and a comparatively unique surviving example of its kind. It was also, however (and somewhat cynically), just a shield, a single item of armoury, one of thousands deployed across the Roman army, which by chance had been cast aside in Doncaster. And it wasn't even a shield anymore, but rather a lump of faded metal which was once part of a shield. To explain the significance of the shield's backstory would eat up a lot of word space in the bid, and, well, could that really be justified? And if the Danum Shield went in, shouldn't we also include other local Roman finds? The Norton Hoard, for example, was a haul of over a thousand silver coins, spanning almost 200 years of Roman rule, unearthed by metal detectorists in the village of Norton in 2018. The earliest coins of Mark Anthony dated to 32BC, and the hoard also included coins from eras of Hadrian and Nero. An amazing find without doubt, but does a big bag of old, albeit impressive, coins make Doncaster more worthy of city status? In fairness, I wasn't aware of the Norton Hoard when we wrote the bid so the question never came up, but, like the Danum Shield, it very likely would not have made the list. We could literally have showcased every historically worthy museum piece in Doncaster, but I'm not sure that any stood sufficiently head and shoulders above the artefacts of our rival towns. Let's not forget too that we were bidding against Colchester, the first Roman capital of Britain; steeped in the remnants of Roman walls, churches, temples, theatres, and the only chariot-racing circus in the UK. I imagine too that it was a hothouse of explicit toga parties and wantful orgies of such a graphic nature that the eager partakers would make the future cast of *The Only Way is Essex* look like inhibited prudes. The Danum Shield was no defence at all against that!

Whilst there were plenty of suggestions made by colleagues as to deserving things we might include in the bid, they didn't always pack the necessary city status punch, and a few asks were politely declined. Doncaster's councillors, however, were the primary advocates for the inclusion of Sir Cornelius Vermuyden, the Dutch engineer commissioned by the Crown to drain the Hatfield Chase wetlands in the 1620s, re-routing the mouth of the River Don, and applying land reclamation and flood protection methods years ahead of their time. I was initially a little on the fence about Vermuyden, as his innovations were difficult to explain without getting lost in the detail, and a drained wetland didn't exactly scream city status. But his achievements really were pioneering, and formed the basis of the River Don Navigation Canal, creating a navigable link between Sheffield and Humberside, a critical trading artery of national significance during the industrial revolution. This was a rare instance of where my editorial arm was twisted, but I think more for the better.

The old saying of "you don't know what you don't know" is acute in the field of proposal writing, and something I remind my clients about all the time. Companies very commonly take some of their best sales collateral for granted. They just assume their customers already know the important stuff, an assumption which is often wrong. You may have a stack of glowing endorsements, business awards, accreditations, and market leading performance figures, but if the person writing your bids doesn't know about them, then they won't get a mention, and the sales leverage they offer is lost. The risk was even more acute with the Civic Honours competition. It's impossible for any single person to know everything that might be sales-worthy about a locality, so you are naturally relying on everyone else to shout up and ensure that nothing is missed.

For example, nobody mentioned that Ford had an assembly plant at Carr Hill in the 1950s, and manufactured 155,000 Ford Populars in Doncaster, the cheapest car on the market at that time, a forerunner to the Escort and Fiesta, so that didn't go in the bid. Likewise, nobody mentioned that *Kes*, Ken Loach's cultural coming of age classic and BAFTA winning film, had its world première in Doncaster in 1969. Whilst our approach worked well overall, and our bid really was bursting with wonderful facts and stories, it was inevitable that a few gems like this would slip through the net.

Perhaps a more notable omission, and one of almost unforgivable significance, was the absence of the name of the late George Porter. Porter was born near Thorne in 1920 and became an eminent chemist. His Wikipedia page[35] states that his research focused on "developing the technique of flash photolysis to obtain information on short-lived molecular species which provided the first evidence of free radicals". Despite having a GCSE in Chemistry, I must confess that I don't really understand what that means. But despite the limits of my own knowledge, Porter was a luminary in his field. He became both a Fellow and President of the Royal Society and held directorships across a variety of other eminent scientific institutions and committees. He started his own company, Applied Photophysics Ltd., in 1971, to further pioneer his work, and that business, based in Surrey, is still going strong today. He delivered the BBC's iconic televised *Christmas*

---

35   https://en.wikipedia.org/wiki/George_Porter

Lectures series from The Royal Institution in 1976. He was
awarded with multiple scientific medals and awards, honorary
doctorates, and a knighthood. He became a life peer in 1990,
earning him the title of Baron Porter of Luddenham. He has
buildings named after him at both the University of Leicester,
where he was Chancellor, and the University of Sheffield. But
the real cherry at the top of his CV was that he was awarded the
Nobel Prize for Chemistry in 1967 for his work on chemical
reactions triggered by light. You heard me right, Doncaster has
its very own Nobel Laureate, and we didn't put his name in our
bid! Porter's achievements were on par to those of Marie Curie,
perhaps the best known of the Nobel Laureate chemists. Those
in the scientific community would rightly view his omission as
sacrilege. His achievements are hardly a secret. All I can say in
our defence is simply that his name was never raised during our
campaign; I only stumbled across him sometime later. I offer
my apologies to his family and to the scientific community
more broadly. Hopefully the mention here goes some way to
make up for it, and I promise I will try my best to work out
what exactly flash photolysis is (albeit please don't get your
hopes up too high on that front).

A more familiar name to many people will be Edward Elgar,
the world-famous composer, whose *Pomp and Circumstance
Marches* are a staple highlight of *The Last Night of The Proms*
at the Royal Albert Hall. No, Elgar is not a Doncastrian (he was
born in Worcestershire), but in 1909 he conducted a performance
by The London Symphony Orchestra at Doncaster's Corn
Exchange. Yep, Edward Elgar, live in Doncaster, for one

night only! I stumbled across this fact literally only a week or two after the bid deadline, and I nearly fell off my chair. Our bid had listed several contemporary music legends who had all performed in Doncaster, such as Buddy Holly (1958), The Beatles (1963), David Bowie (1973), Bob Marley (1973), The Sex Pistols (1977) and Ed Sheeran (2012). That's a world class line-up by anyone's standards. But to omit a visit from a man universally regarded as one of the ten best British classical composers of all time (maybe even top five), was nothing short of calamitous. His appearance in Doncaster is perhaps the most culturally important musical event the town had ever hosted, yet this was another forgotten gem.

The qualifying standard for sportspersons to be included in the bid was to be a sporting legend (step forward Kevin Keegan), a ground breaker (Arthur Wharton, widely considered to be the world's first ever black professional footballer), or a world champion, and Doncaster has produced more than a few of these. Doncaster's Jamie McDonnell, Terri Harper, and Maxi Hughes, all became world champion boxers, whilst Bradley Sinden and Sarah Stevenson MBE achieved the same in Taekwondo (all named in the bid). Other notable names were on the cusp of inclusion, and had achieved more than respectable sporting careers, perhaps even national champions, but who didn't quite make the cut. Less deliberate though was the omission of Doncaster's own Gillian Coultard MBE, former captain of the Lionesses, the England women's football team, who made a then record of 119 appearances for her country between 1981 and 2000. As a Doncaster Belle's player, she also won the women's FA Cup six times. Perhaps not a world champion, but a phenomenal achievement in an era when international level women still played as amateurs, and an inexcusable omission.

Today I still cringe in the knowledge of just how many important people we failed to mention in our bid. People like Tommy Simpson, who grew up in Harworth on the Doncaster/ Nottinghamshire border, and who was the first Briton to win cycling's elite men's World Championships and to wear the Tour de France's yellow jersey. Oh, and he also won the BBC's Sports Personality of the Year Award in 1965. But there was no mention for Simpson or indeed for Sir Michael Parkinson. Parky, the legendary king of television chat, had worked in Doncaster as a young journalist and met his wife here. Two giants of English literature, Charles Dickens and Wilkie Collins, who came on a road trip to Doncaster together in 1857, also missed out. Dickens, then 45, was in amorous pursuit of his soon to be mistress, an 18-year-old actress called Ellen Ternan, who was performing at Doncaster's Theatre Royal. Dickens took Ternan to the St. Leger and published an account, co-authored with Wilkie, of his time in Doncaster and his wider travels to the north, titled *The Lazy Tour of Two Idle Apprentices.* His wife divorced him shortly after. How on earth could I not know this!

Then there is the hellraising actor Oliver Reed, who appeared in more than 30 movies including Oscar winners *Women in Love, Gladiator* and *Oliver!.* It turns out that he had more than one boozy night in Doncaster's Clay Lane Social Club in the 1990s. David Copperfield (not the American magician, but the

Doncaster born comedian who appeared in the 1980s sketch show *Three of a Kind* with Lenny Henry and Tracy Ullman) was Reed's mate and local drinking buddy. On one visit to the club, when Reed was looking especially dishevelled, the regulars held him down on the pool table, and jokingly pulled out razors in a bid to give him an impromptu shave. Taking the whole thing in his stride, the unkempt star slammed £50 on the bar and told the barman to get a round in for 'all the northern working-class pigs.' £50 went a bit further at the bar back then. Doncaster is haemorrhaging with wonderful characters and stories like these, but none of what you have just read was included in our bid. I could argue that, because I didn't grow up here, I couldn't be expected to be familiar with all these stories. It feels like a lame excuse though. What I can say is that Doncaster's history is littered with the most amazing people. And I am quite certain that, even now, I don't know who they all are.

So, what does all this teach us? Well, I suspect that this wasn't a unique experience for Doncaster alone. I imagine that, if I had the time, I could probably research at least one city-worthy fact for every entrant in the competition which didn't feature in their bids. And whilst Doncaster (or rather I) failed to mention its Nobel Laureate and its BBC Sports Personality of the Year, it still won city status. It stands to reason that other contenders likely had some highly impactful facts, figures, stories, and personalities who didn't make it into their bid pages. For some, that may have been the difference between winning and losing. It is not simply a need for good research, but it's also about knowing what to look for and where to find it. There isn't a singular, easy to find website that's teed-up to hand you all the answers on a plate. Nevertheless, I suspect there may be some Doncastrian's reading this chapter with their head in their hands, utterly shocked that we completely missed George Porter, Tommy Simpson, Gillian Coulthard, Charles Dickens, and Edward Elgar. For me, I think, this underlines the importance of having the right people around the table. We didn't have a local historian, an archivist, or a journalist on our Project Board, and I think, with the benefit of hindsight, that was an error. You need people who have a rich and deep knowledge of the locality, people who know more than the obvious. This doesn't mean you have to include everything that they bring to the table, but you can at least be a little more confident in that all the salient stories and historical figures are under consideration.

Having said that, we couldn't realistically pack a lot more detail into the bid. It was already bursting. To add something else would probably have meant that something already in would have had to have come out, and that is always a constant dilemma for bid writers in working with tight word and page count limits. Sometimes it's inevitable that good material ends up on the cutting room floor, and the skill sometimes is in knowing what to keep and what to let go. I continue to learn new things about Doncaster all the time. Writing this book hasn't helped. As I have industriously researched each chapter I have inevitably stumbled upon a burgeoning mound of new information. I typically still wince and recoil with a degree of shame when I read something new that I know would have been a dead certainty to have been included in the bid, but I smile too. There is a sense of real pride in that Doncaster has such a rich menu of accolades to choose from. I apologise if we left something or somebody out that you are personally passionate about, but perhaps this chapter has redressed that balance just a little. We really were spoiled for choice!

Runners and Riders

Whilst many of the city status bidders had run public campaigns, including press events to mark the submission of their bids, a definitive list of all the bidders was not published by the Cabinet Office until two days before Christmas. Prior to this, there was no way of knowing for certain exactly which, and how many, localities had entered the contest. This is not unusual in proposal writing; you rarely know with certainty who all the other bidders are at the point of submission, and it is not unusual to never know this, even after the result is declared. The publication of the list of entrants did, however, give the Cabinet Office an opportunity to sustain the momentum of the contest and keep it in the public eye. By presenting a dynamic list of entrants, the contest could be shown to be relevant and popular, emphasising that city status remained a coveted title in modern Britain, and that the competition was a valued component of the Platinum Jubilee celebrations. The declaration of bidders was also arguably in keeping with the spirit and nature of the competition, epitomising the concept of civic pride. If your town was proud enough to enter, then it should relish appearing on this list.

It turned out that there were 39 bidders in total, a few more than I had personally anticipated. There were 22 localities from England, 8 from Scotland, 3 from Northern Ireland, and Wrexham, the single entrant from Wales. Alongside these were Peel and Douglas on the Isle of Mann, Stanley in the Falkland Islands, Gibraltar, and George Town in the Cayman

Islands. The media coverage primarily focused in on some of these more exotic locations, as well as other surprise bidders, most notably the sleepy seaside port of Marazion in Cornwall. Marazion was the smallest entrant in terms of population, home to around 1,500 people, making it barely a town, let alone a city. Outside of Yorkshire, there was comparatively little coverage of Doncaster's entry; we were arguably lost in the mix and just another name on the list. This absence from the spotlight didn't unduly bother me though. Whilst both mainstream and social media were having a field day poking fun at the list of entrants, some of which was less than gracious, I was content in the knowledge that none of these opinions really mattered. Fortunately, we weren't trying to win a national popularity contest on Twitter or Facebook.

The heavyweight competitors who we'd been keeping an eye on, like Middlesbrough and Reading, were all present and correct. There were, however, several names who hadn't previously been on our radar, and whose campaigns up until now had been relatively low key. I had perceived, as it turns out wrongly, that Doncaster was not facing any competitors on its immediate doorstep. The appearance of Bolsover in the north of Derbyshire, only around 25 miles south of Doncaster, was therefore an irritating surprise. Bolsover's bid had not been publicly launched and had been flying beneath everyone's radar, the local community included. This small market town had shown no previous desires to become a city. Whilst it has a splendid 17th century castle, and a history of coal mining akin to that of Doncaster, its credentials as a prospective city were less than obvious. Of far greater personal annoyance, however, was the appearance of the port town of Goole on the list, at an even closer distance to Doncaster of just 17 miles from town centre to town centre. Doncaster had traded on being the only bid from Yorkshire, with our unanimous signed letter of backing from all the local authorities in the county via the Yorkshire Leader's Board to that end. The East Riding of Yorkshire Council, in whose borders Goole resides, still have some questions to answer from me here! To say that I was decidedly irked was an understatement. In fairness to Goole, they were a previous bidder and had made a little bit of noise publicly about their latest campaign, it just hadn't registered with me before that date. So, rather than being able to draw a large circle around Doncaster and say "hey, why not put a new city here?", we instead had to endure two smaller local upstarts setting up their stall on our doorstep.

Aside from Bolsover and Goole, the entry list threw up a surprisingly high number of other local derbies, with two different towns entering from the same locality. This included Alcester and Warwick (both in Warwickshire), Warrington and Crewe (both in Cheshire), Dorchester and Bournemouth (both in Dorset), Douglas and Peel (both on the Isle of Mann), and Dunfermline and St. Andrews (both in Fife). These head-to-heads were curious, as the odds of two entrants from the same local area winning were debatably slim. If anything, there was a risk that the local rivals could weaken each other's chances, diluting the uniqueness of their respective identities. You would imagine that, had one of the pair dropped out and rallied behind the other, then the chances are that the surviving bid may have fared better. This was partially arguably borne out by the results. Whilst Douglas and Dunfermline went on to win, all the entrants from Warwickshire, Cheshire, and Dorset ultimately went home empty handed. In most cases, these rival bids were submitted by different authorities, perhaps going some way to explain how so many head-to-heads arose. For example, whilst both sit under Warwickshire County Council, the bids for Alcester and Warwick were submitted by their respective district and town councils. As a result, whilst the two towns are only 15 miles apart, there was possibly little if any co-ordination between their campaigns (not unlike Doncaster and Goole). The bids for Dunfermline and St. Andrews, on the other hand, were both submitted by Fife Council, notably the first and only individual authority to make separate entries for two different towns in the same Civic Honours contest. It's an interesting first, as it could encourage more councils with multiple towns to play the numbers game and submit multiple entries in future contests. Essex, for example, has over 30 towns, meaning that Essex County Council could, in theory, submit a bid for each of them.

But what chances did all these places really have? Well, prior to the results of the Diamond Jubilee contest in 2012 being announced, Reading were the standout bookies favourites with impressive odds offered by Ladbrokes at 8/11[36]. They were followed by eventual winners Perth at 5/1, Medway at 8/1,

---

36   https://www.readingchronicle.co.uk/news/13394999.reading-city-its-an-odds-on-certainty-say-bookies/

Tower Hamlets at 9/1, with Doncaster (punching up, I feel) and Bournemouth both at 10/1. Alongside Perth, the other winning cities in 2012 were priced attractively, with Chelmsford at 16/1 and St Asaph at 33/1. Goole sat at the bottom of the list, a long shot outsider at 50/1. Except for Perth though (and perhaps Goole), the bookies had seemingly got their odds completely wrong, which may explain why no bookmakers were taking bets again in 2022. Picking city status winners really was a seeming lottery. More the pity really, as I would have had a flutter on Donny if it had been priced at 10/1 again. I did email William Hill to see if I could put a bet on, but I never heard back from them.

It would take far too long for me to give you an in-depth perspective on all the entrants, and it would take us some way away from the core purpose of this book. There are, however, a few places that I think are worthy of singling out for a specific mention. Let me start with Reading, in Berkshire, claimed to be the largest town in England (albeit Northampton's bid claimed that it was the largest town in Europe, so I'm not going to take sides). The largest town in England tag was, however, both a blessing and a curse when it comes to city status. Reading has so much to shout about asides from its population, with its eminent campus university, a 24,000-seater stadium, and an original Banksy adorning the wall of Reading Gaol. It has great connectivity, positioned on the M4 and with a Great Western Mainline station, and that's now been further enhanced by the newly opened Elizabeth Line. The cherry on the top for Reading is surely that it is the birthplace of Catherine, Princess

of Wales, a future Queen, and mother of a future King. As if
that wasn't a good enough royal trump card, the now ruined
Reading Abbey is also the last resting place of King Henry I.
As royal associations go, Reading is right up there. In poker
they call it a throne if you are lucky enough to be holding both a
King and a Queen in your hand, but Reading has never yet been
dealt that all important full house. It is the perennial bridesmaid
of the city status contests, and it's hard to put a finger on the
reason why. They take the competition seriously, their bids are
strong, and local people seem to genuinely want city status. I
wonder perhaps though, if you are the favourite, the judges feel
a need to apply a more exacting yardstick to your entry? Maybe
Reading is a victim of its own hype. Who knows? I know that
I may come to regret these words, but surely it is only a matter
of time before Reading gets the reward it has coveted for so
long. Surely?

Middlesbrough was perhaps Doncaster's most obvious
direct competitor in terms of a northern England head-to-
head. There are no cities in the Tees Valley, and the potential
elevation of Middlesbrough would place it on what many felt
would be a deserved level pegging with nearby Newcastle and
Sunderland. The threat to Doncaster was, however, seemingly
less about the locality and more about the politics. The Tees
Valley Combined Authority had been created in 2016, and with
it the position of an elected metro Mayor. In 2022 there were
10 elected metro Mayors in England, but only two of those
were Conservatives, and one of those was Ben Houchen in the
Tees Valley. I've heard Houchen speak at a conference, and

he is a formidable policy thinker, and a political poster boy of Boris Johnson's Blue Wall. Houchen's success in Tees Valley was no mean feat when you consider that Middlesbrough is a traditional blue-collar town, with a history of deprivation, and, as a constituency, a safe Labour seat. The temptation for Minister's to give Middlesbrough the nod to further bolster the Conservative's standing in the Tees Valley, and applaud Houchen's achievements, must have been profound. Thankfully for Doncaster, that nod never came. Houchen was, however, recognised in Boris Johnson's infamous Prime Minister's resignation honours list, receiving a seat in the House of Lords and the title of Baron Houchen of High Leven, which I guess is not too bad a consolation prize.

Next up is Rochester in Kent, which has the unfortunate distinction of having previously held city status for almost 800 years, but then having lost it. It's a story that would leave Rochester's forefather's turning in their graves. In recent times this former city has been a victim of several local authority boundary restructures, resulting in its Letters Patent having been updated in both 1974 and 1982. This frequent rewriting of the city's governance created a likelihood of confusion, and a greater risk of the inevitable disaster that followed. In 1998 a further restructure led to Rochester-upon-Medway City Council and Gillingham Borough Council being merged to become the new unitary authority of Medway, named after Kent's famous river which runs through the locality. The 1982 Letters Patent required the new unitary authority to appoint new charter trustees to preserve Rochester's city status. Straightforward enough, you would think. But no trustees were appointed, and thus when Rochester-upon-Medway City Council was abolished, Rochester's 800 years of city status were lost with it. Put simply, no-one remembered to fill the form in! More bizarrely, it would take several years before anyone at the new council even realised the error.

If Rochester were to put in a standalone city status bid now though, it would surely be a very strong contender, with its imposing Norman cathedral and an equally impressive 12th century castle. It's almost nonsensical to think that a former city with almost a millennium of history would not be a shoo-in to recapture its status. There has, however, never been a city status bid made by Rochester. Instead, four back-to-back bids, in 2000, 2002, 2012 and now 2022 have all been submitted by the unitary authority, tabled as the city of Medway. There are those in Rochester who take great exception to this. Whilst Rochester, they feel, has a rightful and historic claim to city status; Gillingham most certainly does not. Medway Council has a difficult dilemma here; a bid for Rochester alone may have a better chance, but would it alienate Gillingham if they were left out? After four failed bids though, I think they must accept that Rochester perhaps deserves its chance to have a standalone bid next time around. If it did, it would be one to watch.

If Rochester's story of losing its city status is strange, then Gibraltar's story of entering the competition despite already being a city is perhaps stranger still. Gibraltar has been a British overseas territory since 1713, when it was ceded to

Britain following the War of the Spanish Succession. Despite this, its future sovereignty continues to be a touchy point between London and Madrid. In its bid Gibraltar described itself as 'the symbol of Britishness', adding some fresh fuel to the flames of that particular argument. Gibraltar is famous for its strategic naval port at the gateway to the Mediterranean; its Barbary macaque monkeys, the only wild monkey population in continental Europe; and for the Rock of Gibraltar, the 426m high monolithic limestone outcrop which dominates its skyline. The outpost at the southwestern tip of the Iberian Peninsula missed out on city status when the Platinum Jubilee Civic Honours winner's list was announced. All, however, was not lost! Research in the National Archives latterly revealed that Queen Victoria had, in fact, already granted the status to the City of Gibraltar in 1842. The award had been made under Diocesan Letters Patent and not under the normal City Status Letters Patent, therefore the City of Gibraltar never ended up on the Home Office's official list of recognised cities. The folks in Gibraltar were seemingly blissfully unaware of this too; there was no claim in their bid to suggest that they were already a city. Gibraltar's city status was nevertheless belatedly re-affirmed by the British government in August 2022, some 180 years late! I am sure that Rochester followed that story with keen interest. If Gibraltar could get its city status back on a seeming technicality, then why not Rochester too?

It would be remiss of me not to give Crawley in Sussex a shout out. My parents have lived in Crawley since 1989 and my sister, Tricia, settled there too after she graduated. It's where she met her husband, Ady, and raised Mathew and Nathan, my nephews. I lived in Crawley too between 1989 and 1991, when I was studying for my A-Levels, and then on-and-off again between my university years and before Anne and I moved in together. Crawley going head-to-head with Doncaster for city status therefore led to some inevitable and interesting family banter. I probably watched Crawley's campaign with a keener eye than some of our other rivals, and, when I finally got hold of a copy of Crawley's bid, I had a far more informed perspective of its strengths and weaknesses. Of all our rivals, it was the one place I knew almost as well as Doncaster, if not perhaps more so.

Crawley was a debutant to city status biding in 2022. It was designated as a new town in 1947 and, as such, was one of the youngest contenders. As with other new towns, Crawley was earmarked to play its role in the post-war housing boom, with 5,000 acres set aside for new homes. The thing though which arguably sets Crawley apart from London's other commuter belt towns is the presence of Gatwick Airport, whose runways, terminals, and ground infrastructure occupies a giant swathe of the northern end of the borough. Catering for around 80,000 flights and 10 million passengers per year, Gatwick is undeniably a city standard asset. But, regardless of Doncaster's prospects, I never really saw Crawley as a likely winner. Their campaign played to the fact that 2022 was Crawley's own 75th anniversary as a new town, which was a nice touch, but I think the borough lacked the depth of history and assets of its stronger rivals in southern England. Gatwick was a blessing and a curse.

On the upside, it is the UK's second busiest airport and a major international hub. On the downside, its association with being a London airport ultimately risked detracting from Crawley's own identity. I'm glad they took part though, and I hope that they will have another go when the time comes. And in terms of my family, much as I love them all, I obviously fully enjoyed the bragging rights that came with Doncaster succeeding where Crawley had failed!

North of the border, South Ayrshire was posing a very different question. Sitting to the south of Glasgow, the locality covers around 80-miles of coastline along the Firth of Clyde and stretches all the way inland to the beauty of the Galloway Forest. The modest town of Ayr, which sits at its northern end, had previously bid by itself to win city status, so this tactic to include the wider locality was something new. But whilst South Ayrshire was fully eligible to enter, it plainly doesn't comply with what many people would think of as a city. There is no discerning or dominating metropolis. It is instead an unending semi-rural swathe of moorlands, beaches, fields, and forests, peppered with the occasional small town, harbour, or village. One of South Ayrshire's chief claims to fame is that it has hosted golf's Open Championship 14 times, shared between two of Britain's best golf courses, Royal Troon and Turnberry, the latter now owned by former US President Donald Trump. Plainly and simply, this is the countryside! The pitch for city status was therefore clearly ambitious, and the prospects may have been slim, but arguably this bid added to the debate as to what a city could or should be.

In recent times the term "polycentric city" has been coined by academics, broadly defined as a locality with multiple urban centres but which are not necessarily connected by continuous development. Many established cities, such as London, Los Angeles, and Washington DC, have already been described as polycentric (and a potential city of Medway would also fall under that definition too), but the term arguably lends itself to more unconventional candidates. For example, the Council in Moreton Bay, a region comprised of both towns and countryside in Queensland, Australia, is actively attempting to reclassify itself as a city. Yes, Moreton Bay has a much more significant population that South Ayrshire, but it also has a much longer coastline, is home to more than half a dozen state forests and offers picture postcard views across the Glasshouse Mountains. Neither place looks nor feels like a conventional city, but the idea of polycentric regions such as these being recognised as cities is gaining traction. So, whilst Britain may not quite be ready for a polycentric city just yet, it may only be a matter of time before we get one. South Ayrshire may have been an outlier this time, but it could just be the shape of city status bids to come.

I could go on and give you a synopsis of all the other entrants, but by now you are probably getting the general idea. By way of a mop-up, I will instead list for you a few of the choice city-worthy credentials described in the bids of some of the other contenders. As was the experience of Doncaster, it is hard to determine which facts to include, but here are just a few of my personal favourites which all evoke plentiful joie-de-vivre. I will let you pick your own favourite.

- Dudley is apparently home to 28 species of waxcap mushrooms, giving it the fourth richest grassland in England for such fungi. I don't know where the top three are, or how many different species of wild mushroom grow in Doncaster.
- According to its bid, houses in Oban range from five-bedroom detached houses in countryside settings and cosy bungalows, to town centre studio flats. This, however, isn't true. I have just checked on Zoopla and have immediately seen several properties for sale in Oban with six or more bedrooms. Larger families should not be deterred.
- The bid from Guildford tells us that, whilst there are a few car showrooms near the Ladymead Retail Park, the majority can apparently be found at Slyfield, a couple of miles beyond the town centre, and where there are also several storage companies. The people of Surrey clearly pride themselves on their attention to the small details.
- Crewe Day is on July 4th, the date when the first steam train arrived in the town in 1837, leading their bid to proclaim: 'Who knows, maybe one day July 4th will be more readily associated with Crewe rather than the USA!' Well, you never know.
- And finally, I'll return to Goole, whose bid tells of a case of mistaken identity. It claims that if you search for the name of Goole on Google, the search engine believes that

you have misspelt its own name by mistake. I tried this, and it does. The bid goes on: 'Let's hope that this works in reverse and that many Google users' chance upon our vibrant town'. I tried this too, and it doesn't.

This all hopefully gives you a sense of who we were up against. It was an eclectic mix of localities of all shapes, sizes, and backgrounds; the good, the bad, the ugly, and everything in between. I may quip a little here, but we were never complacent about any of our rivals. Doncaster may be a lot of things, but it's certainly not the sort of lordly place that holds itself aloof, sits on a pedestal, and dotes upon its own self-reflection. To the contrary, Doncaster was a glasshouse, with many imperfections of its own, and in which the throwing of stones was very much ill advised. At the same time, we didn't allow ourselves to get too distracted by our competitors. We all had the cards we were dealt, with our own histories and heritage, and we had to make the best of ours. We couldn't control their bids, but we could control our own, and that was our only real focus. There was, however, one final noteworthy thing about the list of entrants published by the Cabinet Office. It wasn't a concern about any of the names who were on the list, but rather a bemusement at some of the names that weren't.

The No Shows

hilst there was a high amount of media interest in the towns that had entered the Civic Honours competition, there was far less focus on the longer list of towns that could have entered but didn't. Many towns had entered the various Civic Honours competitions over the decades, but a surprisingly high number of previously unsuccessful bidders, 18 in total, chose not to enter again this time around. With more than 20 past bids between them, the combined absence of Bolton, Croydon, Stockport, Ipswich, Shrewsbury, and Luton from the competition must surely be a worry. Bolton, Croydon, and Stockport had all competed in the previous four successive campaigns. Ipswich, Shrewsbury, and Luton were similarly former three-time bidders, whilst Maidstone, Dover, Swindon, and Aberystwyth were amongst those locations who had entered twice. Notable, and arguably formidable, former one-off entrants included Telford, Greenwich, and Gateshead. It was a glaring and uncomfortable list of absentees.

Don't get me wrong, when potential rivals opt out of a competition, that is usually welcome news for bid writers. If credible competitors step back, and the field narrows, that can only usually improve the prospects of your own bid. In this respect, the absence of northern playmakers like Bolton, Stockport, and Gateshead was not a development that the people of Doncaster were likely to lose too much sleep over. But, in looking at things objectively and dispassionately, the overall competition would have been better had these towns have entered. To prove their worth, bid writers are a bit like sportspersons; they want to compete against, and hopefully beat, the best competition that is out there. The reasons for such drop out, and active non-participation, of major towns from the Civic Honours contest should therefore rightly be a concern for both the Cabinet Office and Buckingham Palace. If a town perceived itself of worthy of city status in the past, its credentials are hardly likely to have materially weakened in the years since. It is surely in the best interests of city status competitions for localities to count themselves in, rather than count themselves out. So, why had all these big hitters decided to take their ball home and not play again this time?

Without talking to Council leaders in all these localities, and assuming that they would give me candidly honest answers if I did, there is no way of knowing the reasons for absenteeism with absolute certainty. We can though perhaps speculate to a degree. It's plausible, for example, that for some local administrations the competition was genuinely overlooked. No one grabbed the proverbial bull by the horns and said 'hey, I think we should be entering this city status thing'. It's not, after all, compulsory to enter. This could well be the explanation in a few exceptional cases, but I suspect that most of the absent past entrants took a conscious, if not necessarily always formalised, decision not to enter. It is hard to believe that any of them would have consciously ignored it.

Of all the no shows, Merthyr Tydfil in Wales arguably did the most due diligence in reaching a decision not to bid. A Full

Council Report, running to 12 pages in detail, was tabled in October 2021, forensically weighing up, with what I would say was a balanced tone, the comparative pros-and-cons of bidding. The Merthyr Tydfil & Rhymney MP, Gerald Jones, had already made a speech in the Commons in support of a bid, securing the wider backing of some other South Wales MPs. The local Council also seemed initially intent to bid. An informal public poll was, however, run through Facebook, Instagram, and the Council's own website. Whilst only around 3% of the community took part, those favouring not to bid were in the strong majority (quelle surprise). This seemed to sway the Council vote; 10 councillors were in favour of bidding, but 21 were against. Despite seemingly only having to outbid Wrexham to win city status for Wales, that was the end of Merthyr Tydfil's campaign.

The Covid-19 pandemic was clearly a factor influencing others in 2021. In terms of the absence of Shrewsbury, Lezley Picton[37], leader of Shropshire Council leader said: 'Given the current focus on post Covid-19 recovery we have decided that our resources are best concentrated on economic and social recovery and delivering important local services. We simply do not have the capacity or finances to spend time bidding.' A similar rationale was put forward by Bolton[38], where a spokesman said: 'On this occasion, following discussion with

---

37   https://www.countytimes.co.uk/news/19493515.no-powys-towns-will-bid-city-status-2022/

38   https://www.theboltonnews.co.uk/news/20006031.bolton-decision-not-bid-city-status-queens-jubilee-competition-made-secret/

the council leader and other cabinet members, it was decided not to submit a bid so we could prioritise the council's core services, the response to the on-going pandemic and the substantial regeneration going ahead in the town centre'. Bolton's decision not to bid was, however, met with something of a local backlash, with the Conservative council leader being accused by opposition councillors of having made the decision not to bid in secret and behind closed doors.

On one hand it is hard to argue with the rationale not to bid put forward by the likes of Shrewsbury and Bolton, and they should be accepted at face value. On the other, almost forty other councils, Doncaster included, all equally challenged by the aftermath of Covid-19 and undeniably stretched in terms of resource, still decided to bid. Yes, there will be some locality specific context behind all these decisions, made by both the bidders and the non-bidders, and the challenges faced by one Council, whilst potentially similar in some characteristics, are by no means identical to that of any other. I doubt, however, that any of the Councils who went ahead with bids for city status in 2021 did so at the cost of a markedly poorer recovery response to the pandemic than those councils who chose not to bid. And whilst the Covid-19 pandemic was an undeniably unique event, several of the former city status competitions also took place at times of economic uncertainty. The Ruby Jubilee competition, for example, which Bolton and Shrewsbury both entered, took place amid the immediate aftermath of the 1990/91 recession. Again, different times and different circumstances clearly must be accounted for, and I'm using Bolton and Shrewsbury here solely for the purposes of illustration, but at the very least these issues raise the question as to whether every Council who could have bid in 2021 but didn't, gave a full and complete account as to their reasons why.

Furthermore, there are several large towns, with populations comfortably over 100,000 people, who have never competed to win city status. This surprising list includes the likes of Blackpool, Watford, Huddersfield, Eastbourne, and Cheltenham; all more than credible names if they were in the hat. Like Bolton and Shrewsbury, some of these places similarly saw their Covid-19 response as the greater priority in 2021. When interviewed about city status, the Mayor of Watford, Peter Taylor, said: 'My instinctive reaction is to ask, will this benefit us? My focus is making sure we recover from Covid by supporting local people and businesses to adapt and grow. That is key for everyone in our town.'[39] But the Covid-19 recovery was not the only factor which kept traditional non-bidders away. Unlike towns who have bid in the past, those who have never entered can more justifiably argue that city status isn't worth bidding for without sounding like hypocrites. Whilst, for example, Cheltenham has at least toyed with the idea of bidding for city status, it has chosen instead in recent years to prioritise investment in its visitor economy strategy. In 2017 Cheltenham Councillor Flo Clucas said: 'While a future bid for [city status] is not ruled out, it's more about getting potential visitors to realise what a significant and visit-worthy place Cheltenham

---

39   https://www.watfordobserver.co.uk/news/19371146.mayor-watford-no-plans-watford-bid-city-status/

is, with its Regency architecture, its major cultural festivals and the best week of horse-racing in the world.'[40] Whilst she makes a good point, I'm not sure that the people of Doncaster would necessarily agree with that final claim.

This all leads me to the central premise of this chapter, a term that I will coin as Civic Honours apathy, and one which I will be very smug about should it ever be referenced in somebody's PhD thesis at some point in the future. It's a simple notion; we all like to spend our time doing things we are good at. If we play a few games of football, or chess, or sudoku, or whatever, and find that we lose every time, or just can't solve the puzzle, then sooner or later it stops being fun. A few will persevere, but many will just give up, and try something different in the hope that they will be better at that instead. I, for example, have always been hopeless at playing team sports like football, but I have always enjoyed running, and the only sports trophy I ever won at school was for orienteering (runner-up, The Hobbs Parker Kent Schools Orienteering League, 1987, thank you). And therein lies my point; if Bolton, Croydon, and Stockport have all bid for city status on four occasions without success, the appetite and enthusiasm to make a fifth attempt must surely and understandably start to wane. No town wants to have a record of being a perpetual loser. But, if city status becomes perceived as little more than a lottery, where success hinges on the worth a select few written pages, rather than the full depth of a town's history and heritage, is there enough of an

---

40   https://www.gloucestershirelive.co.uk/news/cheltenham-news/how-cheltenham-plans-become-city-191803

incentive to participate? Is it less painful to simply not bother?

It would be wrong to suggest that city status apathy is the only factor. Sectarian divides are, for example, a very different consideration in Northern Ireland. Ballymena, Bangor, and Coleraine, the three entrants from Northern Ireland, notably all have predominantly protestant populations. It is perhaps less surprising that a Platinum Jubilee Civic Honours contest would appeal most to unionist leaning towns, and this probably saved some headaches in Whitehall in picking Bangor as the eventual winner without leaving anyone's nose all that out of joint. No towns with a majority catholic population, those traditionally with a more republican persuasion, chose to enter. Omagh, Strabane, Downpatrick, and Enniskillen are all on that list. There could be several reasons for their absence; like most towns in Northern Ireland, they are all comparatively small, and maybe Covid-19 was a factor too. It's hard to believe though that an ideological pushback isn't an influencing factor to some greater or lesser extent. These catholic towns may well all aspire to become cities, but perhaps preferably not on the say-so and bequest of a British (and dare I say English) monarch.

And what about London? The Platinum Jubilee competition was, at face value, open to any local authority; but should, in the case of Greater London, cities be created within cities? By virtue of already being part of London, don't these places already have city status? There is precedent, of course, in that Westminster has city status in its own right, as does the City of London, the ceremonial county and financial business district in the heart of the capital. But if more boroughs become cities, would this damage London's brand, and turn it into a more peculiar oddity, a city of cities? This rationale suggests that bids from London boroughs are unlikely to be successful and may go some way to explain the general lack of bids historically put forward from within the capital. Back in 2018, John Hickman, a local historian and city status advocate from Croydon, acknowledged that his borough's 'big disadvantage is we are too close to London to be a city'[41]. Let's also not forget that, following a failed city status bid in 2002, Greenwich was subsequently awarded Royal Borough status in 2012. Not a city perhaps, but still a meaningful civic recognition, and perhaps enough to keep the good people of Greenwich content. There is still a level of support for city status in both Croydon and Tower Hamlets (bidders in 2012), but the London factor is clearly an ongoing obstacle to traverse. A new city within London is perhaps an unrealistic prospect for now.

In some localities there were split views in terms of city status ambitions. Blackpool's two Conservative MPs, Paul Maynard and Scott Benton, encouraged a bid to be tabled by the town[42], but no bid was ultimately forthcoming from the Labour controlled council. Perhaps that decision was influenced by a splash of political gamesmanship? A similar scenario played out in Ipswich, albeit with the roles reversed. Here the local Conservative MP, Tom Hunt, was against the idea of the town bidding, even though the Labour controlled

---

41   https://www.croydonadvertiser.co.uk/news/local-news/isnt-croydon-city-heres-reasons-1845614

42   https://www.paulmaynard.co.uk/campaigns/city-status-blackpool-0

Council was enthusiastic. There is some irony here, as the Council technically didn't need Hunt's endorsement or consent to submit a bid. They presumably nevertheless felt that, without the local MP on board, the prospects of an Ipswich bid succeeding may be far reduced. Hunt felt that any bid should be subject to some form of local referendum, and ultimately that the people of Ipswich should decide. As I've already discussed, this was effectively making a no bid decision a fait accompli, as it would be effectively impossible for any council to justify the resource for such a referendum, even if they were confident of winning it.

In an interview with *The East Anglian Daily Times* in June 2021, Hunt personally set out his position[43]. He had carried out his own poll on social media, as well as highlighting a similar poll undertaken by *The Ipswich Star*, which had returned results of 66% and 70% respectively against an Ipswich city status bid (shocking!). That said, a poll is a poll, and these results both gave power to the elbow of Hunt's position. Hunt also cited that city status was rarely an issue that came up on the doorstep when he was out campaigning. I am sure that's true, but city status is probably never at the forefront of anyone's mind when a politician randomly turns up at their front door. I suspect too that most people don't voluntarily tell politicians on their doorstep that they would prefer not to see a reintroduction of capital punishment, but their likely silence on the matter shouldn't be taken to imply the opposite. If Hunt

---

43   https://www.eadt.co.uk/news/21277692.tom-hunt-mp-opposed-ipswichs-city-status-bid/

had specifically and proactively asked people about city status on the doorstep, I wonder if the message he heard back would have been different?

But are the people of Ipswich more apathetic towards city status compared to those from other towns? Well, there is one factor which is more specific to Ipswich that may go some way to explain this. It has nothing to do with Covid-19 or cynicism towards the perceived economic benefits of city status. No, one of the biggest stumbling blocks for city status in Ipswich is much more straightforward; it's a matter of football, the beautiful game. Ipswich's football team has a proud history. They won the English League title (what is the Premier League today) in 1962. Alf Ramsey was their manager then, his last club before he became England coach in 1963 and engineered the World Cup win of 1966. Under the legendary management of Bobby Robson in the 1970s and 1980s Ipswich were a footballing tour de force, finishing as runners up in the league in both 1981 and 1982, winning the FA Cup in 1978, and the UEFA Cup in 1981. In 1980 several Ipswich players appeared alongside the actors Michael Caine and Sylvester Stallone, and the footballing royalty of Bobby Moore and Pele, in the wartime era football movie *Escape to Victory*. To this day Ipswich holds the unusual record as being the only British team to have never lost a home game in European competitions. Their fortunes have slipped in recent times, dropping to the third tier, albeit they were promoted back to the Championship in 2023. Football remains a matter of deep-seated pride in Ipswich. And the name of the team? Why, it's Ipswich Town Football Club, of course!

There are 19 different suffixes which appear in the names of English league football teams. You have Albion, Athletic, Rangers, United, and (of course) Rovers, to name but a few. In most cases, these team names have little if any bearing on city status ambitions. But there are two suffixes which have the potential to polarise opinions, perhaps more so than any other factor: Town and City. If you think it would be a simple thing to just rename Ipswich Town and turn them into Ipswich City, think again. The identities of football clubs are sacrosanct, they are entwined in the helix of a community's DNA. Just ask the people of Cardiff. In 2012 Vincent Tan, the Malaysian billionaire who had bought Cardiff City FC a couple of years beforehand, replaced the bluebird on the team's crest with a dragon and changed the team's colours from blue to red, colours they had worn for over a century. The move was considered as sacrilege by the Cardiff faithful, and Tan was reviled. He eventually yielded to the relentless backlash from supporters and reinstated the original strip in 2015. It was a cautionary tale; you just don't mess with football clubs. If Ipswich needed a reason not to bid for city status, they wouldn't find a more popular one locally than the prospect of renaming their team.

The issue is not unique to Ipswich. Platinum Jubilee bidders Crawley and Northampton, and former city hopefuls Swindon and Shrewsbury, all have teams with the Town suffix. With no disrespect to any of these teams though, none have matched Ipswich's historic accomplishments on the pitch. When a team wins trophies, its name is written in the footballing history books. But is it all just a storm in a teacup, making mountains out of mole hills? After all, Swansea Town successfully renamed to become Swansea City in 1969 to reflect the award of city status. Let's also not forget that the Milton Keynes Dons were only established in 2002, when 1988 FA Cup winners Wimbledon FC were lured to the town and rebranded. These things seemingly didn't ruffle too many feathers for too long. And Ipswich Town doesn't necessarily have to become Ipswich City. They could simply become Ipswich FC or, if they really wanted to double down, just keep the name Ipswich Town. Would that be any more of a bizarre team name than that of Sheffield Wednesday or Tottenham Hotspur? Or maybe a new breakaway Ipswich City FC may emerge all by itself, a bit like Reading City FC which arrived in 2001, perhaps more in hope than expectation of city status. Thankfully Doncaster's team is, and always will be, the Rovers, giving us one less problem to contend with.

Ipswich Town supporters may take some comfort from nearby Colchester. Colchester has two train stations, one named Colchester and the other, more contentiously, named Colchester Town. Despite Colchester's newfound city status, Greater Anglia trains, who manage the station, have so far declined from renaming it as "Colchester City", despite local voices calling for the change. Apparently it would all be disproportionately expensive. In reply, Sir Bob Russell, the High Steward of Colchester, said: 'The Dutch-owned company have made their decision and if they want to insult Colchester and not take accord of the wishes of our late Queen, to make

Colchester a city, then there's nothing I can do about it.'[44] Feisty words indeed, with a little nationalistic spice on the side, but perhaps it's not obligatory for everything in a city to be renamed. Then again, I wonder if Sir Bob is aware that, north of the border, Scottish-owned Scotrail agreed to rename Dunfermline Town station to become Dunfermline City[45]. Who would have thought that the names of railway stations could be so contentious?

The ironic twist in Ipswich's story is that, since the Platinum Jubilee competition concluded, the local momentum for city status has undergone a notable U-turn. The "Future City Ipswich" campaign was launched in February 2023, spearheaded by Sophie Alexander-Parker, the Chief Executive of Ipswich Central, the town's Business Improvement District. The campaign created its own dedicated website, garnered renewed support from local stakeholders and politicians, and gained coverage with the BBC and local media. A couple of months later the University of Suffolk hosted a panel event, chaired by Omid Djalili, the well-known comedian and actor (albeit perhaps lesser known as being a resident of Ipswich), to urge the locals to look beyond the name of the football team, and unite behind a future city bid. This was the level of investment and campaigning that would likely have given Ipswich some serious city status momentum had they applied

---

44   https://www.gazette-news.co.uk/news/23337192.greater-anglia-will-not-rename-colchester-town-station/

45   https://news.stv.tv/east-central/dunfermlines-railway-station-set-for-name-change-to-reflect-city-status-after-kings-visit

it during the Platinum Jubilee contest. The contest had also seemingly inspired some other prospective bidders. In October 2022, for example, there was a call from Berwick upon Tweed, a town that has hitherto never put its name in the hat, to be declared as Northumberland's first city[46]. Building on all of this, perhaps we may see a wave of fresh impetus for the next city status contest.

The problem for Ipswich and Berwick, of course, is that no one knows when exactly that could happen. Both were perhaps hopeful that there would be a new contest to mark King Charles' coronation, but that didn't happen. Perhaps this was because it fell so soon after the Platinum Jubilee competition, which had already rewarded a record number of winners. So when could the next contest be? Well, the first meaningful jubilee for Charles would surely be at least 10 years into his reign, in 2032, albeit that would either be classed as a Tin Jubilee or an Aluminium Jubilee, hardly the most treasurable of elements. He would be 83 by then, and wouldn't reach a Silver Jubilee until he was 98, in 2047. Given the trend for royals to live to ripe old ages, you wouldn't bet against him reaching that milestone, but that seems like an awfully long time to wait before Britain may have its next new city. If, God forbid, Charles didn't live that long, then a coronation contest for King William in the medium term may be appropriate. But, either way, a new contest to find the next British city seems unlikely to occur anytime soon. Ipswich and Berwick may just have to bide their time.

---

46 https://www.northumberlandgazette.co.uk/news/politics/berwick-councillor-calls-for-town-to-seek-city-status-3894374

Our process for elevating cities may well be peculiar, but for now that appears unlikely to change. It may be quirky, subjective, and idiosyncratic in a uniquely British way, but it is what it is. I hope nevertheless that the absentees from this most recent competition, and especially the heavyweights with a point to prove, will return for the next outing. And I hope too that those in Whitehall who are ultimately responsible for these competitions will take heed of their recent absence. Worthy would-be cities need a clear and realisable pathway to be elevated. If we don't rethink this, we may be destined to become a country that is littered with giant towns, who may indefinitely boycott any future contest.

Freedom of Information

You may never have heard of Tucktonia unless you happened to have grown up or holidayed on the Dorset coast in the 1970s and 1980s. As a forerunner to modern day theme parks, Tucktonia was the quintessential tourist attraction of its day. Located in the village of Tuckton on the outskirts of Bournemouth, it was a picture-perfect seaside destination. The brainchild of former British Formula 3 motor racing champion Harry Stiller, Tucktonia was centred around a model village of England's most famous landmarks, over 200 models in total, each painstakingly and perfectly recreated in 1:24 scale. The many models included Hadrian's Wall, Buckingham Palace, Stonehenge, the Houses of Parliament, Tower Bridge, Windsor Castle, a Cornish village, and Westminster Abbey. Holidaymakers congregated in their thousands, exploring the little buildings, buying keepsake souvenirs, and taking blurry family photos. Costing a reputed £2 million to build (around £10 million when inflated to 2022 prices), the park was opened by wartime comedy legend Arthur Askey in 1976. Jon Pertwee and Una Stubbs, visiting in character as their popular TV personas Wurzel Gummidge and Aunt Sally, topped out the NatWest Tower, Tucktonia's tallest model. Meanwhile, Keith Chegwin and Maggie Philbin presented a live edition of the BBC's *Multi-Coloured Swap Shop,* the staple Saturday morning kids show of its era, from the park. In terms of seventies prestige and swagger, this was as good as it got. Indeed, I am a little perplexed as to why my sister and I, as young children, hadn't relentlessly pestered our own parents to take us there.

But Tucktonia's bubble burst almost as quickly as it had been inflated. In 1980 a new theme park opened a few miles to the east of Stoke on Trent. Whilst Harry Stiller had originally tried and failed to build a rollercoaster at Tucktonia, with planning permission denied, his new northern rival had succeeded in achieving just that. Named after its infamous double inversion turns, which twice turned its riders upside down, and defined by its imposing yellow track and sleek red, white, and blue striped cars, The Corkscrew was a white-knuckle attraction like no other in the UK at the time. As quaint as Tucktonia was, it never really stood a chance against the arrival of Alton Towers and its showpiece rollercoaster. Chessington Zoo and Thorpe Park, jumping on the bandwagon, also evolved into theme parks in the 1980s, raising the bar and reinventing the British family day out. By 1986, just a decade after it had opened, and in the face of rising operational costs, rapidly dwindling visitor numbers, and increased competition from its newer nimbler rivals, Tucktonia closed its doors for good. The models were put into storage, with most lost in a subsequent warehouse fire. Only Buckingham Palace still survives, which was rehoused at Merivale Model Village, near Great Yarmouth.

By now you will probably be wondering what any of this has to do with Doncaster's bid for city status. Well, I first came across the story of Tucktonia when I was trying to track down the identity of a man called Alex McKinstry. On 10th December, two days after the bid submission deadline, Mr McKinstry sent a

Freedom of Information Act request, sometimes abbreviated to an FOI request, to Doncaster Council via the whatdotheyknow. com website, asking to be provided with a copy of our city status bid. A copy of this e-mail eventually found its way to my own inbox later that day. The Freedom of Information Act came into law in the year 2000 and gives the public right of access to information held by public authorities. Whilst commercially sensitive information can be withheld, proposals and tender responses submitted by suppliers for publicly funded contracts fall within scope of the Act. In my experience it is generally viewed to be a little ungentlemanly to submit an FOI request to secure a copy of your competitors bids, and, if you do, there is a good chance that large swathes of the documents may be redacted. That said, in the cut and thrust of public outsourcing, there are plenty of suppliers out there looking for a competitive advantage, and who wouldn't hesitate to use the Act to get their hands on their rival's tenders and bids.

This wasn't the first FOI request we had received. We'd had another a few weeks beforehand requesting a copy of Doncaster's 2012 bid, which we believe came from a marketing agency working on behalf of one of our competitors. I won't name names, but we were pretty sure of which rival was behind the request. We weren't too precious about the old bid though, and happily shared it. A request for our live bid was, however, something different. My immediate reaction at the time was to try and work out who Mr McKinstry was, and what his intentions might be in relation to seeking a copy of our bid. Could he be a local objector against Doncaster attaining city status, and possibly looking to make mischief for our campaign? Perhaps he was contemplating a forensic review of our bid document, fact checking every detail to expose some unforeseen inaccuracy, or contemplating some form of public tomfoolery to unmask a notable omission? If that were to be the case, perhaps we should apply caution, and not rush to share our bid with him. Maybe we should reject his request outright, and with good reason! Instinctively my defences were up.

A quick search revealed, however, that Mr McKinstry was not local to Yorkshire at all, heralding instead from far away Dorset. I breathed a sigh of immediate relief. McKinstry was a local historian and committee observer of the Bournemouth Civic Society, who had written a book entitled *The Village of Tuckton 35,000 BC – 1926*, which seemed paradoxically like both a very specific and unspecific time frame for a history book to cover. He had also written a series of articles about Tucktonia on the Christchurch Eye website. Indeed, McKinstry appeared to be the definitive authority on all things Tucktonia related. More pertinent though than any of this, Alex McKinstry was clearly a vocal opponent against Bournemouth's campaign for city status. He hadn't just issued a request under the Freedom of Information Act for Doncaster's bid, McKinstry was a man on a mission, seemingly aiming to acquire a copy of every bid in the competition. In doing so he had posed, albeit perhaps a little unintentionally, an important question about the transparency of the competition.

Prior to receiving McInstry's request, the topic of whether we should publish our bid had never come up. I think we had a moment of hesitation, but the collective view that was quickly established was that we had nothing to hide. We were all proud of our bid, and whilst we didn't really know what McInstry's specific interest was, there was a realisation that the people of Doncaster should, at the very least, have access to it. It was, after all, just as much their bid rather than ours, if not more so. The only adjustment we made was to add a one-page preface to the publicly published version. This was perhaps a little overzealous, but we thought that people perhaps needed a little context about the rules of the competition and the specified response template to view the bid in the right light. It might otherwise have been too easy to compare Doncaster's bid to the glossier and shinier documents prepared by some of its rivals and conclude that it was, for want of a better word, rubbish. I'm not sure if anyone took that level of interest in practice, but it was better to be safe than sorry. The final version was duly published in full on the Team Doncaster website a few days after the deadline.

I made direct contact with Alex McInstry sometime later, in February 2022. I was keen to further understand why he had requested Doncaster's bid, as well as all the others, and what he had planned to do with them. To use his own words from his very open and kind reply: 'My thinking at the time was to see how Bournemouth's application shaped up in comparison with all the other bids as well as having a genuine interest in these other areas. My father was a ground-hopper and visited every football ground in the country at one point or other but took as much pleasure imbibing the architecture and the ecology of each individual town as he did in the actual football. I inherited that interest.' I thought that was a nice story, and I wagered that his father had more than a few good tales to tell from all his travels.

Not every local authority needed the stick of an FOI request to publish and share their bids. Reading surprisingly published theirs the day before the official submission deadline. I had to say that this threw me off completely. In nearly twenty-five years of bid writing, I have never had a copy of a competitors bid in my hands the day before the deadline. It was a slick, well written and well-presented bid too. In my opinion it set a strong standard, and cemented Reading in my mind as one of the most likely winners in waiting. Reading's bid had, however, diverged slightly from the official application template, with a smart cover page, a few choice graphics, and photos of people as well as places – all things that the Doncaster campaign had consciously avoided. Indeed, the silkiness of Reading's bid was one of the reasons why we added a preface to the published version of our own. But, should we have changed anything in the Doncaster bid at the last minute in response to this shiny, self-assured document that Reading had so unexpectedly placed in front of us? For a moment it was very tempting, but we stuck to our guns. We had a plan and a format which we had all bought into, and any eleventh-hour edits were as likely to dilute the quality of our own bid as much as they might add to it.

In many respects, Alex McIntsry had done us a favour. By submitting FOI requests for all the bids, he had saved Doncaster, as well as all the other bidders, any potential embarrassment from making any similar requests. The whatdotheyknow.com website not only publishes FOI requests made, but also the submissions given in response. Thereby, for each of McInstry's requests which were successful, anyone else could access the bid in question too. As such, I started to anonymously collect up copies of all our competitors' bids. Boston, Milton Keynes, South Ayshire, and Northampton all joined Reading in publishing their bids at the point of submission. Almost half of all the bids were in the public domain before Christmas, and, by the time the result of the competition was announced in May, only a handful were still unpublished or otherwise undisclosed.

At the end of January 2022, with well over half of the city status bids now available in the public domain, I thought I would try to secure copies of the bids submitted by localities outside of the home nations, the applications from Gibraltar, Stanley in the Falkland Islands, Georgetown in the Caymans, and the two bids from the Isle of Mann. There is no equivalent piece of legislation to the Freedom of Information Act in these places, so this was more of a good-natured appeal on my part. I hit a bit of a blank with Gibraltar and Georgetown, as I wasn't even sure who to contact, but Rhian Burgess, Head of Communications for the Falkland Islands, was very prompt and replied straight away. She wasn't willing to share the bid at that time, as it turned out with very good reason. It is probably easier here for me to use Rhian's own words, from an e-mail that she sent me at the time. 'Unlike locations in the UK,' she began, 'their applications being made public won't result in yet another assault on their sovereignty. 2022 is the 40th anniversary of the Falkland Islands war and almost everything that we put out is being carefully monitored because of the inevitable and resultant hostility from across the water, as well as the 'rewriting' of our history. We have to be extraordinarily careful with what we say because the Government of Argentina will use our words to further their claim on our home. It's a unique situation but hopefully you understand why we won't jeopardise either our application or our broader ambitions for this year by giving potential grist to the mill of a government that bullies us (there is no other word) on a daily basis.'

Although I had only just turned nine years old when it happened, I still remember the television news coverage of Argentina's invasion of the remote Falkland Islands in 1982. It was the first overseas conflict involving British armed forces that I lived through. The imagery of the flotilla of our naval ships setting sail for the South Atlantic to liberate the islands remains in my memory, alongside the gritty explosions of the Battle of Goose Green, and the enduring footage of the controversial sinking of the Argentine naval vessel the General Belgrano. Even though Argentina lost the war, their claim on the Falklands, or the Islas Malvinas as they call them, has never gone away. Whilst the attention of most people in Britain has long since moved on, Argentina continues to this day in lobbying the United Nations to bring about sovereignty negotiations over those small islands at the foot of South America. Whilst another war is exceptionally unlikely, an awkward geopolitical stalemate persists, with growing support in Latin American countries for Argentina's cause. The decision for Stanley not to immediately publish their bid is therefore more than understandable, albeit I was pleased that they ultimately decided to do so once their city status was confirmed. As an aside, in case you were interested, the South Yorkshire Aircraft Museum, located in Doncaster, is also home to the largest permanent exhibit dedicated to the Falklands War in Britain, featuring a Westland Wessex helicopter and aircraft that were flown during the conflict.

The bids from Gibraltar and George Town proved to be the hardest of all to get copies of. Like the last couple of the rarest stickers of football players that you need to complete a Panini World Cup album, they had eluded for me for too long. So, I made my own FOI request to the Cabinet Office on 23rd June 2022 to obtain them. This was notably after the competition winners had already been declared, thereby at a relatively uncontentious point in proceedings. The Freedom of Information Act requires that a response to a request must be given promptly, and in any event within 20 working days. The Cabinet Office therefore advised me that they aimed to reply at the latest by 22nd July. When the 22nd July came, the Cabinet Office sent me a letter by email, advising that a response to my request would in fact be delayed until 22nd August. To quote from that letter: 'Information you have requested is exempt under Section 35 of the Act, which relates to protecting the government policy-making process in order to maintain the delivery of effective government'. Well, that sounded a bit strong. I wasn't altogether clear how the bids from Gibraltar and

George Town were somehow interwoven with the government's policy making process, and Lord forbid, I certainly didn't want to be an obstacle to the delivery of effective government! The letter went on: 'Section 35 is subject to a public interest test and the Cabinet Office has not yet reached a decision on whether the balance of the public interest favours disclosure of this information.' Good grief! I wondered if they may have perhaps got my request mixed up with someone else's, perhaps asking for the launch codes for Britain's nuclear arsenal, or something of equal magnitude, rather than just a couple of unsuccessful Civic Honours proposals.

On the 23rd August (a day later than promised) the Cabinet Office wrote again, sending what was essentially a duplication of the letter I had been sent in July. They had still not reached a decision in relation to a public interest test (how hard could that be) and had advised that they were delaying their disclosure decision again until 20th September. By now I was very curious as to exactly what Gibraltar and George Town had written in their bids to result in so much fuss. Of course, in August 2022 we were just days away from Liz Truss being confirmed as the new Prime Minister, and the resultant cabinet reshuffle which would see Edward Argar appointed as the new Minister of the Cabinet Office. Perhaps the civil servants at the Cabinet Office wanted to let him get his feet under the desk and give him the final say in deciding what was and what wasn't in the public interest when it came to all matters concerning the Civic Honours competition. Anyhow, eventually I got copies of the bids, with the only things redacted being the identities and contact details of the officers who had submitted them. It seemed like a lot of fuss about nothing!

If a Civic Honours competition is to be the vehicle through which cities in British Overseas Territories and Crown Dependencies are elevated, then that must be as open and transparent as the process for mainland UK candidates. It was an inclusive idea to welcome these places into the Platinum Jubilee competition, but, as demonstrated by the Falkland Islands, some diplomatic eggshells still need to be stepped over. But you can't have a city status contest on one hand, but then treat certain entrants with kid gloves, just because you might accidentally offend Argentina, or Spain, or any other country where Britain's historic presence in the world has stepped on the toes of other nations. Most of Britain's surviving territories and dependencies are the relics of our former empire. Many are small Caribbean islands, annexed and exploited through the forced migration of West African slaves, a legacy that is increasingly uncomfortable to this day. Whilst slavery has long since been abolished, an implied culture of subservience remains, where prospective new cities on some Caribbean islands may only be elevated on the say-so of the British Monarch. I suspect, in the long term, this approach will only fuel a desire for more of these territories and dependencies to become independent republics, and that is maybe not such a bad thing.

My main takeaway from all of this is that there should probably be a rule requiring entrants to publish their bids immediately after the submission deadline. If a locality thinks it has a strong case for city status, a case that it believes is compelling and worth taking pride in, then there really is no reason not to make that public. The people from that place have an expectation, if not a right, to see that case with their own eyes should they so choose. Having seen them all, I can tell you with all sincerity that there is nothing of any sensitivity or confidentiality in any of the Platinum Jubilee bids. I would be amazed if there was anything in any of those bids which wasn't already in the public domain somewhere or other. To resist publication, and shun FOI requests, suggests to me that there is a nervousness about the application, and a concern from those submitting it that it may not really be in the locality's best interests. Either that, or there is genuine, deep seated, and sincere local resistance to the campaign which they are afraid of. Such a disclosure rule might make a few places step back from entering, which would be a shame, but I think they would be acceptable losses. On the other hand, if localities knew that their bid must be published, maybe this would push the standard of the bids on to greater and higher levels. Localities would be more conscious of the risk of public scrutiny and criticism if their bid falls short, so maybe they would all try that little bit harder. The bar would be raised, and surely that is a good thing overall. We shouldn't really need the Freedom of Information Act at all.

The Expert Panel

In late December 2021, when the Government published the full list of entrants for the Platinum Jubilee Civic Honours competition, they also made another big reveal. In a first for a Civic Honours competition, an Expert Panel had been appointed to work with Ministers to make recommendations in terms of winning cities, before the proposed winners were ultimately approved by the Queen[47]. I took this as largely positive news. An Expert Panel should be relatively independent, and not swayed by political horseplay, applying a more objective lens to the decision-making process. With recommendations coming from such a panel, and not just Conservative ministers in isolation, Doncaster's history of being a traditional Labour party stronghold was seemingly now less likely to count against it. The whole notion of introducing an Expert Panel added a layer of additional transparency and integrity. Entrants were more likely now to be judged first and foremost on the strength of their applications, and not by wider and often less favourable prejudices and stereotypes.

The Expert Panel was made up of eight people, five men and three women. Whilst that ticked at least one box for diversity, it is probably also worth adding that the panel were, in most cases, white, middle-aged, and heralding from the south of England. That is perhaps a little surprising given the emphasis

---

47   https://www.gov.uk/government/news/full-list-of-places-aiming-to-become-jubilee-cities-revealed

on diversity and multiculturalism that is otherwise so prominent in modern Britain. That said, the panellists were all, without doubt, high achievers in their respective fields. Most were seasoned, long serving senior civil servants. Forgive me, as the next couple of paragraphs will read a little like a slightly musty biographical extract from *Who's Who*, the annually published goliath sized reference book of Britain's most noteworthy movers and shakers. It's only fair though that I give a little background context on who the Expert Panel were, and their credentials to do the job. There are some very weighty job titles here; Presidents, Directors, and Chief Executives, each of which no doubt involves doing very important and clever stuff of distinct public benefit.

Ben Dean, for starters, was Director for Sport, Gambling and Ceremonials at the Department of Culture, Media & Sport (DCMS). He had previously held positions at the Home Office, the Foreign & Commonwealth Office, and the Number 10 Policy Unit[48]. Alongside him there was Peter Lee, Director of the Cabinet Office's Constitution Group and formerly a Director at the Department for Environment, Food and Rural Affairs (Defra) [49]. Meanwhile, Catherine Francis was another civil service heavyweight, the Director General for Local Government & Public Services at the Department for Levelling Up, Housing & Communities (DLUHC), which is more than a mouthful for anyone's CV. Her inclusion may have suggested

48 https://www.linkedin.com/in/ben-dean-696bb72/

49 https://www.gov.uk/government/people/peter-lee

that the government was thinking politically about which towns might be promoted, just as much as it might be concerned with heritage and royalty.

The panel also included a champion for each of the home nations. Roger Lewis was President of Amgueddfa Cymru, or National Museum Wales, in Cardiff. He had previously held an eclectic mix of senior executive positions at the BBC, ITV, and Classic FM, amongst others, as well as serving as the chair of the Royal Liverpool Philharmonic Orchestra and Cardiff International Airport[50]. Representing Northern Ireland there was Kathryn Thomson, Chief Executive at National Museums NI. She was an accountant by trade who previously worked in the senior finance team within NHS Greater Glasgow[51]. Laurence Rockey was Director at the Office of the Secretary of State for Scotland. He was formerly Head of Strategy & Communications at the City of Edinburgh Council, and earlier still had worked at The Cabinet Office[52]. England was represented by Kate Mavor CBE, Chief Executive at English Heritage, who had also previously headed up The National Trust for Scotland[53].

The final panellist was Lord Neil Mendoza, Commissioner for Cultural Recovery and Renewal, a Secretary of State appointed role aimed to draw on his experience in the culture and financial sectors, to advise the Government on how the culture sector

---

50   https://museum.wales/trustees/

51   https://www.nationalmuseums.org.uk/members/nmgni/

52   https://www.gov.uk/government/people/laurence-rockey

53   https://www.english-heritage.org.uk/about-us/our-people/

might best recover from the Covid-19 pandemic. Mendoza's career background was in banking and enterprise, but he had more latterly headed up two Government reviews focused on museums and had also become Provost of Oriel College at Oxford University[54]. This was, by all accounts, a formidable group of panellists, and a group of people whose reputations would warrant that all appropriate due diligence would be brought to bear through their decision-making process.

The announcement of the Expert Panel resonated with me on several levels. Whilst I welcomed the development, it would have been helpful to have known about it before the application deadline. A simple rule in bid writing is to know your audience, what makes them tick, and what their key decision drivers might be. For example, a key pillar of Doncaster's bid was geared to setting out the economic case for city status, so it was perhaps then surprising that there wasn't a leading urban economist on the panel. I'm not saying that our more economically focused content was necessarily wasted on deaf ears, but in recognising that several panellists had a primary interest in culture and heritage, we may have dedicated more content and word count to this particular interest set. Case in point, Doncaster is home to two properties managed by English Heritage, these being Conisbrough Castle and Brodsworth Hall. Both featured in the bid. With the Chief Executive of English Heritage sitting on the Expert Panel though, we may have played to the gallery a little harder with these two key assets. Similarly, Professor

---

54   https://www.gov.uk/government/people/neil-mendoza

John Beckett of the University of Nottingham, the only man to have written a detailed book about the city status in the UK, and who knew the ins-and-outs of all the former competitions better than anyone, was another questionable omission. If you are going to have an Expert Panel, surely you would include the most qualified expert of them all? To use Beckett's own words though, his 'phone remained silent'.

The reveal of the Expert Panel was a real fascination for me. This was such a critical group of individuals holding sway over our bid. If we could sway the opinion of just one of them, we had the potential to put Doncaster's bid in a winning position. I didn't know exactly, of course, how the panel would function in practice, or the specific process they would go through in making their recommendations. This has never been made public and, in the interests of integrity, perhaps never will. My assumption was that each panel member was provided with a set of bids from all the entrants to read and reflect upon. They would then perhaps have come together through a series of meetings, or more likely videocalls, to moderate their recommendations, and reach a level of collective consensus. Alternatively, they may have individually scored the bids, with the Cabinet Office then tallying up the results using some form of points system. I'm speculating here, as you can tell. I imagine though that Ministers were heavily led by the recommendations of the panel. After all, why have a panel at all if you are not going to follow their recommendations? Equally, the creation of a panel gave Minister's a get-out when it came to the final decisions. The people of Middlesbrough and Reading couldn't really take umbrage at Ministers for snubbing their applications if the decision was ultimately based on the recommendations of an independent panel. I surmised that Doncaster's prospects of becoming a city really did rest squarely in the hands of these eight individuals.

Suffice to say that I started pondering how I might capture their attention of the panel in a more effective way than our competitors might and raise the profile of Doncaster's bid by doing so. Inappropriate lobbying of evaluators and decision makers during any tender competition is, quite rightly, a no-no. Offering to buy them a pleasant lunch, treating them to some corporate hospitality, or, heaven forbid, directly handing them a brown envelope with a wedge of bank notes inside, would normally be grounds for a bidder to be automatically disqualified. You can't bribe your way to a win. It wasn't as if I had a stack of cash stuffed envelopes anyway, not that I would ever consider such a tactic. Bid writers need to have to be beyond reproach when it comes to personal integrity. You only need to get that wrong once and it can quite literally end your career. No, a more nuanced strategy was called for if I was to successfully influence the panel, but to do so within the rules and protocols of good behaviour. This was a conundrum. I pondered it over Christmas, looking for inspiration, before some plans started forming in my head.

I didn't know any of the panellists personally, and I was certain that no one else in Team Doncaster was likely to know them either, so there was no obvious or immediate way to engage them. So, in the first instance, I decided to try and connect with each of the panellists through LinkedIn, the social media platform for professional networking. Connecting through LinkedIn was hardly contentious; there are lots of suppliers to government who are connected to public sector purchasers on this platform. Being connected via social media is not a conflict of interest in anyone's book. Most of the panellists had LinkedIn profiles and it wasn't too hard to track them down and send them an invitation to connect with me. I didn't necessarily expect any of them to accept my invitation, after all they didn't know me from Adam, but at least they might be curious to know who I was and check out my LinkedIn profile.

With my invitations sent, I sat back and waited, and waited, and waited. Days went by, and there was no reaction at all. My tentative engagement efforts through LinkedIn had seemingly come to nothing. I clearly needed to make a bigger statement to get their attention, but what? I wanted to send the panellists something that would really elevate Doncaster's prospects, but something that could not be accused of breaking any rules. I couldn't send them anything that might have a monetary value, or something that might be accused of unfairly gaming the competition. No gifts, no favours, nothing that gave them any additional information about Doncaster over and above our bid submission. Nothing of any impropriety whatsoever. Not even a small box of Doncaster made butterscotch. What on earth could I give them that met such an exacting criterion? I was lying in bed one evening, staring at the ceiling, struggling to go to sleep, and looking for inspiration, when the answer finally came to me. It was obvious really. The one thing I could legitimately send them all was the one thing that they all already had. I decided that I would send them each a copy of Doncaster's city status bid.

Now, I appreciate here that I may have confused you a bit. If they already have the bid what would be the point of sending it again? It's a fair question. I wagered, however, that the panellists had only received electronic copies of all the bids. It is possible that The Cabinet Office may have sent them hard copies, but that would translate as 312 documents to be printed, bound, and dispatched (39 locations x 8 panellists). It struck me that this would have been a bit of a faff for The Cabinet Office to orchestrate and was, as such, unlikely. Similarly, would the panellists all determine to print a hard copy of each bid they had been sent to review? Again, that seemed unlikely too. In this respect, the panellists had, most likely, only ever seen the bids on a computer screen. Now, if you are reading a document on a laptop, you most typically only have about half a page of content on screen at any one time. You can't appreciate the layout of a full page. You don't naturally leaf backwards and forwards. You don't run your fingers over each page, feeling its texture. You don't scribble notes on the pages or fold their corners over to mark your place. You don't feel the physical weight of the work that you are reading, holding it tangibly in your hand. Reading a document on screen is simply a far less tactile means of engaging with a piece of writing (forgive me though if you happen to be reading this on an e-reader). Remember here too that the panellists were all primarily culturalists. They were probably people who typically read books in their spare time, or at the very least broadsheet newspapers. They were probably readers who preferred the physical touch and feel of paper. As I stared up at the ceiling, lying in my bed, a broad smile crept across my face. I rolled over and fell soundly asleep.

The next day I was stoked and ready for action. After around an hour of Googling I had readily determined a plausible postal address for each of the panellists, in most cases the head office or primary location of the organisation that they worked for. Anne has a good relationship with a local printer in Retford, and I readily got a quote for them to print and bind some copies of the Doncaster bid. The quality of paper is based on a thing called gsm, or grams per square meter, and I wanted the very best paper, and the very best print quality, that they could offer. Wire bound, with a stiff piece of backing card and a transparent PVC cover. Other than that, the printed copies were not enhanced in any way. There were no extra design motifs or added copy. It was the same document that we had submitted to The Cabinet Office, but with one small distinction; it was a printed hard copy. When the box arrived with the printed copies I was in silent awe. Creating the Doncaster bid had already been a labour of love, but holding a plush, professionally printed copy gave it extra potency. It looked slick. You could readily flip through the various sections in a far more accessible way. The photo section really stood out. On screen you could only really look at one photo at a time, but in the printed version you could absorb four sharply printed photos across each double page spread. It was more like leafing through a magazine or a photo album. Who knew that such a simple thing as printing the bid would make such a difference? I promptly stuck copies into eight separate envelopes and mailed them to the panellists. The only thing I added was a very brief covering letter, so that they knew what was in the envelope and who had sent it to them. Job done!

I must confess at this point that I didn't share what I was up to with either Lee at the Council or Dan at the Chamber. This was deliberate. I was 99.9% sure that I was doing nothing untoward by posting copies of our bid to the panellists. There was no explicit rule written down anywhere saying that you couldn't do this, and I was as confident as I could be that I was legitimately colouring inside the lines. That said, my intention was clearly and undeniably an attempt to garner favour with the panellists, which could, at the very least, raise some questioning eyebrows. As such, just in case The Cabinet Office deemed this to be a yellow card offence, it would be better if everyone else had plausible deniability, and I could rightly be the sacrificial lamb to take the blame if it all went sideways. As the saying goes, sometimes it is better to ask forgiveness, rather than seek permission. As it turned out though, no-one complained about my little stunt, so all was good. What I didn't know, of course, is whether all the copies had made it to the desks of my intended targets and, even if they had, had they even been opened? I sat back again, and I waited, but this time I didn't have to wait too long.

On the morning of Friday 28th January, Kate Mavor from English Heritage accepted my invitation to connect on LinkedIn. Bingo! I duly sent her a message, thanking her for linking-in, and daringly asking her if she had received the copy of the bid I had posted. For good measure, I added that I hoped she liked the photos in the bid of Doncaster's two English Heritage properties, Brodsworth Hall and Consibrough Castle. Almost immediately Kate replied, saying: 'Thanks Jim – yes. Full pack received. Very impressive and I loved seeing Conisborough there (and on the mural!).' It was only a handful of words, but I was elated. She'd received it, she'd looked at it, she'd been very impressed by it, and she'd loved seeing the castle. The mural, in case you are wondering, is a piece of public art titled *Future's Past and Present*, created by acclaimed street artists Nomad Clan, which was unveiled in 2021 opposite Doncaster Station. At 108 metres long, it is the UK's longest mural, and celebrates Doncaster's heritage through a montage of images, including a coal miner, an NHS nurse, the St. Leger Festival, and, of course, Conisbrough Castle. Kate's reference to the photo of the mural in the bid was especially satisfying, as it wasn't something I had highlighted in my own message. It meant her reply wasn't just lip service, she had clearly taken a little time to digest and enjoy the hard copy version.

It was at this point I came clean with Dan and Lee, sharing Kate's message as a vindication of my strategy, and all was good. If Kate had been as impressed as I had hoped, then maybe she would positively advocate for Doncaster with the other panellists. Shortly after, in mid-February, and a goodly while after my original invitations were sent, two more panellists, Laurence Rockey and Peter Lee, both viewed my LinkedIn profile. I had notifications to that effect, even though neither was yet to accept my invitation to connect, and, unlike Kate, neither replied when I messaged to see if they had received the postal copy. The first thing, however, that they would have hopefully both noticed was the swanky #GoingforitDN Doncaster city status banner at the head of my profile. They may have only taken a fleeting look at who I was, or they may have read my biography in detail, that I don't know. But I took the very fact that they were looking me up as a good thing. The fact that both checked my profile concurrently was also perhaps a sign that deliberations about who might win city status were well underway. My most recent post on LinkedIn at the time was, fortuitously, a photo of the banner from the recent Business Showcase, blazoned with over 100 signatures of local folk who had pledged to support our bid. I really hoped that they had both looked at that! Laurence Rockey went on to accept my invitation to connect at the end of February, which is around the time I believe the panel concluded their work. Peter Lee never accepted, and I had no communication at all from any of the other panellists.

But had my ploy to post out hard copies of the bid really made any difference? The truth is I have absolutely no idea. I'd like to think there was at least a little discussion amongst the panellists about it. If there was, I'm not suggesting that it was, in isolation, the critical clincher that sealed the deal for Doncaster. It is, nevertheless, another good example of a Critical Non-Essential. I didn't need to send the panel hard copies, it wasn't asked for, but if it delivered us even just a 1% advantage then it was worth doing. I would wager too that, despite the slick design of some of our rivals, none of them played the same tactic, adding further strength to Doncaster's elbow. You don't need to have the best printed proposal if yours is the only printed proposal. The irony, of course, is that the early Civic Honours contests all occurred before the age of e-mail and the internet, and would have required a physical, printed bid to be delivered and read. How times change!

Whatever the process, my thanks to the panel for having the faith to back our proposal. It can't have been an easy job, and I doubt there was unanimous backing for any individual candidate. I suspect there was probably a little horse trading required to get to the final list. In the interests of objectivity, I hope too that the involvement of a panel is retained as a feature of future Civic Honours competitions. It's a good idea and it helps to bring independent objectivity to the process. I apologise in advance, however, if the future panellists should be deluged with printed proposals from candidate cities in the post. I will own responsibility for that one!

The Schools' Competition

Actively involving local young people in the city status campaign had been a hard-wired principle of our Project Board from the outset. It was hardly rocket-science. Making Doncaster a city was not an ambition geared solely to benefit the population of today, but rather to create a legacy for the next generation, and every generation thereafter. Like most places, people in positions of importance and influence in Doncaster tended to be middle aged, or older still. We didn't want the campaign to be remembered for being a parade of the generally older faces of councillors, politicians, businesspeople, and such like. Less focus on grey hair and wrinkles, more on youthful exuberance and aspiration. City status was a gift and an opportunity for young people, and this was readily seized upon.

Samuel Finn, at just 15 years old, was a member of the Project Board and was the closest thing we had to a poster boy for the campaign. Sam was an active scout, a member of Doncaster's Youth Parliament and latterly a Doncaster Youth Councillor. The UK hosted the 26th UN Climate Change Conference of the Parties (better known an COP26) in Glasgow, falling over the end of October and start of November in 2021, bang in the middle of the city status campaign. The "parties" refers to the signatories of the Paris Agreement and the UN Framework Convention on Climate Change. As global political events go, COP26 was on a comparable footing to the G20. It was a window of opportunity for global leaders to make accords to tackle our global climate emergency. Over 100 countries were represented by heads of state and senior officials, with former US President Barack Obama arguably the star draw. Through his scouting connections, young Samuel also got to deliver a speech during the conference programme too. This earned him a deserved mention by name in the city status bid, the only member of the Project Board to be singled out in the bid. Alongside Sam, the Project Board also enlisted a couple more youngsters, Courtney Helsby, another of Doncaster's Young Advisors, and Owen Marshall Dungworth, who was a student at Hall Cross Academy, and has also gone on to become a Young Advisor. The role of the Young Advisors is to help organisations and local services improve their offer to make them more young people friendly. All three made a valued contribution to the city status campaign.

Having young people on the Project Board was, however, just the start. There was a concerted effort to try and get schools engaged in the campaign. Letters were sent, via the Council, to all the schools in the borough to that end. This offered suggestions such as encouraging schools to taking creative photos and sharing them on social media using the campaign hashtag, or developing an artwork, creative writing, design, or poetry contributions. The idea was pitched in a way that would hopefully not create an undue additional burden for teachers or add any extra costs which schools hadn't otherwise budgeted for. Nevertheless, it was a tough ask, and most schools didn't pick up the ball and run with it. Maybe it was just one ask too many upon an already overstretched education system, or maybe we hadn't quite found the right way to engage with them. In hindsight, I think we could have developed some form of downloadable city status lesson plan with accompanying resources, or something along those lines, most probably targeted on primary schools. Something involving puzzles, colouring-in, and making things, that would save teachers' time, and that could have been a bit of fun for the children too.

I can't remember who first suggested it, but a competition for local schools to get involved emerged as the main hook for youth participation, giving every school in the borough a distinct opportunity to contribute. The focus rapidly evolved into a film making competition, whereby local schools could create their own short video celebrating Doncaster and its campaign. At its most simple level, making a movie only required access to a smartphone, which presented zero barriers for any school to enter. You didn't need any fancy cameras or editing software. This was key, keeping with the principle of making participation easy for schools and teachers. The brief was also appropriately loose, enabling schools to bring as much or as little creativity to the party as they so wished. Extravagant staging, props, and costumes were not required. Besides, schoolrooms are generally great for making anything on a low budget using just empty washing up liquid bottles and sticky-back plastic. This all felt straightforward enough and was perhaps a better way to focus the involvement from schools. Making it happen, however, once again turned out to be a bit more complicated.

Whilst the originally intended idea was for the videos to

feature as a backdrop to the "City for a Day" deadline day event, the fact that the event was abandoned was not reason enough to cancel the schools' competition too. It did however present some difficult questions. Without the launch event we weren't sure where the videos might be shown, on how the winning school might be recognised and celebrated. City for Day created the prospect of the winning school having a day out at the Yorkshire Wildlife Park on the same day. Happy, smiling children and exotic, fluffy animals; it was a perfect for media coverage. But the schools' competition in practice was simply adding to the complexity of delivering City for a Day. We rapidly ran out of time to give schools enough opportunity to produce entries, as well as giving the winning school enough notice to attend the City for a Day event, taking account of such things as arranging transportation and securing parental consent. Remember, this had been originally planned for the bid deadline day, and that date was locked in the calendar. If City for a Day and the schools' competition were to work in tandem, it all had to come together on the 8th of December. When City for a Day was finally canned, it solved part of that problem, by buying extra time for the schools' competition, but the competition still needed its own finale.

The solution presented itself in the form of Opportunities Doncaster LIVE. Opportunities Doncaster LIVE is an annual showpiece event organised by Doncaster Chamber for local school children. It takes place each spring at Doncaster racecourse, with around 100 local employers exhibiting, and around 3,500 children from across the borough coming along to meet with them. The idea is to raise the aspirations of local children, giving them a better idea of the careers that may be available to them within their own community, as well as giving them a better idea of the qualifications and experience they may need to pursue their dream job. It's also a lot of fun, and the participating employers usually go out of the way to make their stands interactive and participative for all the kids. This also usually involves collecting a bag-full of branded corporate freebies – pens, stress balls, keyrings, water bottles, and such like – to take home with them at the end of day. Opportunities Doncaster LIVE ticked all the right boxes. It was an event that was already scheduled and paid for, so there was no new monetary ask of the campaign. It was aimed specifically at children, it had ready made profile and prestige, and it was nested perfectly timewise to cater for next phase of the campaign. The winning school would still get their day out at the wildlife park, but Opportunities Doncaster LIVE was the perfect stage to announce the winners.

Only five schools entered the competition in the end. Being candid, I don't know why we had so few entries given the overall number of schools across Doncaster. But whilst the response was disappointing, what we lacked in numbers we more than made up for in terms of the quality of the entries that we received. Alongside me, a couple of other members of the Project Board put their hand up to volunteer to do the judging. A simple scorecard was devised, enabling us to award each film points based on its creativity, the extent to which it celebrated civic pride and Doncaster's heritage, and how well it demonstrated the reasons why Doncaster should become a city. When you are marking children's work you naturally want to give them all the best scores, but the process was robust enough to determine a winner fairly and squarely.

Outward Primary Academy made a film with different children each holding up an A4 image, with each image representing a different Doncaster asset, and each asset representing a different letter in Doncaster's name. So, there was D for the Doncaster Dome, O for the Outlet shopping at Lakeside, N for the National rail interchange (a bit tenuous that one, but you get the idea), and so on and so forth. It was a cute, simple, and effective idea. The next entry was from the Coppice School in Hatfield, which specifically supports children with severe learning difficulties and Autism, so it was wonderful to see the effort that their children had made in making their film. Their entry featured a couple of students visiting sites across Doncaster, from the centre of town all the way out to the airport. If there was a prize for distance covered in making the film, then the Coppice School would have won. Next up was Doncaster School for the Deaf, part of the Doncaster Deaf Trust, who made an equally impressive film with the children using British Sign Language (BSL). It was a simple, short, and direct message which the three children delivered in unison using BSL: 'We're from Doncaster School for the Deaf, and we support Doncaster becoming a city.' Enough said!

The Film Club from Bessacarr Primary School get a special mention for their excellent cinematography and production values. The fact that this primary school had its own film club was impressive. If we had awards for camerawork, scripting and editing, they would have been theirs. The film which they made fittingly paid homage to two of Doncaster's lost cinemas, the former Picture House Cinema on the High Street, and the Gaumont Palace Theatre in Hall Gate. The children filmed at the locations where the two cinemas previously stood, as well as visiting the Gaumont Freeze, the last surviving remnant of the Palace Theatre, which has now been relocated to the civic quarter. I had to say I learned a few things I didn't know about these forgotten picture houses of Doncaster from watching the film. The children also paid tribute to the St. Leger race, including some stop frame animation they had made of a Lego horse race. It was a great little film, and a more than worthy runner up in my book.

It was Kingfisher Primary School from Wheatley, however, who made the winning film. Each year group in the school had contributed, with each telling a different aspect of the Doncaster story. One year group were dressed up as Romans with brightly painted Danum shields, another was taking part in a hobby horse race to represent the St. Leger Festival, and another still had made a mock-up of The Flying Scotsman. Other children had made models of Conisbrough Castle and of Doncaster Sheffield Airport. Year 11 had produced a giant painting, featuring a pit wheel from the coalmines, a Vulcan bomber, a lion from the Yorkshire Wildlife Park, and the Doncaster Rovers emblem. Each individual activity would have taken time to organise, and the sheer scale of effort right across the school was immense. Their entry included a montage of all these things, narrated by the children reading out a self-written poem all about Doncaster. It was a great video in that all the children in the school appeared to have had the opportunity to take part, and it also reflected so much of Doncaster's different history and symbolism. In the end it was an easy choice to award the school the prize.

I was invited to declare the winner of the schools' competition at Opportunities Live, which would involve me making an announcement on a small stage in front of the children. I have presented at quite a few conferences over the years, with up to as many as 500 poor souls in one sitting having to endure me talking at them, so I had some experience here. I don't get undue stage freight when I'm stood in front of an audience, although I always want to be better at presenting than I am. The best presenters have both wit and warmth, neither of which come naturally to me when I have a microphone in my hand. I tend to be guilty of over scripting what I'm trying to say, to the extent that I come across as if I'm reading out a telephone directory page-by-page, with a delivery that has the hallmarks of a bad impression of a monotone newsreader. More than once I have attempted to drop what I thought to be a humorous quip into a speech or presentation, expecting a polite ripple of gentle laughter to seep across the room, only to be met instead by deathly silence by the wall of faces in front of me. It's an awful feeling. Luckily for me though, at many of the conferences I go to, a lot of the other speakers are as hopeless at presenting as I am, and a few are indeed a goodly bit worse. In this respect I don't think my performances stand out too badly.

This was a different gig altogether though. As the saying goes, never work with children or animals. Presenting to adults was one thing but standing up to speak to a group of children was not something I am used to at all. As we got nearer to the allotted timeslot for the announcement, groups of children from the various schools who had entered the competition began to amass around the stage. As the wider exhibition hall was mainly filled with older secondary school children, the younger and much smaller primary kids huddling in around the stage stood out, especially as some were clad out in high-vis vests to help the teachers keep tabs on them. There were easily fifty or so kids around the stage when I was finally handed the microphone and went on. Whilst there was some inevitable fidgeting, most of the kids were carefully eyeing the suited, middle-aged, slightly awkward looking bald man who now stood before them. The fact that I was the guy who was standing between them all and a potential day out at the Yorkshire Wildlife Park was not lost on me. That was, after all, what they were mainly interested in finding out. My brief was to say a few words about city status, the schools' competition, and the different entrants, before revealing the winner. The occasion clearly got to me, as I inexplicably found myself going into pantomime mode. 'Who's hoping to win a day out at the wildlife park?' I asked. There were a few positive, yet generally inaudible murmurs from the children. 'What was that?' I teased, pretending I couldn't hear them. 'It doesn't sound as if anybody wants to go. Let me check that again. Who wants a day out at the wildlife park?' This time I got the volume I was hoping for, with all the kids screaming 'yes'!

I did my piece, talking briefly about each of the entrants, building up the anticipation as best I could, before finally announcing Kingfisher Primary as the winners. The news was greeted by Kingfisher kids with predictable whoops and hollers, whilst the kids from the losing schools were visibly crestfallen. There was one particularly steely eyed little girl in the front row, no more than 10 or 11 years old, who I think was from Bessacarr Primary, and who gave me a look of utter indignation. It was as if we were at the Oscars ceremony. She was the established big studio name and hot favourite to carry away the Best Actress statuette, only to be upstaged at the last minute by an up-and-coming starlet making her debut in some highbrow, avant-garde, indie arthouse nonsense. Her impassive stare, which followed me right across the small stage, left me in no doubt that I was to blame. If looks could kill! I would be hearing from her agent and, rest assured, she would see to it that I never worked in Hollywood again!

Undeterred, albeit perhaps also a little bit scared, I duly invited up representatives from each of the runner-up schools to collect their book tokens (£100 for each school), offering commiserations to them, and congratulations to the winners. Some of the Kingfisher kids were then invited up to a VIP lunch in one of the executive suites at the racecourse, hosted by Damian Allen. The lunch was an opportunity for a second announcement to confer Kingfisher as the winners, and to formally bestow their prize. I suspect that the kids enjoyed the buffet of nibbles and treats a bit more than all the speeches and presentations, but the lunchtime session included a special screening of their film, greeted with a round of warm applause, which left them all with beamingly proud smiles.

Looking back, I have mixed views about the schools' competition. I think our campaign priority to involve young people was right, and I am full of praise of all the kids who took part. I guess I'm frustrated though in that the campaign didn't inspire more schools and more children to get involved. I'm not sure what the answer to that is. Perhaps we needed to reach beyond schools, and involve youth clubs, scout and guide groups, youth sports teams, and other bodies that bring young people together? Maybe we should have engaged more with parents as a more direct route to children? Maybe we didn't have the right angle, and a video competition wasn't the thing? Maybe city status is just a bit too dry to inspire the young? As I say, I really don't know. As a small consolation, I don't think any of the other entrants managed to materially engage with young people any better than we did, so I don't see this as challenge limited to just Doncaster. I do, however, take a little hope and a little faith from all the schools who turned up to see the King deliver Doncaster's Letters Patent. There were a lot of little people cheering and waving flags on that day, and at least a few schools who had taken the kids out of their usual lessons to witness a slice of local history in the making. They didn't seem to need a nudge or a heads-up from the campaign team to come along; they just came. Maybe, in the end, it was the winning of the thing that was the real inspiration for the next generation? And I won't deny, seeing all those children smiling and waving their flags, that I felt a small pang of pride. Ultimately it will be their city, and it will be fascinating to see what they do with it and where they take it.

Farewell Marazion

There is always something of an anti-climax after a bid is submitted. The long hours have all been put in, the hard work has been done, and the finish line crossed. Then the waiting begins. 162 days, about 5 full months, would pass between the submission deadline of the city status competition, and the date that the bidders would find out the result. This isn't all that uncommon. Most evaluations on public sector tenders typically take at least two or three months as standard. The proposal writer's best practice playbook would suggest that you use this time wisely to apply a pre-implementation strategy in anticipation of a winning bid, planning for all the necessary new staff, resources, and systems. That's clearly logical, but the reality for 99% of bidders is that they just put everything on ice. Hopefully we will win, but we'll cross that bridge when we reach it. We'll kick that can along the road, stick it on the back burner, and take a rain check. And, most often, this strategy generally plays out just fine. Even from a position of relative unreadiness, most bidders have a knack of pulling out all the necessary stops to get their services promptly up and running once their winner's status is confirmed. In the meantime, everyone goes back to the day job. They move on to other projects and other bids. So, inevitably, after all the hiatus of the city status submission day, things in Doncaster calmed down and went a little bit quiet.

The national headlines reverted to the growing spread of the Omicron Covid-19 variant, and the extent to which restrictions and lockdowns may be re-imposed over the Christmas and New Year season. England had taken a more relaxed stance than the devolved assemblies in Scotland, Wales, and Northern Ireland. Indoor events were allowed, with no masks, and no distancing. This meant that the Doncaster Chamber Business Awards, one of the largest black tie business awards ceremonies in the country, hosted at Doncaster Racecourse, could go ahead as planned. It wasn't a straightforward decision, and it needed an extraordinary meeting of the board before a final green light was granted, even with the official guidance for such an event being on our side. On the night though it was great to see people back together in a physical space. Each table at the awards dinner was garnished with some paper city status campaign flags, and there was a slightly jingoistic moment in the proceedings when the 700 or so guests in attendance all stood up to jubilantly wave them. Most would have little idea of the effort that had gone into the bid, but it was great to see the crowd showing their enthusiasm for the campaign, even if it was fuelled by a few pre-Christmas drinks. It was also a touching moment for me, to see that the campaign had so much implicit support from the business community.

I had a relatively quiet Christmas that year by all accounts. As a treat, I took Anne and the children to Tickhill Alpacas, an attraction I ironically had first discovered when researching the city status bid. Tickhill Alpacas is, as the name hints at, a farm attraction in the village of Tickhill, within the borough of Doncaster, where you can take an alpaca out for a walk. They all groaned when we arrived (my family, not the alpacas), as I had kept our destination a secret until we had got there. Nobody had guessed that alpaca walking was on the cards – as if they would! Even though I had instructed them all to wear clothes suitable for an outdoor walk in a wet and nippy December, Anne had curiously convinced herself that we were all going for a cosy afternoon tea. Her disappointment on arrival was palpable, not a teapot or fruit scone in sight. But once we were all paired up with our animals and off walking, they all got into the spirit of it. After all, what's not to like about taking a fluffy South American sheep-like creature out for an invigorating Christmas country stroll?

Dean and Karen, the doting owners of Tickhill Alpacas, guided us on our walk, peppering us with a wealth of alpaca trivia along the way. Did you know, for example, that the gestation period for alpacas is 11 months and, if it's a bit wet and chilly out, female alpacas can hold their delivery ready babies in for several further days until the weather has sufficiently picked up enough for them to give birth? No, neither did I! And we got to hand feed our animals at the end of the walk too, a little gross having them sloppily scoff their feed straight from our hands, but it all added to the authenticity of the experience. Whilst Tickhill Alpacas didn't make the final cut for a mention in Doncaster's bid (I didn't feel that it quite had the necessary city standard punch) I would nevertheless still give Dean, Karen, and their herd of alpacas a personal thumbs up! An hour or so very well spent.

Christmas drifted seamlessly into the new year, and we beckoned in 2022. We have a family tradition at new year to write a list of predictions for the year ahead; winners of sporting events, outcomes of elections, Oscar winners, royal events, and such like. We also throw in a few family predictions for good measure. Most of our predictions are usually hopelessly inaccurate. For 2022 though I naturally had to add a prediction to the list that Doncaster would become a city. Once written down, the predictions are sealed in an envelope before midnight on New Year's Eve to then be opened again exactly one year later, although I didn't need to wait until then to know that, for a change, I had got at least one prediction right!

A week or so later I was sat at home on the couch flitting through Twitter on my phone when something caught my eye. Much hullabaloo had been made about the boldness of the tiny Cornish coastal town of Marazion having entered the city status race. With a population of less than 1,500, their audacious bid was pitched for the town to become the smallest and most southerly city in the UK. It's a picture postcard destination, with an ensemble of quaint whitewashed cottages, gift boutiques, tea shops, fudge pantries, and sea view bed and breakfasts. Marazion was the surprise package, with a campaign that was perhaps the most intriguing of them all. But, as misfortune transpired, they turned out to be the first horse to fall. The tweet on my phone that morning was telling me that Marazion's bid had somehow seemingly been disqualified. But why? Well to get to the bottom of this breaking revelation, and explain Marazion's surprise exit from the contest, I need to rewind a few weeks, to give you a little more of the backstory for context.

Marazion's bid had been led and masterminded by Richard Stokoe, a member of the town council. Stokoe was not, however, your typical Cornish yokel. In fact, he wasn't Cornish at all. Originally from Kent, his CV included stints as the Head of News at the Local Government Association, as Director of Communications for the London Fire Brigade, as an Opinion Writer for the Huffington Post, and as an Interim Director of Communications at The London Assembly. Marazion might be a small west country backwater, but their frontman was an experienced, well-connected, and serious player who could hold a pen and make it sing. Marazion meant business. Much of what follows over the next few paragraphs was shared with me by Richard Stokoe himself, so credit where credit is due. This bit is his story, far more so than mine. With a background in politics and public relations, Stokoe immediately saw the Civic Honours competition as an opportunity to put Marazion on the map.

The small town was already best known for being joined by a sandy causeway to St Michael's Mount, the imposing rocky island crowned by a medieval church and castle, and a standout national landmark by anyone's standards. Doncaster certainly couldn't trump that for the cultural wow factor. Many who visit St Michael's Mount, however, tend to completely bypass Marazion; a visit to the former does not guarantee money spent in the shops of the latter. Overall Marazion itself is affluent, but there are parts of both the town and the surrounding area that are anything but. If Marazion could, however, market itself as effectively as St. David's, Britain's current smallest and perhaps its most boutique city, then perhaps this could trigger a welcome and sustainable economic boost. Stokoe was also motivated by giving the town a boost more broadly. After the prolonged misery of Covid-19 and all its lockdowns, acutely felt locally in terms of the death rate of a small seaside town with an ageing population, businesses were suffering, and people were generally down in the dumps. A city status campaign might be just the tonic to give local people something else to talk about, and to forget about how awful everything else was.

Despite Stokoe's enthusiasm, a Marazion bid wasn't a done deal. When it came to the vote of the town council to go ahead, it was a close call. Some born and bred locals proudly boast that Marazion is one of the oldest market towns in England. Stokoe's own research suggests it doesn't even come close but, in his own words, 'they like to believe this, and no outsider is going to tell them different.' Nevertheless, with a bit of democratic manipulation on Stokoe's part, securing a deferment of the vote by a fortnight so that two supportive councillor colleagues could return from their holidays, the decision to press ahead was approved by six votes to four. The councillors did, however, stipulate an unusual proviso to get the vote passed. Despite an agreement that a bid should be submitted, Marazion would not become a city, whatever the outcome of the contest. You read that correctly, Marazion was bidding, not only with no actual intention of winning, but to purposefully want to lose.

What had started out as a genuine ambition to become a city, with dreams of boosting long term local trade, had quickly flipped over into a public relations stunt primarily geared to provide some momentary local sunshine through the dark skies of Covid-19, and to drum up some welcome Christmas business for the local traders. So, in early December, just before the submission deadline, Stokoe got out his little black book of media contacts and tapped up a few local and regional contacts with the hope that the quirkiness of the Marazion campaign would feed into the nationals, which of course it did. When the list of entrants was officially announced, the Marazion story was the second most read article on the BBC News site and mustered a full-page story in *The Guardian*. According to Stokoe, the coverage boosted online Christmas sales for the local shops by a fivefold magnitude. Mission accomplished!

Despite the understanding within the town council that city status wouldn't be accepted, Marazion wasn't obviously trying to throw the game. The bid they submitted is actually pretty good. It was well referenced, nicely presented, and articulate in the case it put forward. It was by no means the worst entry on the table and stood up well against the efforts of larger rivals. There was, however, some seemingly subtle mischief afoot. 'As it is often said, size is not important,' Stokoe teasingly jested in the BBC News article,[55] a reference to Marazion's status as a bantamweight contender. In a further video on the *Cornwall Live* website, he described the town as being stacked with weird and wonderful things to do.[56] 'There are snooker clubs,' he began. 'For a town this small that's incredible. Having been

55   https://www.bbc.co.uk/news/uk-england-cornwall-59571276

56   https://www.cornwalllive.com/news/cornwall-news/marazion-tiny-cornwall-town-thought-6453445

brought up in Kent I would have to drive 15 miles to get to a snooker club, so it's great that it's just around the corner.' The delivery seemed sincere on face value, but a campaign that was counting snooker clubs amongst its most city-worthy assets smelt fishier than an Atlantic mackerel freshly hooked on Marazion's seafront.

I don't know if the Cabinet Office had gotten word through their own backchannels that Marazion's bid might not be quite what it seemed, but they had the town's card marked. Just before Christmas, the Cabinet Office contacted Marazion's Town Council to clarify that applications must only be submitted by principal authorities, even though this requirement didn't feature in the originally published rules. What the Cabinet Office meant by this was that only district, county, or unitary authorities could submit a bid; town councils, like Marazion's, could not. The Cabinet Office claim that all local authority Chief Executives were contacted early in the competition to clarify this, but I have no real way to verify that. The entry guidelines published online were certainly never updated, continuing to state the contest was open to any elected local authority, with no mention of non-principal authorities being excluded. It felt to Marazion like this was an unfair, belated change in the rules which was more than a little against the spirit of the competition. There was seemingly no obvious incentive to single out and kill off Marazion's bid. If the government, for whatever reason, particularly didn't want Marazion to win, they could just have vetoed their bid in the final evaluation. Taking all that into account, I'll leave it for you to decide how straight you think the Cabinet Office's bat is.

So, applicants who had entered but hadn't secured permission from the principal authority were given the grace of five days to secure such consent, literally in the days immediately before Christmas. For Marazion, this would mean securing authorisation from Cornwall Council, but from whom specifically? 'So, was it the leader?' Stokoe questioned. 'Full cabinet? Full council? The Chief Executive? The ward councillor? A local binman?' Cornwall Council would very likely have been juggling several important priorities in the days before Christmas: calculating council tax levels and budgets for the next financial year, managing their ongoing Covid-19 response, unwrapping each other's Secret Santa gifts, and so on. Cornwall Council had not thus far been involved in the Marazion bid, and their own councillors were hardly likely to set down their mulled wine and mince pies at this late hour to debate its merits and reach a consensus as to whether it should be endorsed. Five days quickly came and went. No endorsement came. And just like that, in the first week of January, Marazion was gone from the competition. The pool of 39 bidders had become 38.

Now, we've already established that Marazion weren't all that bothered about winning. So, as a final hurrah, Stokoe had one final stir of the pot, and did a protest piece about Marazion's dismissal with *The Independent,* focused on what he refers to as the 'evil dead hand of central government killing off local democracy'. This got more headlines and helped generate a little more new-year trade for Marazion's businesses. So, was

Marazion's bid ever designed to win? 'Originally yes,' Stokoe told me. 'But then no'. Was it a PR stunt? 'Absolutely'. Did the Cabinet Office force Marazion to withdraw? 'Yes'. Did the town mind? 'No'. Were they pleased with the outcome? 'Probably about 50/50'. Some locals had hated all the attention that was being thrust upon the town, and the very idea of even thinking of becoming a city, whilst others had seen the value that it was having. However you look at it, Marazion's adventure as a city status contender had been quite the story.

The news about Marazion had perked my curiosity though. I had not seen any official announcement about Marazion's removal from the competition from the Cabinet Office. Could therefore other yet unnamed candidates also have fallen foul of the same technicality? Crewe's bid, for example, had been submitted by the Clerk of Crewe Town Council (a non-principal authority), but co-naming Cheshire East Borough Council on its application. Was the Town Council duly asked to provide specific endorsement from the Borough Council in the same way as Marazion and, if so, had it been given? Alcester's bid had been submitted under the name of Stratford-on-Avon District Council, but by the Mayor of Alcester, who was technically a representative of Alcester Town Council. Could they be in the same boat? The application from Dorchester was submitted under the name of "Dorset Council for Dorchester Town Council" by the Chief Executive of Dorset Council, so surely that ticked the right box? There was clearly a lot of questions, but we must assume that the Cabinet Office applied a consistent and even hand across all these permutations.

The Platinum Jubilee year officially began on 6th of February, the date that marked the 70th anniversary of the death of King George VI, and the ascension of his eldest daughter as monarch. The day before the anniversary, the Queen held a reception at Sandringham House in Norfolk. She cut what was likely to be the first of many celebratory cakes and released a message, patriotically reminding the British people that 'as we mark this anniversary, it gives me pleasure to renew to you the pledge I gave in 1947 that my life will always be devoted to your service.' It is poignant to think that she would only be with us for just a few more short months, but she was nevertheless steadfast in that pledge until the very end.

On the same day that the Queen was at Sandringham, the government launched a new competition that was set to keep Team Doncaster preoccupied for a goodly chunk of 2022. The Department of Transport were behind the contest to find a home for the proposed headquarters of Great British Railways, the new body to oversee, as its name suggests, Britain's railway network. The contest was open to any locality outside of London who had until the 16th of March to table an Expression of Interest to participate, and naturally it was a competition where Doncaster fancied its chances. After all, why wouldn't the town that had given the world The Flying Scotsman and The Mallard be a steadfast contender? I didn't have the same opportunity to be directly involved in this bid. Even though, through my day job, I had plenty of other bids to be involved in, I still strangely felt a little left out. This bid was a little different as the decision as to which town or city would win was based on a combination of both technical merit and a public vote. 42 places put their names in the hat, including some formidable localities like Manchester and Edinburgh, as well as the slightly less obvious, such as the small town of Camborne in Cornwall. Doncaster nevertheless persevered to the shortlist of the final six, alongside Birmingham, Crewe, Derby, Newcastle, and York. These were all strong contenders, all strategically positioned and with great railway heritages. The final six would progress to a final stage of having a Ministerial visit and the public vote itself. Readying for the visit, canvassing for votes, and broader lobbying for Doncaster's campaign dominated the local agenda. There was a quiet confidence in that Doncaster could pull off the double, winning both city status and the GB Rail HQ competition too.

The city status bid wasn't completely forgotten about though. February also saw the staging of Doncaster's annual Business Showcase staged at Doncaster Racecourse. The Showcase, run by Business Doncaster, is one of the biggest local business exhibitions in the country. The 2022 event, returning for the first time after the Covid-19 lockdowns, attracted over 250 exhibitors and more than 2,500 visitors. Business Doncaster has given a free stand for the city status campaign to use, so Scott McFarlane, Ginny Lindle and I put our heads together in terms of how we could best exploit the opportunity. For starters, we still had a bag full of city status pin badges which we liberally gave away to attendees. Then, for a relatively small budget we had a couple of pop-up banners made up, as well as a customised selfie-frame board. One of the pop-up banners was intentionally left blank, with an opportunity for attendees to sign it with a Sharpie pen to show their support for the campaign. We collected over 100 signatures during the day, including those of Mayor Ros Jones and Nick Fletcher MP. Plenty of people were cajoled too in having their picture taken with the selfie-board, and Scott had brought his own camera along to take some quality photographs. All of this gave us a fresh bank of eye-catching collateral to push out through our social media channels. It also helped to maintain the local buy-in and momentum for the campaign. Most people who visited the stand were happy to sign their name on the banner, but not quite everyone. It was interesting to meet a few people who were against the campaign in person. No one was in anyway impolite, but there were a few who were steadfast in their view that Doncaster should remain as a town. Me being me, I did my best to sway their opinion, with more success in some cases than in others. But fair play, at least these folks were not afraid to have a sincere debate.

All in all, though, it was a frustratingly long Spring though. Hopes and aspirations for winning city status continued to bubble away, but we had no real idea of how our prospects were shaping up. We just had to sit it out. Within my business we'd had a bit of a recruitment drive, and our new starters were coming on board. That led to the suggestion of having a team away day to welcome the new arrivals, do some teambuilding activities, and set out our stall for the year ahead. Having deliberated a few venues, we booked an off-site meeting room just down the road at the Mount Pleasant Hotel in mid-May and we set about making plans for the day. Not that it had any obvious significance at the time, but that would turn out to be the 162nd day since Doncaster's city status bid was submitted. Destiny was literally waiting for us just around the corner, we just didn't know that yet.

The Winning Post

There was no set date for when the outcome of the city status competition would be revealed. The working assumption was that it would be announced before the double bank holiday weekend in June, which was earmarked for all the official Platinum Jubilee festivities, but exactly how much before was anyone's guess. As we moved into May 2022, I started to monitor the parliamentary diary on-line in the hope of identifying any clues, on the basis that results of previous competitions had first been announced via a Ministerial statement in the House of Commons. On this basis, the 26th May looked like the most promising date. Nadine Dorries, the then Culture Secretary, was scheduled to take questions from fellow MPs at the dispatch box on that day, which had all the trappings of a potential announcement. It was also the last day the House was due to sit before the bank holiday weekend. As that date grew nearer, the parliamentary calendar was further updated to include an address from the Prime Minister himself in the Commons on the same day to celebrate the Platinum Jubilee. That sounded like it had a city status announcement written all over it. Yes, the announcement would come on the 26th of May, I was certain of it. I could switch off from the distraction of fretting over the news. You can therefore imagine my surprise when, on the 19th of May, a week earlier than I expected, I took the call from Dan Fell at the Mount Pleasant Hotel during our team building day. But although I was wrong about the date, my intuition about the result was right.

The news of the outcome of the contest was technically embargoed until midnight, but with several of us in the loop, Dan Fell shared The Cabinet Office press release with the project board and other key contributors that evening. After all, who else were we all going to tell at that point apart from each other? When I got home Anne had already bought me a congratulatory card and a bottle of red wine. We ended up sat out in Kings Park in Retford with our daughter Alice a short while later, eating take-out pizzas in the evening sunshine courtesy of The Saucy Pizza Co. (which I highly recommend if you ever find yourself in Retford). I was mentally pinching myself all evening, trying to process the news. We really had just won and turned Doncaster into a city. How crazy was that? There was also a slightly humbling realisation that, in all the bids I had ever written, and all the bids I had yet to write, this would probably be the one that would most likely define my whole career. If I might be remembered for anything in a professional capacity, something vaguely worth recording as a footnote on a Wikipedia page, then this bid was it. Best of all, at that point the people of Doncaster didn't even know it yet. They would all be going to bed that evening for the final time in a town and waking up the next morning in a city. Some people quite probably couldn't have cared less, but I just sat there in the evening sunshine, inwardly marvelling at the whole thing.

It normally takes me a minute or two to come too when I first wake up, but the next day I was instantaneously wide awake the second my eyelids opened. The very first thing that I did as I lay there in bed was to check the BBC News app on my phone.

I don't usually keep my phone next to the bed, but I had made a rare exception to help me get to the news that little bit quicker. And there it was, the very top story, accompanied by a smiling library photograph of the Queen! Doncaster was a city for all the world to see. Seeing it on the BBC News website somehow made it that little bit more real. It wasn't a secret anymore. A career full of bids, and this was the first one, and probably the only one, to make the BBC headlines. People waking up all over Doncaster, all over Britain, and tuning into the news that morning would all be hearing and seeing the same thing. I clicked off the BBC News app, then I immediately clicked back on it. The story was still there! I think I did that a few more times. It wasn't in my imagination, it was real. It was such a surreal experience.

There was one small error on the BBC News website. In providing a pen picture profile of the each of the winners, the BBC proclaimed Doncaster as the home of the famous rail locomotive, The Flying Dutchman. Shiver me timbers! The Flying Dutchman is, of course, a mythical ghost ship, which first appeared in popular literature in the 18th century and was most recently seen in Disney's *Pirates of the Caribbean* movies. To the best of my knowledge the ship has never visited Doncaster, perhaps because Doncaster is landlocked from the sea, but mainly because the ship is a complete work of fiction. The BBC News website was updated shortly after with the correct title of The Flying Scotsman (a real train, which has never been driven by a crew of peg-legged ghost pirates). I guess confusing Scotland and the Netherlands is an easy mistake to make in the cut and thrust of the BBC newsroom.

Dan Fell did the rounds on the media circuit, and the story of Doncaster's winning bid naturally got a lot of coverage through BBC *Look North*, ITV's *Calendar News*, the *Yorkshire Post*, and the other local outlets over the course of the day's news cycle. Ros Jones offered some soundbites too. Of course, the outcome of the city status competition didn't remain as the top national news story for very long. The story quickly gave way to updates on the brutal fighting between Russia and the Ukraine in the besieged city of Mariupol, the conclusion of the "Wagatha Christie" celebrity libel trial between Rebekah Vardy and Coleen Rooney, the confirmation of fixed penalty "partygate" fines for Boris Johnson and a host of Downing Street officials, and the glamorous images of the Duchess of Cambridge taking the hand of Hollywood star Tom Cruise on the red carpet at the premiere of his new movie, *Top Gun: Maverick*. C'est la vie! As big as city status was for Doncaster, and for me personally, it was never going to keep pace with all of that. The news cycle kept on turning, as it always does, but for a fleeting moment at least the eyes of the country had been upon us.

There were eight winning cities in the end, a new record for a Civic Honours competition. Wrexham, perhaps unsurprisingly, was successful as the only Welsh bidder. I was personally surprised that Colchester was a winner, not because they had a poor bid, but because it meant that Essex had now been granted three cities in relatively quick succession, following Chelmsford in 2012 and Southend in 2021. Milton Keynes was the other winning city in England, and Dunfermline won the battle to become Scotland's eighth city. Bangor in Northern Ireland became a city, which means that there are now two British cities with that name, the other being in Wales. Outside of the home nations, Douglas, the capital of the Isle of Mann, made the list, as did Stanley, the administrative capital of the Falkland Islands. Whilst I was pleased for the other winners, the only success I was really interested in was Doncaster's.

Finally, now content to leave the BBC news app alone, I got ready for work. I had already bought a life-size cardboard cut-out of the Queen for a Platinum Jubilee street party planned for the bank holiday weekend, but she was going to make her debut a little sooner than planned. I bundled the Queen into the back of my car, which doesn't sound right at all, and drove her to Doncaster where she would grace our office for the day. Social media was buzzing on that Friday. Various people who had been involved in the bid posted their celebratory thanks to each other. The #goingforitdn hashtag had been joined by a new #wewonitdn hashtag. I have no idea exactly how many posts were made by people that day, but at one point "Donny" was trending on Twitter. There were lots of posts and comments too from Doncaster's previously silent majority, ordinary people who perhaps hadn't posted anything during the campaign, but who were now a welcome part of the celebration. I joined in, posting a photo of me with my cardboard Queen, holding my campaign launch edition of the *Doncaster Free Press*, and it's Back the Bid headline. I also fielded more than a few congratulatory emails and messages. Any other work plans which I had for that day pretty much went straight out of the window.

Dan Fell and Ros Jones did the rounds on the media circuit, and the story of Doncaster's winning bid naturally got a lot of coverage through BBC Look North, ITV's Calendar News, the Yorkshire Post, and the other local outlets over the course of the day's news cycle. Of course, the outcome of the city status competition didn't remain as the top national news story for very long. The story quickly gave way to updates on the brutal fighting between Russia and the Ukraine in the besieged city of Mariupol, the conclusion of the "Wagatha Christie" celebrity libel trial between Rebekah Vardy and Coleen Rooney, the confirmation of fixed penalty "partygate" fines for Boris Johnson and a host of Downing Street officials, and the glamorous images of the Duchess of Cambridge taking the hand of Hollywood star Tom Cruise on the red carpet at the premiere of his new movie, Top Gun: Maverick. C'est la vie! As big as city status was for Doncaster, and for me personally, it was never going to keep pace with all of that. The news cycle kept on turning, as it always does, but for a fleeting moment at least the eyes of the country had been upon us.

As a bid writer you rarely get mementos when your proposal wins, there are no trophies or medals to be handed out. That normally doesn't bother me too much, but this competition was always a little bit different. I'd always promised myself that I would get a Doncaster Rovers shirt with Doncaster City 2022 printed on the back of it if we won, and that was one of the personal mementos I rewarded myself with. I had hoped to buy it at the stadium shop on my way home from North Yorkshire, but US rock band The Killers were set to play a concert there a few days later, and as a result the whole stadium was off limits as they set up the stage. Although I didn't go to the concert myself, it looked like an amazing gig, with a crowd of around 25,000, all singing in unison at the top of their voices with frontman Brandon Flowers to *Mr. Brightside*. It was a more than an appropriate curtain raiser for Doncaster to start its new life as a city. It did, of course mean, that I had to wait another week before I got my shirt. When the stadium shop re-opened I went straight round. I naturally posted a picture of myself wearing the shirt as soon as I got it. I've yet to find a proper opportunity to wear it again, but that was never really the point of buying it. Driving home from work on the Thursday after the announcement, I also stopped off at the newsagents in the village Ranskill and bought their last three copies of that week's edition of the *Doncaster Free Press*, celebrating the success on its cover. The title banner had been subtly changed to read as the *Doncaster City Free Press*, an inspired touch. I don't really know why I bought all three, and the guy behind the counter clearly thought I was a bit strange, but these were all my own personal little trophies.

The celebrations kept going strongly for several days. Heather Wheeler MP, Parliamentary Secretary for the Cabinet Office, visited the Doncaster Gallery, Library and Museum the following week for a congratulatory reception with local councillors and members of the Project Board. The reception was held in the Railway Heritage Centre in DGLAM, where the imposing steam locomotives the No. 251 and the Green Arrow are on display, a fitting backdrop. The event was hosted by Ros Jones, Damian Allen, and the Civic Mayor, Ian Pearson, and a nice buffet spread had been laid on. Wheeler did the rounds, shaking hands with as many people as she could. When it came to my turn, she asked 'what did you do?' I smiled, and simply said that 'I had done a bit of the writing'. Content with my answer, she briskly moved on to the next person. Whilst it was cut from published video footage of her visit, as part of her address to those assembled, she advised us that Doncaster's was the 'Number 1' bid in the competition. I don't know if that was true or not. I remember the late Bruce Forsythe on the BBC's *Strictly Come Dancing*, telling every competing couple that they were his personal favourites, albeit always somewhat tongue in cheek. Maybe Wheeler was just stroking our egos, and all the new cities received similar praise. Then again, maybe, just maybe, we were the very best of the bunch. The fact that the Council and local press were asked not to show that footage is perhaps telling; a little backtracking so as not to put any noses out of joint elsewhere. But I promised you a truthful story, and what was said was said!

I've offered all sorts of personal views throughout this book as to why I believe Doncaster's bid was a success. Of course, I have no idea for certain if any of my theories on this are correct. There may well be some civil servants left in stitches reading this, snorting and guffawing at just how wide of the mark I am. To understand more, I reached out to the some of the Expert Panel members again to see if they might be willing to offer any practical feedback from their own musings on our bid. Ben Dean at the Department for Digital, Culture, Media & Sport, replied via LinkedIn to say that Doncaster's was "a strong bid and fully deserving of selection", but went on to suggest that I contact the Cabinet Office's dedicated Civic Honours email address to request more insightful feedback. So, I did just that, dropping in that it was Ben's suggestion to make contact, which I felt may hopefully improve my prospects of receiving an informed reply. Victoria James, a Constitutional Policy Advisor at the Cabinet Office came back to me a short while later. The brief feedback she gave was largely a bit of a playback of our executive summary. It was reassuring to a point, but it also felt like a very safely worded reply and only a skin-deep justification for our success. This is not uncommon with bid feedback more broadly; sometimes as a proposal writer you never get a fully satisfactory answer as to why your bid won or lost. Here is what Ms. James said though, and I'll leave you to make up your own mind:

It was assessed that Doncaster gave a very strong bid, meeting all the criteria and showcasing that the town has a distinct identity with a proud Yorkshire culture and identity and a rich history in record of innovation. It was also noted that the bid was formally backed by the Lord Lieutenant of South Yorkshire, The Bishop of Sheffield, and The Yorkshire Leader's Board. Further to this, it was also assessed that Doncaster is in a good position to benefit from city status. It was noted that over £150m has been invested over the past decade in civil and cultural facilities, education institutions, and transport infrastructure.

Another successful aspect of the bid was the demonstration of the support from the people of Doncaster, showing the lengths to which the council had gone to involve Doncaster's communities in making the application. It was noted that residents have appeared in the #GoingForItDN videos sharing personal reasons why Doncaster should be a city.

I mean, these are all very kind and gracious words, but you could be forgiven for thinking that we should have just submitted the executive summary and nothing else. Or maybe we just had a world class executive summary? Either way, there surely had to be more to explain Doncaster's success than just this alone. What about the other 18 pages? Perhaps one day a Cabinet Office whistle-blower will write a full expose as to how city status bids are really evaluated. In the meantime, let's just enjoy the fact that Doncaster won, without necessarily getting too bogged down in the reasons why.

The other winning cities were all enjoying their moment too. One of my favourite stories came from Dunfermline which received a message of congratulations from none other than the country singing legend Dolly Parton, sent all the way from her home in Nashville, Tennessee[57]. Mirroring the spirit of Parton's global hit, *9 to 5*, Dunfermline had literally tumbled out of bed, stumbled to the kitchen, and poured itself a cup of ambition. It's the birthplace of Andrew Carnegie, the philanthropist, entrepreneur, and all round Scottish national treasure. Carnegie

---

57   https://www.thecourier.co.uk/fp/news/fife/4150867/dolly-parton-letter-dunfermline/

led the expansion of the American steel industry in the 19th century, becoming one of the richest men in US history, but also one of history's greatest benefactors. Having recently been awarded the Carnegie Medal of Philanthropy in New York in respect of her own charitable work, Parton had a newfound connection with both the great man and the people of Fife. 'I want to congratulate Dunfermline on becoming Scotland's newest city!' she said. 'Scotland holds a special place in my heart, and I wish I could be there in person to celebrate this wonderful recognition and our connection through Andrew Carnegie!'

As might be expected, the government of Argentina was less than amused to see Stanley in the Falkland Islands on the winner's list[58]. Santiago Cafiero, the Argentine Foreign Minister, said that the 'decision has no effect but confirms that the UK does not respect international law. The announcement from the British Crown on Puerto Argentino [the Argentine name for Stanley] simply exposes the colonial character of the illegal and illegitimate occupation by the British of our Malvinas Islands.' Unflapped by this condemnation, the Falkland's government readily purchased a new street sign, bearing its coat of arms, which read: "Welcome to the City of Stanley, capital of the Falkland Islands - twinned with Portsmouth and Whitby". If there was ever a thinly veiled two finger salute directed towards Buenos Aires, this sign was surely it. One thing is for certain though, Argentina isn't about to relinquish

---

58   https://en.mercopress.com/2022/05/23/argentine-officials-question-city-status-awarded-to-stanley-falklands-capital

its claim on the Falkland Islands any time soon. There are more chapters in that story yet to be written.

Doncaster Chamber's "What's Next?" conference took place less than a fortnight after the city status winner's announcement in May. As you might expect, the feel-good factor was still being strongly felt, with buckets of bravado dripping from the stage. With city status secured, we were riding high, and the world was our oyster. There was talk, for instance, that Doncaster might bid to become the UK City of Culture in 2029, but Bradford was announced as the 2025 winner shortly after and having back-to-back winners from Yorkshire seemed like an unlikely ask, regardless of our ambition. Nevertheless, it was latterly announced that Doncaster had won the right to host UK Pride in 2024, the focal point of the LGBTQ calendar nationally. That was a big deal. Doncaster was also mooted as a potential future host of BBC Radio 1's *Big Weekend* festival. Well, why not? We were so cocksure of ourselves back then that we could have bid for Doncaster to host the Olympic Games and expected to win it. But whilst we all revelled in that moment of victory, there was a bigger question waiting in the wings. How would Doncaster celebrate and mark this historic milestone? After all, its not everyday that you become a city. As with everything else about our campaign though, this was to prove to be a less straightforward question to answer than it first appeared.

Celebrating the City

Although the results of the Civic Honours competition were announced in May 2022, Doncaster didn't officially become a city until 1st of November 2022. After the euphoria of the initial announcement, everything inevitably went a little quiet again. The dust settled, and the onward responsibility for Doncaster's transition from a town to a city fell back to the Council. For a bid writer, this experience is not unusual. My job has always been to write a proposal to win the contract; the implementation and delivery of the contract once it has been won inevitably falls to others. This situation was no different. Whilst I may have written a winning city status proposal, I am in no respects qualified to run a city. Usually this doesn't bother me that much; winning the bid is the high, and the natural end point of my involvement. This wasn't just any bid though, and the job didn't yet feel fully done. The bid was won, but Doncaster wasn't an official city yet.

Some aspects of city status celebration happened of their own accord, without the need of any intervention from Team Doncaster. The Doncaster Half Marathon, for example, organised by local events firm Curly's Athletes, was due to be run on the 12th of June. When the news of Doncaster's city status first broke just a few weeks previously in May, the team at Curly's Athletes had literally just enough time to rebrand the event as the first ever Doncaster CITY Half Marathon, and to re-design the finishers' t-shirts in the same vein. June also saw the formation of a new football team, Doncaster City

FC. The team was backed and sponsored by national retailer Sports Direct, owing in part to their Chief Executive, Michael Murray, heralding from Doncaster. I'm not sure if Doncaster has the fanbase and wherewithal to support and sustain two league clubs, but this was no deterrent to the new "blues". The new club joined the Sheffield & Hallamshire County Senior Football League Division Two in their inaugural campaign, in the thirteenth tier of English football, which they won at the first attempt. You may recall earlier that I talked about the Treaty of Durham signed in 1136, under which Doncaster became a ward of Scotland, with the Treaty never being repealed. Well, as Doncaster City FC were ineligible to play in the English FA Cup, they applied instead to play in the Scottish FA Cup in 2023, citing the Treaty as the basis for their inclusion. It was arguably something of a publicity stunt, and the Scottish FA didn't bite, but it would have been quite something if Doncaster's new team had played at Ibrox or Celtic Park.

The city status Project Board wasn't reconvened until August, and I had gone into that meeting expecting that some interesting plans from Team Doncaster to celebrate our success would already be in motion. By that point Milton Keynes had already held a city status celebration cycle ride and was now scaling-up its autumnal light festival to include a free concert headlined by Sam Ryder, who had finished in second place for the UK at the Eurovision Song Concert earlier in the year, bringing some much-restored British pride after a long run of poor results. Meanwhile Wrexham was on track to be the first of the Platinum Jubilee cities to receive its official Letters

Patent on 1st September, with a city fun day planned, and a package of other community events lined up. Colchester's Council had set aside a budget of £50,000 to support a year of city status celebratory events[59]. The headline event was a re-enactment of the 1648 Siege of Colchester, staged in August 2023, involving more than 500 costumed participants and lord knows how many horses, muskets, and cannons. This was probably the biggest, and most elaborate, city celebration event staged by any of the winners. Whilst Southend had gained its city status under different circumstances, they had also been audibly blowing their own trumpet. They had hosted a "City Week", kicked off with an inaugural city performance for Sir David Amess, witfully titled the *He Built this City* concert, and headlined by local lad and West End star, Lee Mead. Like Colchester, Southend had also launched a dedicated city status website and a £25,000 city celebration fund to help residents celebrate.

I had anticipated that Team Doncaster may have spent the early summer devising some similar schemes, riding on the crest of the city status wave. As it transpired though, Doncaster's plans were still largely on the drawing board. It was only when the Project Board reconvened, three months or so after city status had been announced, that attention turned to how Doncaster might celebrate its newfound title. Central to this was the receipt of the Letters Patent, the document officially confirming city status from the Crown Office, which

59   https://www.gazette-news.co.uk/news/23349502.siege-colchester-city-status-plan-part-commemorative-events/

would formalise Doncaster's city status. We had been given a confirmed date for this, the 1st of November. It wasn't clear at that time whether a member of the royal family would present it, or whether the Letters Patent would be delivered less formally, but at least the date was set, or so we thought. A new working group was set up to deliberate and steer these onward celebrations, which I seemed to become the unofficial chairperson of.

The other main order of business for the Project Board when it first reconvened in August was to discuss the renaming of the council. Two options were on the table: Doncaster City Council or the City of Doncaster Council. The council were proposing a community consultation to inform the decision; not a binding vote per se, but near enough to all intents and purposes. Council colleagues were, off the record, largely backing City of Doncaster Council, as this was perceived as being more reflective and inclusive of the whole borough. Doncaster City Council was perhaps a little more casual, but equally more of a plain speaking and Yorkshire-like title. A poll was duly opened for three weeks on the on-line Doncaster Talks Platform, and project board members were duly encouraged to promote the poll through their networks. Illustrative logos capturing what the Council's new brand identity might also look like, put together by Steph Cunningham's team, were also on display. The result of the poll would be put to a full meeting of elected Council members who would ultimately decide upon and ratify the new legal title, albeit they had the option to ignore the result of the public poll if they so wished (as precarious as that might be in the eyes of residents). The short window for the poll was deliberate, as the consultation, poll, and Council ratification all had to wrapped up before the Letters Patent arrived, and there was a specific timeline of opportunity to get this all done in time for the full Council meeting scheduled for the 8th of September, the last full meeting before the 1st of November.

More than 12,497 people took part in the poll, which I think is an impressive response on the issue. 7,764 (62%) of respondents opted for the City of Doncaster, thankfully sparing the blushes of Council colleagues who preferred that option too. If you are interested in statistics, then I can tell you that 10,573 of those polled gave a Doncaster postcode, albeit that doesn't necessarily mean the others didn't live in the borough. Perhaps less surprising is that the poll had a proportionately slightly higher engagement rate with those aged over 45, and slightly lower engagement with the under-18s. The response rate was also slightly higher amongst women then it was men. Statistics aside, the poll result was convincing, and papers were duly drawn up for the Council meeting on afternoon of the 8th of September to ratify the new legal title. Of course, that meeting never got to take place, and 8th September 2022 would end up being remembered in history for a very different reason.

On the morning of that Thursday there were widespread news reports that the Queen was under medical supervision at Balmoral Castle in Scotland after doctors had become concerned for her health. All four of the Queen's children, along with Prince William, were travelling to be with her. Princess Anne was already staying on the Balmoral estate, Prince Charles arrived in the morning from nearby Birkhall, whilst a plane carrying the Duke of Cambridge, Duke of York and the Earl and Countess of Wessex touched down at Aberdeen Airport in the late afternoon. Their cortège of cars rolled into Balmoral around an hour later, but by that point the Queen had already passed away. The news coverage, across every channel, was intensively sombre, with broadcasters dressed in dark suits as a foreboding omen of the seemingly inevitable news that was about to come. Then, at 6.30pm that evening, the news of the Queen's death was publicly announced, and the union flag atop of Buckingham Palace fell to half-mast. The entire nation came to an abrupt halt. All things relating to city status didn't seem all that important in the days that followed. The Council meeting scheduled for that afternoon was quite rightly called off.

Books of Condolence were opened for the public to sign at Doncaster Gallery, Library & Museum, as well as an e-Book of Condolence via the Council's website, where almost 1,200 people left messages. A Service of Commemoration was held at Doncaster Minster, floral tributes were laid in Sir Nigel Gresley Square, and a photo of the Queen appeared on the giant display board on the side of the Frenchgate Shopping Centre. The death of the Queen also coincided with the St Leger Festival weekend, meaning that the race cards for Friday and Saturday were cancelled. The "Celebrating the City of Doncaster Nursery Handicap Stakes", a race named in honour of our successful city status campaign, was ironically one of the casualties, albeit the showpiece St Leger Stakes were still run on the Sunday. A period of silence was observed prior to the opening race, and the jockeys all wore black armbands. The official race day programme and form guide had been hastily reprinted; the cover showed a black and white photograph of the Queen, jubilantly cheering on the horses from the stands. Further tributes to the Queen had been added inside. Some from Doncaster made the trip to London, joining thousands of others, to queue to see the Queen's coffin lying in state at Westminster Hall. The local reading of the Proclamation of Accession of King Charles III was made on the steps of Doncaster's Mansion House on 11th September; jointly given by Ros Jones, Damian Allen, and Ian Pearson. Then, on Monday 19th September, in unison with the rest of the country, as well as the rest of the world, Doncaster watched on as the Queen was finally laid to rest.

The passing of the Queen left everything, inevitably, a little up in the air. Operation London Bridge, the codename for the Queen's funeral plan, covering every protocol and detail with exacting precision, was first devised in the 1960s, albeit updated several times since. No plan could, however, cover everything. At the time of her death, the country was already somewhat upside down in the wake of Boris Johnson's resignation as Prime Minister. The literal final engagement that the Queen fulfilled in person, two days before her death, was her meeting at Balmoral with Liz Truss, inviting her to form a government as our new Prime Minister. Seven weeks later Truss herself would also resign, having committed economic suicide with an ill-considered mini budget, becoming the shortest serving British Prime Minister in history. A ministerial merry-go-round was in full swing, alongside a new monarch,

King Charles, easing himself into the public consciousness in taking the place of his mother. How and when Doncaster might receive its Letters Patent was, understandably, a question that was nowhere near the top of anyone's to-do list in Whitehall or at Buckingham Palace.

Local plans to celebrate city status were getting somewhat bogged down. There was no specific money being pledged from the Council for a celebration, and with no budget there was no easy way that any plans could be made. The debate swung back and forth. Should, for example, there be a particular signature event or a series of smaller events? Should we focus on the Autumn, dovetailing with the showpiece Rugby League World Cup fixtures that were already scheduled to be played in Doncaster, or plan something for the warmer climes of summer 2023? Given the cost-of-living crisis, there was a view that any celebration shouldn't be too extravagant, whilst equally acknowledging that being awarded city status was a significant moment for the borough. From this a couple of ideas gained some traction. Front and centre, there was an idea for a staged celebration event in Elmfield Park. Doncaster Pride was already due to be staged there in August 2023, so the same staging and infrastructure could be utilised for a city celebration event, helping to keep the costs down. Logistically though this would all take a lot of organising, and way beyond the time commitment that I, or anyone else on our steering group, could readily make alone. With no money or project management resource forthcoming from the Council, and no alternate funders waiting in the wings, any prospect of organising a celebratory event quickly stalled.

The situation was somewhat overtaken by the hastily arranged visit from King Charles in November 2022 to proclaim Doncaster as a city (which I'll return to in detail shortly). Suddenly the Council's purse strings were loosened a little, in ensuring that an appropriate reception was staged. It was obviously a great event, and a day to remember for everyone who took part. Staged on a Wednesday lunchtime, and arranged with only a few days' notice, the event was nevertheless out of reach for many ordinary Doncastrians. I suspect that many more locals would have liked to have come along, but couldn't get the time off work, or faced similar barriers. In this respect it was a great celebration, but perhaps not a celebration for all. Nevertheless, the consensus following the King's visit was that it was a day that would be hard to top and, as such, all talk of any other city celebration event readily withered on the vine.

A further idea was tabled to devise a full year programme of associated city celebration events. Again, in a bid to keep things simple and affordable, this was primarily intended to leverage the programme of events already planned in the borough in 2023, such as the St Leger Festival, Armed Forces Day, and Doncaster Pride, but to give each event a city celebration twist. Grass roots events could be added to the online programme and community organisers would have access to a city status logo and other resources to tie everything together. There was even talk of the new Letter's Patent featuring as an exhibit in Doncaster's Moving Museum; essentially a converted transit van with various built in display cases, which travels to schools and various community events around the borough. It was sensibly concluded, however, that the Letter's Patent was probably too valuable to be paraded in such a way. Whilst rival Colchester managed to execute a Year of Celebration, Doncaster, again, didn't quite get there. Visit Doncaster instead ran a "Summer in the City" programme of events, which was broadly the same idea, but critically, at least for me, wasn't an explicit celebration of Doncaster's new city status. That said, there were some notable, and in some cases unexpected, highlights within the 2023 calendar. Markedly, it saw the second visit by King Charles III to Doncaster in less than a year. The St Leger has always enjoyed a patronage of royal spectators, but, unlike Ascot, hadn't had one in many years. In Queen Elizabeth II's first year as monarch she came to the Doncaster to watch her own horse place third in the St Leger Stakes and, low and behold, Charles did the same. His horse, Desert Hero, also placed third having started out, just like his mother's, as the favourite. The royal visit was a welcome shot in the arm for the St Leger, helping to reassert its credentials as a highlight of the racing calendar. With the 2022 St Leger overshadowed by the Queen's death, the 2023 race shone even more brightly by virtue of having the King return to greet the race going crowds.

Earlier in the year a special ceremony had been held to plant an oak tree sapling in the grounds of the Danum Gallery, Library, & Museum to celebrate the visit of King Charles III and Queen Consort in bestowing city status. The ceremony was hosted by the Civic Mayor, Ian Pearson, with invited guests from a variety of local organisations and communities. The tree itself was planted by Lord Graham Kirkham, with the help of school children from across the borough, and a small plaque was unveiled. Kirkham is another famous born and bred Doncastrian who was named and featured in the city status bid. He is the veteran entrepreneur behind DFS, the sofa giant. It is one of Doncaster's great business success stories, which currently has over 100 stores nationally and a turnover of more than £1bn per year. Whilst not every DFS sofa is still made in Doncaster, its headquarters remain in Adwick-le-Street, and Lord Kirkham still lives in the borough. He reportedly furnishes his own homes, which include Cantley Hall, a Grade II Georgian mansion set in 400 acres, with both reasonably priced DFS sofas alongside a very expensive private collection of masterpieces by likes of Constable and Gainsborough. Each of the schools represented at the ceremony were presented with a miniature spade inscribed on the handle as a souvenir of the day.

2023 also marked the centenary of the Flying Scotsman, a hundred years since the grand old locomotive first rolled out of The Plant railway shed in Doncaster and into active service. The National Railway Museum in York unveiled an official programme of events to mark the occasion, albeit unbelievably this didn't initially include a visit to its birthplace. After a goodly bit of lobbying led by Ros Jones, an extra stop off in Doncaster in November 2023 for a couple of days was hastily added to the schedule, with free tickets made available for locals to see the engine up close at the Freightliner Railport. This wasn't an official city status event and, by the time the Flying Scotsman eventually got here, it wasn't Summer in the City anymore either. That said, a dedicated visit by the Doncaster's most famous train generated almost as much excitement as the visits made by the King himself. As Bill Bryson once put it, 'there are thousands of men in Britain who will never need Viagra as long as there are steam trains in operation.' And a good number of those men live in Doncaster.

Doncaster's Armed Forces Day in June, another Summer in the City event, was headlined by the marching band if the 1st Battalion Coldstream Guards. With the largest regimental membership outside of London, Doncaster has a long association with the Coldstream Guards, and uniquely granted the regiment the Freedom of Entry of the Borough in 2001. In 1660 the regiment marched from Coldstream, the small town on the Scottish border, to London to assist in the restoration of King Charles II to the throne, stopping off for a brief rest in Doncaster on the way. History has it that the first "Donny Lads" then followed the drum, and a Doncaster man has reportedly served in the regiment in every British conflict since the Boer War (1899-01). Alongside the Flying Scotsman, the Guards were another cultural icon with which Doncaster held a deep-seated bond, so it was somewhat poetic too that they should return to the city in its inaugural year.

Some other celebratory ideas were floated but didn't take off. The team at Doncaster Racecourse, for example, came up with the concept of creating a City Celebration Wall, to be positioned in the Grandstand Enclosure, and unveiled at the

2023 St Leger Festival. The plan was for the wall to be made up of a series of commemorative plaques, some celebrating the most memorable events and race winners at the racecourse, as well as others that could be purchased and personalised by the public and local businesses to record their own messages and tributes to the city and the racecourse. It was a novel concept, but sadly it didn't sufficiently capture the imagination of the people of Doncaster, and ultimately not enough plaques were sold to make it happen. There was also some talk that one of the LNER engines running on the East Coast Mainline would be named as the "City of Doncaster", albeit I'm not aware that anything further ever became of that. Both brilliant ideas, but also healthy reminders that having city status doesn't mean that everything you touch turns to gold.

Now that Doncaster has marked its first anniversary as a city the impetus for further celebration has, understandably, waned. Sooner or later the party must end. There will, of course, be anniversaries in the years to come. Many of Britain's newer cities have staged cultural programmes to mark their tenth, twentieth or thirtieth anniversaries and in time that will switch up to centenary celebrations. I have no idea what these future festivities will hold in store for Doncaster, but I hope they will do the city proud. Perhaps too Doncaster will one day enter a future Civic Honours competition, but this time to win the accolade of a Lord Mayoralty. It stands to reason that it will happen sooner or later (probably later). I doubt the first Lord Mayor of Doncaster has even been born yet, and I wonder what they might be like. Young or old, man or woman, black or white, straight or gay? Maybe even, dare I say, a southerner? Whoever it is, I hope it is someone surprising! And I hope too that Doncaster continues to grow into, and find comfort within, its new city status skin. As I've said before, Yorkshire is a proud place, and it can be rightly proud of Doncaster. Its city status has been hard earned. It's taken a long time to get here, and it really is worth celebrating.

Letters Patent

The ceremony held in December 2021 to confer city status on Nakuru in Kenya was quite the thing. The event was held in a giant marquee specially erected in the Nyayo Gardens, a municipal park and green oasis in the heart of the new city. Whilst some of the attending dignitaries had donned their best suits and ties for the day, the Kenyan President, Uhuru Kenyatta, was one of several to opt instead for just a flamboyantly coloured and vibrantly patterned shirt. Whilst he may herald from one of the country's richest families, Kenyatta has been described as a man who easily mixes with ordinary Kenyans, eagerly getting down on the dance floor, and joshing in the local youth slang. An energised crowd had amassed around the marquee, keen to be part of the celebration, and there was a deafening chorus of whistles and vuvuzela horns as the formal declarations were signed. A formal plaque on a nearby wall was unveiled by Kenyatta to commemorate the day, and a sense of hope, renewal, aspiration, and joy was installed into every speech. As the traditional Kenyan music played, with its distinctive tribal beats and harmonies, everyone was up and dancing, including, of course, the President, exchanging celebratory fist bumps on stage with Nakuru's Governor. It was one giant party. And that's how they do city status celebrations in Africa. Suffice to say that, back home in Britain, we do things with a somewhat stiffer upper lip.

Whilst it is usual practice for city status to be conferred by a senior royal, it wasn't a done deal that King Charles III would necessarily come in person to do the honours in Doncaster. Given all the commotion and upheaval of 2022, we certainly didn't presume this would be the case for Doncaster. Indeed, I think our collective view was that we probably wouldn't get a royal visit at all. But, as one of his earliest royal duties, the new King visited Dunfermline, Wrexham, Milton Keynes, Colchester, and Doncaster to deliver the Letters Patent, with his sister, the Princess Royal, fulfilling the duty in Bangor and Stanley. There has, to date, been no equivalent royal visit to Douglas, albeit I'm not altogether sure why. Doncaster's Council only got around two weeks' notice that the King would be coming in person to formally proclaim Doncaster as a city. Having been second guessing when and how the formalities may occur for some time, it all then seemed to happen very suddenly. For the first week, for obvious security reasons, only Damian Allen and his small inner circle of trust within the Council were aware of the imminent visit. Once the corgi was out of the kennel though, there was an immediate wave of anticipation. Logistically there was a lot to be done, making the city centre look spick and span, determining who would be on the guest list and in what capacity, orchestrating crowd control, printing up hoardings and banners, and a host of other things. Street sweepers were summarily dispatched, and barricades were mounted along the High Street. The Mansion House, the venue for the historic visit, had to be readied and prepared, hoovered and dusted. The main ceremony would take place in the Ballroom on the first floor, an appropriately grand room at the top of the imposing main entrance stairway, adorned with portraits of, amongst others, King George III, and Queen Victoria. It was all very prim and proper. The stage was set!

Aside from the King's personal appearance, the other main attraction on the day would be the actual Letters Patent. This is one of three formal documents of state in creating a new city. Firstly, there is the warrant, the monarch's instruction to the Lord Chancellor to prepare the Letters Patent. The Letters Patent itself is the document which confers city status and entrusted to the new city. Finally, there is the patent roll, the record of the warrant held within the National Archives. Doncaster's Letters Patent is a large parchment, written with swirling calligraphy, with the coats of arms of both the Queen and of Doncaster. It comes with an accompany seal and is presented in a big red box a bit like a briefcase. Although the ceremonial formalities of delivering the Letters Patent resided with the King, Doncaster still had to pay for them to be made and had to collect them in person from the Houses of Parliament. As I understand it, the Council paid £2,000 for them to be made up (they don't tell you that in the competition small print!). Paul Bareham was given the honour of travelling to Parliament to collect them. The Council had been advised that one of Ikea's iconic heavy-duty blue shoulder bags was the perfect size and durability, so Paul duly took one to London with him, and carried it back to Doncaster on the train with the freshly scribed historic artefact inside it. It is fitting that the Letters Patent arrived on a regular train on the East Coast Mainline, an unofficial nod of sorts to Doncaster's railway heritage. It would be a much lower key journey than that being made by the King himself.

There are a couple of points that immediately stand out when you read the Letters Patent. Firstly, there is absolutely no punctuation in the document, which makes it very hard to make any real sense of. You certainly need to be a better scholar of history than I am to correctly follow it. Secondly, and much more interestingly, there is the date on which the Queen decreed the Letters Patent. No, it's not the 1st of November 2022, the official date upon which Doncaster's city status is recognised. It is instead the "seventh day of September in the seventy-first year of Our Reign". To put that in further context, it was the day before the Queen died. Technically this makes Doncaster the very, very last of Queen Elizabeth II's British cities. Number 24. Indeed, the approval of Doncaster's Letters Patent may well be the last formal act of any kind attributed to the Queen, on the penultimate day of her record-breaking reign. I'm not suggesting that, lying on her death bed, she shouted out words to the effect of 'Wait! Before I take my last breath I must make Doncaster a city'. There was very likely a little calligraphic licence. Even so, let's still just call this another historical accolade for Doncaster. For reference, Dunfermline's Letters Patent were dated 28th of July 2022, Milton Keynes' were dated 15th of August, and Colchester's were dated 5th of September. Bangor's Letter's Patent were bestowed in the name of King Charles III (dated 22nd of November), ironically making it the first British city to be technically elevated by him. I am sure they will enjoy their kudos too.

I received my invitation to attend only a week before the ceremony. Given the profile of the event, there were specific instructions on what time to arrive, what to wear, and what to bring (primarily a photo identification to pass through security). Donning my faithful blue suit and platinum purple tie one final time, I set off. I had a nervous moment at the security checkpoint on Priory Place, when the chap holding the guest list couldn't find my name. Standing next to him was a burly looking armed police officer who took a moment to eye me up and down suspiciously, which for me felt like an hour, whilst I wondered if the crowning moment of my career was about to be unexpectedly cut short with a surprise bullet to the head. Then the man holding the list finally found my name. It transpired mine was the only name on the very last page, which somehow made it easy to miss (especially as my surname begins with a C rather than a Z). I shared some polite laughter at this "it could happen to anyone" mishap, although the armed officer looked clearly disappointed by not having had the chance to pop a couple of rounds into my forehead. I smiled gingerly and walked past. I turned the corner onto the High Street, in front of the already sizeable crowd, and walked onward to the front door of the Mansion House. A few faces in the crowd turned to look at me, curious to determine if I may be a celebrity or some other recognisable person of importance. After quickly satisfying themselves that I wasn't even a C-lister, they swiftly looked away again.

The invitation was extended to a small number of members of the Project Board which was nice to see. It would have been a challenge to invite everyone, but equally not all the members of the Core Group were invited which I personally think was an oversight, and I am sure a point of personal disappointment to those colleagues who missed out. I don't know who all the actual invitees were, but those present in the Ballroom to listen to the King included the contingent from the Project Board, council members, the local MPs, and (hidden in plain sight) some formidable looking secret service guys. Noteworthy guests included Doncaster war hero Ben Parkinson MBE, the most severely wounded soldier to survive the war in Afghanistan. He lost both his legs and suffered lasting brain damage when his vehicle struck a landmine, but he went on to become a resilient ambassador for disabled veterans, and memorably carried the Olympic torch through Doncaster in 2012. Parkinson was a rarity as someone who was both named in person in the city status bid, as well as being invited to attend the Letters Patent ceremony. Unsurprisingly the King would take a moment to share a few words with him.

The King, alongside the Queen Consort, had started his day in York. He attended a short service at York Minister where he also unveiled a new statue of his mother. As he undertook a walkabout to greet the crowds in York, Patrick Thelwell, a 23-year-old student, took it upon himself to try and pelt the monarch with eggs. Thankfully Thelwell was a terrible shot and seemingly, to use a popular basketball metaphor, couldn't throw a ball in the ocean if he were standing on the beach. He missed the King with each attempt, and moments later was duly snatched by the police. He was later convicted of threatening behaviour and sentenced to a 12-month community order with 100 hours of unpaid work. Despite his hopeless lack of aim, Thelwell's stunt still stole the headlines and frustratingly overshadowed the Kings visit to Doncaster. "It's just no yolk being a King" read the cover of the *Daily Express* the following morning (please feel free to add your own cymbal crash sound effect). Ho-hum!

Undeterred by all the commotion in York, the King arrived in Doncaster via a short helicopter ride, touching down at the racecourse. The Royal car carried him along Bennetthorpe, Hall Gate, and the High Street before pulling up at the Mansion House. By the time he arrived, the crowds were at least half a dozen deep on the pavement all along the High Street, with a host of waving union jacks and a chorus of cheers. I don't know exactly how many people came to watch that day, but it must have been comfortably in the low thousands, and more than comfortably outnumbering the naysayers who had previously derided Doncaster's city status ambitions on social media. A surprise face in the crowd was Paul Elliott, better known as Paul Chuckle. Heralding from nearby Rotherham, Paul and his late brother Barry were the Chuckle Brothers, household name children's entertainers who came to fame on the television in the 1980s. Interviewed outside of the Mansion House, Paul said: '70 years ago, when the Queen became the Queen, she toured around and came to Rotherham. I was five years old. I remember waving to her up in the balcony. And now, 70 years later, the new King is coming here, so I had to come.'[60] What a lovely thing to say. I had slight imposter syndrome being inside

---

60 https://www.doncaster.gov.uk/News/a-right-royal-visit

the Mansion House when a celebrity like Paul Chuckle was outside in the crowd. The Chuckle Brothers toured right up to Barry's death in 2018, and we took our kids to see them two or three times at the theatre in Retford when they were younger, once even collecting their autographs. Masters of good old-fashioned slapstick comedy, their shows were always simple in design, but hugely entertaining, and always funny.

Inside the Ballroom it was a little hard to gauge exactly what was going on down on the street below. Alison Jordan, clipboard in hand, was busy organising everyone, making sure we were all sat in the right place. Opposite the Mansion House is the old Nat West Bank on the other side of the street. Looking out from my seat through the Ballroom window, I could see that the bank's staff had congregated on the building's rooftop balcony to get a perfect view of the proceedings unfolding below. I tried to gauge their reactions to get a better sense of what was happening, but the King was seemingly running a little late, so they looked as if they were idly waiting with the same anticipation as the rest of us. Damian Allen hushed everyone to give us all a short briefing on the royal protocol for the event before the King arrived, delivered, I felt, in a style inspired from his days overseeing assemblies as a teacher. He focused on all the important etiquette, reminding us of when we should stand up, when we should sit down, not to have our phones on, and not to take photos. Most importantly though, under no circumstances were any of us allowed to fidget (a big no-no). Shortly after there was a hiatus of activity over on the Nat West balcony, and the sound of cheering below. The King was here!

The Royal couple took a moment to shake hands with well-wishers in the crowd, and thankfully no one had brought any eggs with them. More handshakes followed with the local politicians and Council leaders as they made their way inside the Mansion House. The Core Group members who were there that day didn't get the opportunity themselves to shake the King's hand, which was a shame given that his attendance that day was mainly down to all our own hard work. I know that sat a little awkwardly with one or two people but for me, as a man without any office or standing to speak of, I was just happy and proud to be there. We stood silently as the procession entered the Ballroom, the King of my country and the Queen Consort passing barely an arm's length away from where I stood, making their way to the stage at the front of the room, where the Letters Patent sat proudly on a table just in front of them.

I may have not known or recognised many of the other people in the room, but that didn't really matter. The truth is that none of us had really made the city in which we now stood. Daydreaming for a moment, I imagined that I was in a scene from the BBC sitcom *Ghosts*, only it was the spirits of Doncaster's legends who had gathered and were watching on from the back of the room. Ronnie Barker was there, in the character of Arkwright in his shop overalls, haggling with Samuel Parkinson over the price of his butterscotch. Ted Hughes and Sir Walter Scott were discussing literature, whilst Diana Rigg and Donald Pleasence reminisced about acting together. Thomas Crapper was animatedly explaining his ballcock invention to Sir Cornelius Vermuyden, who seemed genuinely interested. The Roman Emperor Vespasian seemed confused as to why he wasn't the centre of attention on the stage. Shirley Clarkson offered him a Paddington bear to cuddle to make him feel a little better. Sir Nigel Gresley was obviously there, looking like a proud grandfather to us all. And who was that over in the corner? A fella wearing green tights and looking suspiciously like Errol Flynn. Robin Hood! Who the hell had let him in? He wasn't even a proper ghost! He nevertheless gave me a defiant wink and a smile. And, strangely, I found myself smiling back. There they all were. The real heroes who had made this city. Somehow I had developed a strange enduring kinship with them all. And just like that, they all disappeared again, back into the deepest archives of my imagination, with my attention returning swiftly to the front of the room, where the non-imaginary proceedings were getting underway.

The formal ceremony saw speeches made by Ros Jones and Ian Pearson, the Civic Mayor, as well as by the King. It was, however, the Junior Civic Mayor, 9-year-old Evia Shaw-Lewis, who is, like Pearson, visually impaired, who stole the show with her own speech, delivered with an innocent, heartwarming charm. 'When I was lucky enough to be chosen as Doncaster's Junior Civic Mayor only a few weeks ago,' she began, 'I knew that I would get to meet a lot of new people and attend lots of exciting events, but I never dreamt that I would be lucky enough to meet the King and the Queen Consort.' Afterwards, the King told her: 'You did so well,' patting her on the shoulder. The King's speech was, nevertheless, what everyone had come to hear. It was short, yet nevertheless delivered with an earnest warmth and humour. It may have been a traumatic day for him, unveiling statues and avoiding flying eggs, but in that short moment the people of Doncaster were the only ones that mattered. Rather than select edited highlights, it is more than appropriate that I repost the full speech here:

'Ladies and gentlemen,

My wife and I are so delighted to be with you in Doncaster today as you celebrate this historic occasion.

The warmth of the welcome we have received today is all that we have come to expect in a county which is renowned for its sense of belonging and its feeling of community. It is something which all who know this wonderful part of the world will recognise instantly, and can never forget.

Here in Doncaster, you have, of course, a great deal of which to be proud: from your Roman origins two thousand years ago, to your crucial role in the Industrial Revolution and in the creation of this nation's railway network, to the pre-eminent place you occupy in the horse-racing world.

For all those reasons, and many, many more, it is entirely fitting that Doncaster should be chosen as one of the new cities created to celebrate The late Queen's Platinum Jubilee. We mark that occasion now in memory of my beloved mother's lifelong dedication to all that is best about our country. She would, I know, be immensely glad that this honour should be conferred on a place where it is so richly deserved.

It is my hope that your new status will be taken not just as a mark of your community's great achievements in the past, but also of your ambition for the future. Doncaster as a town has played its part in the life of the nation for two millennia, and I know that this very special community will approach the future as a city with the same enterprise, the same resilience, and the same good old Yorkshire spirit.

So, ladies and gentlemen, nothing could give me greater pleasure than to offer you my most heartfelt congratulations as you celebrate your new-found status, and to wish you all every possible success for the next two thousand years!'

With that, the King and Queen Consort were shuffled away into the room known as the Salon, where they posed for a photograph in front of the portrait of his mother, and were duly fed, watered, and refuelled. They signed the Mansion House guestbook, and were presented with gifts of some Sprotbrough Honey and, as is now a Doncastrian royal tradition, a Paddington bear. Beyond this is the old Council Chamber, where various ambassadors from the local voluntary and community sector were waiting in turn to meet the royal couple. Those of us still in the Ballroom had the opportunity to take some selfies with the Letters Patent, which of course I did. We were then escorted to the old kitchens on the ground floor which served as a temporary holding area, and where a welcome cup of tea was on hand. I had taken a pocketful of the campaign pin badges with me, not sure quite when or how they may be called into service. There were, however, some school children there who were more than happy to accept one each as a souvenir of the day, as were their accompanying teachers.

Once the King and Queen Consort had left, and were on route back to their helicopter, we were allowed back upstairs for some lunch in the Salon. In a particularly nice touch, all the floristry and catering were provided by students from Doncaster College. A generous buffet spread had been laid on, which the King had obviously gotten first dibs on a little earlier. The savoury treats included Yorkshire ham and Doncaster ale chutney sandwiches, as well as slightly more exotic options, such as char-grilled chicken, peppers, and pesto on a brioche slider. The sweet menu had similar local influences. There was Danum gin bramble trifle, Yorkshire parkin with stem ginger and Doncaster honey glaze, Yorkshire curd tarts, and fresh fruit scones. It was, in every sense, a feast fit for a King. It was all delicious.

I enjoyed my plate of food and networked with a few familiar faces. There was a real sense within the building that it had been a special day, and everyone was upbeat. Talk of a wider community celebration event rolled on for a little while, but there was a school of thought emerging that, whatever we might plan, we wouldn't top the King's visit. We were certainly unlikely to attract any celebrity of greater calibre, but I still personally believe Doncaster missed a trick here. Not everyone had the freedom to come and see the King on a blustery midweek lunchtime in November with just a few days' notice, and there was never a specific event afterwards for the community at large to be part of the celebration. I think that is a shame. I nevertheless dined out on my date with the King for a while ('The King you say? Well, I spent the day with him only last week!'). By the time I left the Mansion House the crowds had gone, the staff at Nat West were back at their desks, and the King was away in his helicopter. But as I walked back to my car, I was smiling all the way. We had just bought the King to Doncaster. How wonderfully crazy was that!

The Future of Civic Honours

It's June 2023, the hottest June in Britain since records began. Whilst the country has been basking in sweltering temperatures, today is a little fresher with a veil of light cloud drifting over the Nottinghamshire countryside. I'm at the White Post in Farnsfield, a pub that is roughly equidistant between my house and the city of Nottingham. It's a deceptively large place, with lots of tables, albeit on this summer's lunchtime it is comparatively quiet. There is small group of diners at the far end of the restaurant who are celebrating something, perhaps a birthday or a colleague moving on to pastures new (I can't really tell), and then there is my guest and me. The man I am dining with is a sagacious, softly spoken character in his early seventies. He is sporting a lively wave of grey hair, a matching beard, and metal framed glasses. He's wearing a short-sleeved lilac shirt, his beige linen jacket draped over the back of his chair. If you didn't know him, you might readily walk past him on the street without a second glance. But this man is arguably the Don Corleone of city status, in a gentle godfatherly kind of way. Today I am having lunch with John Beckett who, up until his recent retirement, was Professor of English Regional History at the University of Nottingham. If you've been paying attention, you'll recall too that he is the only person to have written a book about Britain's history of city status, just one of a dozen history books he has authored and edited. If he ever appeared on *Mastermind* there is a good chance that city status would be his specialist subject, a topic on which he would achieve a commanding score.

We order fishfinger sandwiches, which have come a long way from being a quick-and-cheap student meal to these days being reinvented as a quasi-gourmet staple on gastropub menus. Whilst we tucked in, I asked John about how he first became bitten by the city status bug. It transpires he was editing a book entitled *A Centenary History of Nottingham* in the late nineties. Nottingham had received city status in 1897, but John had struggled to initially unearth exactly how or why the accolade had been bestowed. It turns out that Bradford and Hull had both petitioned strongly and developed applications to attain city status at that time, whilst Nottingham hadn't pursued this avenue at all. Nottingham was, however, the nucleus of the Victorian lace manufacturing industry. There was as such a view in Whitehall that if Bradford and Hull were to become cities, which were considered of no greater industrial significance, then Nottingham should be a city too. So, all three duly became cities in 1897 as part of the Diamond Jubilee celebrations of Queen Victoria. Nottingham though is perhaps unique as being a British city which never actually applied for the honour. To get to the bottom of all this, John had visited The National Archives in Kew, where he discovered that there was a file documenting Nottingham's elevation to city status. And there was another file for Bradford. And another for Hull. And another for each of all the other British cities elevated up to that point (and probably now one for Doncaster too). Very soon John found himself ferreting through them all, unearthing all sorts of facts and stories which would shape and influence his further works. Pandora's Box was well and truly opened.

I asked John for his view on which currently unsuccessful bidder most deserved city status. In line with my own thoughts, he immediately suggested Reading. He was, however, a little more critical about opening the competition up to British Overseas Territories and challenged whether Stanley in the Falkland Islands really was a more deserving winner than some of England's largest towns. I only partly agree with John here. I think the capitals of overseas territories, such as Stanley, have a valid case for city status regardless of their size. John is right though about city status becoming a mockery of itself if awards are made on a quota basis. This is where the principle of Civic Honours sits uneasily with that of basic population demographics. The largest British towns (i.e., not cities) outside of England are Paisley in Scotland (population 76,000), Newtownabbey in Northern Ireland (65,000), and Tonypandy in Wales (62,000). There are around 70 towns in England which have larger populations than any of these. Without a rethink, we will increasingly have a wealth of disproportionately small cities outside of England, and a dearth of disproportionately large towns within it. Blackburn, Croydon, Dudley, and Sandwell were four of the nine city-worthy candidates which made the shortlist for the very first Civic Honours contest in 1977. Almost half a century later they have all further grown and evolved, but they are all still waiting to become cities. That can't be right. It just can't be! I'm English, and you may therefore think I'm biased, and maybe I am, but it should be perfectly reasonable to elevate many more cities in England, without this offending people elsewhere in the UK. This doesn't mean that Scotland, Wales, and Northern Ireland are any less deserving of civic praise, but that shouldn't be measured solely in terms of the comparative number of cities which each country has.

We perhaps should also pause to think about what it means to be a city in the 21st century. In this regard, Civic Honours contests are not the only game in town. Many UK localities are vying to become "Smart Cities", including Belfast, Bristol, Hull, Glasgow, and Peterborough. Smart Cities use big tech solutions to capture data on how people live, work, and travel, and use this data in turn to shape and improve local policy making, but you don't need to be an actual city to be a Smart City. Similarly, 19 UK localities received recognition as being "Tree Cities" in 2022 for their commitment to effective urban forestry management, even though several, such as Chesterfield, Solihull, and Welwyn Hatfield, aren't cities. The European Union has invented "Access Cities", recognising places with a population of over 50,000 which have undertaken outstanding work to become more accessible for people with disabilities. UNESCO, on the other hand, recognises "Learning Cities", which promote education and lifelong learning opportunities. "15 Minute Cities" is the latest policy buzz-term, an urban planning concept whereby most daily necessities (work, shopping, education, healthcare, leisure) can be reached by a 15-minute walk or bike ride from any point in the said city. Basically, if you want your town to become a city, just come up with your own similar scheme or name. Aberdeen is the Granite City, Sheffield the Steel City, Oxford the City of Dreaming

Spires, and the City of London is, well, just plainly *The* City. If you are looking for options, maybe you might choose something like a Faux City, a People's City, or a Goddammit-Will-We-Ever-Be-A City (Reading, I'm speaking directly to you now).

I enjoyed my lunch with John, and I even cheekily asked him to sign my copy of his book which I had taken along with me, which he thankfully accepted to do. The conversation really got me thinking about the future of Civic Honours. I fully subscribe to the concept, recognising and rewarding places, rather than people, for their contribution to Britain's culture, history, and heritage. We should rightly celebrate different places and their respective contributions to British life. I equally think, however, that as a country we are missing so many opportunities to fully exploit this idea. In recent times we have rewarded just a select handful of places with the accolade of city status, typically once per decade. This is wonderful, but it also means that so many other places have gone silently unrecognised. It begs the question as to whether we should do more to celebrate and recognise the achievements of Britain at large, not just those few towns who aspire to become cities.

A few places have, of course, already earned special designations by virtue of their historic associations with royalty. These are not Civic Honours per se, but they are nevertheless regal distinctions that carry their own certain swagger, and in most cases, like city status, they are enshrined through formal Letters Patent. Take, for starters, the majestical prefixes afforded to the towns of Royal Tunbridge Wells and Royal Leamington Spa; to the London boroughs of Royal Kensington & Chelsea,

Royal Greenwich, and Royal Kingston upon Thames; to the historic county of Royal Berkshire; and to the modern borough of Royal Windsor & Maidenhead. Such accolades are only usually proffered for localities with an exceptionally strong royal connection, such as places where past monarchs may have been born, lived, or been coronated, meaning that we are unlikely to see Royal Doncaster anytime soon. Likewise, Regis (Latin for 'of the King') is a title only bestowed where there is historical ownership of lands or manors by the crown. Examples include Lyme Regis in Dorset, Beeston Regis in Norfolk, and Houghton Regis in Bedfordshire. The most recent bestowment of the Regis title came in 1929, when, in a break from convention, the seaside town of Bognor on the south coast became Bognor Regis, after King George V spent time recuperating from illness there.

If city status is hard to attain, then these more regal accolades are even harder and rarer to come by still. Whilst Queen Elizabeth elevated a lot of cities during her seventy-year reign, her regal accolades were awarded far more sparingly. Greenwich's elevation to Royal Borough came in 2012, as part of Elizabeth's Diamond Jubilee celebrations. Caernarfon, where King Charles III was formerly invested as the Prince of Wales, became a Royal Borough in 1963, and latterly a Royal Town following local authority restructuring. Royal Hillsborough, in County Down, was granted its Royal prefix in 2021, in recognition of Hillsborough Castle being the official royal residence in Northern Ireland. Like I say, it's a very select list. For me, though, the one place that truly earned its designation during Elizabeth's reign is Royal Wootton Basset in Wiltshire, which became a Royal Town in 2011. I single it out because Wootton Basset has no especially significant historical association with royalty. Instead, the town achieved its royal status because of the unique service of its people, which for me feels like a much more relevant, modern-day basis for considering civic recognition.

Britain's entry into the 21st century began with bitter military conflicts in both Iraq and Afghanistan. The bodies of many servicemen and women killed in these faraway battles were repatriated to RAF Lyneham, a few miles from Wootton Bassett. The coffins, each covered with a Union Flag, were transported to nearby Oxford, passing through the town on their way. In 2007, local members of The Royal British Legion became aware of the repatriation and lined the kerbside of Wootton Bassett to pay their respects as the hearses drove by. Gradually more and more residents joined them, standing in tribute. Sometimes there was applause, sometimes flowers were thrown, and sometimes there was just poignant silence. The locals described their role as standing proxy for the grief of the nation. As each cortège approached, the tenor bell of St Bartholomew's Church began to toll. Business stopped, allowing shoppers and shopkeepers to join the crowds, and the former servicemen lining the route tendered their salute. In July 2009, when a convoy of eight hearses drove through the town, each carrying the coffin of a fallen serviceman who had died in Afghanistan, over 4,000 people lined the route. The High Street became affectionately known as the Heroes Highway.

RAF Lyneham closed in 2011, and subsequent repatriations have since moved to RAF Brize Norton, but there was a wave of support for Wootton Bassett to deservedly receive a legacy of royal recognition. Notably this call didn't primarily come from the townsfolk themselves, but rather from the relatives of the fallen, other servicemen, and the wider public at large. If this isn't the very epitome of a deserving civic honour, then I don't know what is.

These hard-to-come-by royal accolades and designations aside, city status, alongside the appointment of a Lord Mayor or Provost, are currently the only official Civic Honours that a place or locality can win, but these honours are effectively out of reach for the smaller towns and villages which make up most British communities. Now, it would be overzealous (and perhaps a bit too American) to upgrade every small town into a city, but perhaps the civic pride of smaller places can be recognised in other ways. Rather than looking to the Royal Family for inspiration, a great idea of this approach in practice came from a slightly less obvious source, the Royal Mail. To celebrate the British gold medallists of the London Olympics and Paralympics in 2012, the Royal Mail painted a gold letterbox in each of their hometowns. The cyclist Sir Chris Hoy has a gold letter box in his honour in Edinburgh, whilst the heptathlete Dame Jessica Ennis-Hill has one in Sheffield, and world champion boxer Anthony Joshua has one in Watford. There are almost 100 such gold letterboxes in total, spread across the length and breadth Great Britain, in a diverse mix of cities, towns, and villages. Although this was initially conceived as a temporary initiative, the gold boxes became permanent, with a plaque added to celebrate the athlete in question. A simple and comparatively cheap idea, yet incredibly symbolic and bursting with civic pride. An unofficial civic honour, but still a civic honour nonetheless.

It would be remiss here not to mention Britain's blue plaques, the little circular blue signs affixed to buildings up and down the country to commemorate famous residents who were born or who lived there, or some similar historical provenance of the building in question. There are two in Mexborough commemorating Ted Hughes, the former Poet Laureate (1984-1998), one on his former home where he spent much of his childhood in the 1940s, and another at the local grammar school which he attended. Some places, like Sheffield and Birmingham, have Hollywood styled walks of fame, where prominent sons and daughters of the city are celebrated on metal floor plaques in pedestrianised areas. And there is no end of statues of famous alumni associated with different towns and cities up and down the country. Many towns and cities have their own Civic Honours, and the accolade of Freedom of the Town or Borough, warmly bestowed on noteworthy achievers. And this is all great, but it also comes back to, in the main, celebrating people rather than places. Every town has at least a few famous sons and daughters, as well as at least a one or two heritage plaques, memorials, and statues. It may sound hugely cynical, but so what?

When you start to think about it, there is a bucketful of places across Britain that are worthy of a formal civic honour, but for whom city status is arguably not the appropriate reward. And I really do mean places, not people. Let's start, for example, with Civic Honours to recognise contributions to British cuisine, perhaps an award for Melton Mowbray for its pork pies, or for Kendal for its mint cake, or for Bakewell for its tarts? Caerphilly, Cheddar and Stilton could all be recognised for their services to cheese, as could Pontefract and Eccles for services to cake. The list of worthy candidates in this category is longer than your arm, each place being synonymous with the food or drink it has given its name to. How about, as well, Civic Honours to recognise contributions to British music? Glastonbury, with its legendary music festival first staged in 1970, immediately springs to mind. Or the town of Lewes in East Sussex, home to Glyndebourne, the quintessential British opera experience. How about Gretna Green, where thousands of people have married, traditionally sealed by the striking of a blacksmith's anvil? Maybe some honours that recognise Britain's sporting heritage too, such the village of Silverstone, home of the British Grand Prix, or Cowes on the Isle of Wight, with its celebrated annual regatta?

Perhaps we should also consider places celebrated by classic British fiction? Step forward Launceston in Cornwall, whose real-life Jamaica Inn was immortalised to readers worldwide by Daphne du Maurier. Or how about the port of Whitby in North Yorkshire, the adopted home of Bram Stoker's Dracula? The association between Stratford-upon-Avon and Shakespeare is, of course, implicit, as is that between the Yorkshire village of Haworth and the Bronte sisters. Then there is Borehamwood in Hertfordshire, home of Elstree Studios where blockbuster movies have been made since the 1920s, including instalments in the likes of the *Star Wars, Indiana Jones, Harry Potter,* and *X-Men* franchises. I could go on, and on, and on. We are a literally a nation of towns and villages which are simply oozing with civic accomplishments. Many of these places have garnered implicit national, if not international, fame and recognition through their respective achievements, but equally none of the places I have listed here have been recognised with a national civic honour. I can't be the only person to think that this might be wrong!

As a small aside, it's not solely about the little places. Most of Britain's major cities achieved their city status, lord mayoralties, and lord provostships over a century ago, and a goodly bit longer in a few cases. Are we to say that the likes of Canterbury, Leicester, Coventry, and York have therefore exhausted the maximum number of Civic Honours they may ever win? Will future civic achievement in such places go unrecognised and unrewarded? Is the award of a lord mayoralty comparable to the ending of a *Looney Tunes* cartoon, with Porky Pig popping up to say, 'that's all folks!' It all feels just a little bit depressing. If we are going to celebrate civic pride at each jubilee milestone of our monarch, which is already something of a protracted infrequency, shouldn't everywhere be included?

In terms of a model that the UK could potentially plagiarise, let me introduce you to the All-America City Awards. These awards, organised by the National Civic League, recognise the work of communities of all sizes across the length and breadth of the United States in promoting inclusive civic engagement, such as increasing the participation of younger people in voting and policy making. Since the programme's inception in 1949, more than 500 communities in the USA have been named All-America Cities, with currently 10 award winning localities per year. As a civic or community recognition programme, the initiative is not unique, but a key point of differentiation is in its acknowledgement of places rather people. There was a frustratingly half-baked attempt by the British government to do something similar in 2020, when Robert Jenrick, Secretary of State for Housing, Communities, & Local Government, launched a Town of the Year competition. This backfired spectacularly though when the competition was launched in Wolverhampton, which officials had failed to realise was a city, not a town, and had held city status for almost 20 years. As far as I know, a winner was never crowned, and Jenrick's Town of the Year contest was dead in the water before it even started. It's a shame really, as the underlying idea is one of great potential.

No disrespect to Robert Jenrick, but perhaps the responsibility for this shouldn't sit with Whitehall. As with city status, perhaps the recognition of the civic achievements of our towns and villages should be steered from Buckingham Palace. Prince Philip gave us the Duke of Edinburgh Award, King Charles gave us The Prince's Trust, and even Prince Harry gave us The Invictus Games. Perhaps now is the right time for another royal to step up to the plate and create a civic initiative that will equally stand the test of time. That would be quite the legacy. It may be timely too. A poll in 2023 showed that public support for the British monarchy was at an all-time low, especially amongst younger generations, with a growing number believing it should be abolished[61]. Whilst that may be an unlikely scenario for the foreseeable future, a monarch free Britain would have its hand forced in terms of coming up with a new way to elevate cities and celebrate civic pride.

In the meantime, let's have a round of applause for all the wonderful small places in Britain. Many of their civic achievements may otherwise go unsung, but everywhere has something that is worth putting in a frame and hanging on the wall. If we did that, those frames could collectively fill the entirety of Hadrian's Wall, all the way from Carlisle to Newcastle, and we should all be rightly proud of that.

---

61   https://www.bbc.co.uk/news/uk-66707923

Four Letter Words

So, we come to the end of our story. That was how Doncaster won the Platinum Jubilee Civic Honours competition and became a city, all written down and recorded. It has been quite the journey and I hope you've enjoyed it as much as I did. Would I do it all again? Well, never say never (Ipswich, I know you have my number). In the meantime, when I walk through this city that I have, at least in some small way, helped to establish, people still don't know who I am. I doubt that this book will ever change that, but that's still okay. They will at least know how their town became a city, and that's the most important thing. But as the story of the town of Doncaster ends, the story of Doncaster the city is only just beginning. It's fair to say too that Doncaster's first year as a city didn't exactly go to plan; in fact, quite the opposite.

In July 2022, just weeks after the city status announcement, The Peel Group, the owners of Doncaster Sheffield Airport, commenced a consultation exercise with a view to closing the airport for good and repurposing the land for alternate use. The decision came off the back of the Covid-19 pandemic, which had hit the aviation sector especially badly. Peel's announcement nevertheless blindsided the local establishment and was a real body blow for the new city. Now, I'm no expert in running commercial airports, and I am sure it's a complex challenge to operate one successfully and sustainably, but the pace at which Peel moved to close the airport inevitably ruffled feathers. Millions of pounds of public money had been invested, including the building of the Great Yorkshire Way, a £56 million link road from the M18 only opened in 2018, so the decision to close felt like something of a slap in the face. The government on one side, and the Council and new South Yorkshire mayor, Oliver Coppard, on the other, locked horns, waving their fingers at each other and calling out the other side to come up with a rescue plan. Whilst all the jiggery-pokery delayed the closure, it didn't stop it.

As a brief aside, it is ludicrous in my opinion that the owners of a regional international airport can simply decide to shut up shop, without the government having any meaningful legislative powers to intervene or force them to sell the airport on. As I write, the government are planning to spend around £18 billion to obliterate a swathe of outer London to build an extra runway at Heathrow but have committed diddly squat from the Treasury to preserve the existing, longer commercial runway in Doncaster at a fraction of that cost, with enough change to build a rail link from the airport to the East Coast Mainline and a dozen or so new hospitals (maybe even one in Donny). I know I said that I would try to avoid political sentiment but, strewth, give me the actual strength!

On 8th of November 2022 the last commercial TUI flight, a Boeing 737 arriving from Hurghada, Egypt, touched down at Doncaster. The plane took off again a short while later, but this time with no passengers, bound for Manchester. The departing pilot delivered a brief but impactful speech over the radio to the control tower below, as the plane rose into the night sky. 'Doncaster, on behalf of all of us at TUI – thank you for your support and for being part of our team. Together we've delivered wonderful experiences for our customers for the last 17 years. The runway and buildings form an airport, but it's the people who are really the core. God speed and tailwinds all the way.' And with those final few emotive words, the airport was closed. The very next day the King came to Doncaster to deliver the Letters Patent to the new city. The sense of irony couldn't be any more palpable.

The airport closure wasn't the only setback. After several delays, in March 2023 the government finally announced that Derby had won the competition to become the new headquarters of Great British Railways. Doncaster was the unfortunate runner-up this time, a more than respectable achievement given who it was competing against, but, as we all know, there are no prizes for second place. Then, in May 2023, the National College for Advanced Transport & Infrastructure (NCATI), another institution showcased in the city status bid, announced its closure. Formerly known as the National College for High-Speed Rail, the £25m state-of-the-art Doncaster campus had only opened in 2017. Why did it fail? Well, there was plenty more theorising and finger pointing. The government's decision to scrap the proposed HS2 high speed rail extension from Birmingham to Leeds certainly didn't help. You can't really expect young people locally to choose a future in high-speed rail if the government itself doesn't see one. Doncaster had also missed out on a key Levelling Up funding bid, and the Doncaster Royal Infirmary failed in its £1.37 billion bid to be added to the government's hospitals building programme.

And in 2023, just to rub salt in the wounds, the BBC confirmed that it wouldn't be commissioning any new episodes of *Still Open All Hours*. Arkwright's famous corner shop had closed its doors for the last time. Almost everything that Doncaster was trying to achieve was thwarted. So much for city status opening the gates of opportunity!

Beyond Doncaster, the never-ending global race for city status rumbled on. In Saudi Arabia work began to build The Line, an ambitious $500 billion new mega city, which will occupy an area that is 110 miles long, but only 200 meters wide. It's a concept which sounds like something straight out of a dystopian science fiction movie. Each side of The Line will be walled with a continuous 500-meter tall, mirrored building, with a green space in between. Running from the current city of Tabuk all the way to the Red Sea, The Line is planned to house nine million people, and will be powered entirely by renewable energy. It's just one of several major new city concepts being developed around the world. Oceanix Busan, for example, is a proposed floating coastal city in South Korea, which would be built from a self-sustaining bio-rock capable of withstanding rising sea levels. The design of Mexico's proposed Smart Forest City is described as a botanical garden within a contemporary city, integrating 7.5 million plants. South of Beijing, the new city of Xiong'an is billed as an ecologically friendly showcase development, with the biggest high speed rail hub in Asia. Japan's parliament has passed legislation which paves the way for the creation of 'super cities', utilising artificial intelligence and big data to improve mobility, disaster preparedness, healthcare, and education. Meanwhile over in India, the government there are currently evaluating proposals to build no fewer than eight wholly new cities to alleviate population growth pressures.

It's not all about shiny new mega cities and high-tech environmental innovation though. At the other end of the spectrum the Drogheda City Status Group, a longstanding community lobbying body, continues to work tirelessly to secure city status for the towns of Drogheda and East Meath (population 56,527) in the Republic of Ireland. Smaller still is the application submitted in Deschutes County, Oregon, USA, in February 2023 to incorporate a new city called Mountain View. The proposed city would have just 165 residents, barely a street by British standards. And let's not forget that there are still 40 or so towns across Britain who would dearly love city status too. The variety of new and impending cities around the world couldn't be any more diverse. One thing is for sure though; steadily we are getting more and more of them. Doncaster may be one of the newest cities for now, but that mantle won't last forever. In a world full of cities, with one seemingly emerging on every longitudinal and latitudinal intersection, how will Doncaster continue to stand out?

Brighton & Hove, for me, is the epitome of the city status ideal. Brighton used to be referred to disparagingly as Skid Row on Sea, a term coined by *Private Eye* owing to the town's frequent mentions in their "Rotten Boroughs" column. It had become a somewhat run down and neglected coastal resort, looking for a new purpose. But city status, achieved in 2000, changed all that. Brighton & Hove's communities and agencies bonded together with a new mindset, a city mindset. Seafront roads were pedestrianised, and vibrant new bars and clubs opened. In 2002 over a quarter of a million people descended onto Brighton Beach for a free concert performed by Fatboy Slim (aka Norman Cook, Brighton's very own superstar DJ). The 30,000 seat Amex Stadium was approved, built, and opened in 2011. Creatives, digital innovators, environmentalists, and the LGBTQ community were warmly welcomed, as the new city shaped itself as a place where individuality and difference could be embraced. Hardly surprising then that Brighton elected Caroline Lucas, Britain's first, and still only, Green Party MP, in 2010. Described as a comeback Queen, Brighton was readily named in listings of Britain's best places to live, turning the heads of wannabe urbanites as a fashionable alternative to London. My nephews sometimes catch the train down from Crawley, staying out and partying in Brighton all night, having a blast, then catching the first train home again the next day. The lads from Crawley never did that when I was their age. No one refers to Brighton as Skid Row on Sea anymore. But this didn't all happen by chance. It happened because the key people in Brighton understood their opportunity, defined their city's identity, set a high bar for success, and showed a determination to deliver.

This is the challenge for Doncaster. Right now, it is at a crossroads. Is it really a city or still just a town, hidden in a city's clothing? Is there really any difference between a town and a city anyway? They are both just four-letter words, each with one vowel, and three consonants. When John Duffy, the CEO of local business Clean Power Hydrogen, spoke at the "Doncaster, What's Next? Business Conference" in June 2023, he described Doncaster as being 'shabby'. It was one little word, but a brutal and sobering assessment that bristled through the audience. Doncaster's future might entail attracting just enough investment, just enough jobs, and just enough new houses to get by. It could be just above the average in the national league tables of opportunity, of health, of education, and of life expectancy. It could have just enough of its potholes filled in, just enough of its fly tippers issued with fixed penalty notices, and just enough of its discarded chewing gum scraped off the pavement. The people of Doncaster could be more-or-less content with their lot, nothing to necessarily grumble about, but nothing to get too excited about either. Doncaster could wear its bright, shiny new city status badge proudly on its lapel, but in all other respects carry on as the town that it has always been. It could all be just enough. Or, maybe, just maybe, it could be more. We're all familiar with the hashtag saying that #doncasterisgreat, but maybe #doncastercanbegreater.

In December 2023 I was honoured to become the Vice President of Doncaster Chamber of Commerce, meaning that in December 2025 I will, in turn, commence a two-year term as the Chamber's President. It is, in many respects, a largely ceremonial role, which comes with some attractive chains of office hung on a small, mitred neck ribbon and an expectation to make several mildly amusing public speeches. More importantly, it also means that I will have just a little more skin in the game when it comes to Doncaster's future. To be clear, when that term ends in 2027, there will still be a long way to go whatever happens, and I certainly don't have a monopoly on good ideas for civic ambition. The Council, the MPs, the Metro Mayor, the government; none of them are obligated to pay any attention whatsoever to what I think. It's my book though. I've spent a long time writing it and that means I have author's privilege in sharing my opinions about the future of Doncaster, whether any of them (or indeed you) want to read them or not.

Firstly, we need to re-open the airport. Economically, the importance of Doncaster's airport to South Yorkshire cannot be understated; reopening it could deliver £1.5 billion of economic benefit within 30 years (or at least that's what the experts who know about this kind of stuff reckon). It is the singular, most important, game changing priority for the future of Doncaster. After a somewhat higgledy-piggledy initial response to the closure, meaningful headway between all the parties concerned is being made. The Council plans to lease the airport on a 100-year term from the Peel Group and will, in turn, appoint an operator to manage it. This should hopefully see commercial flights return to Doncaster by 2025, and for the airport to set new records for its passenger throughput by 2030. 5,000 direct new jobs are projected, as well as 11,500 more in the South Yorkshire economy. That's the big-ticket item, but it's not the only priority.

We also desperately need to rediscover, restore, and reinvigorate the city's forgotten assets. Doncaster has too many historic buildings which have been left to rack and ruin, such as Dennison House and the Pillar House on South Parade, the Doncaster Grand Theatre, and St James' Baths on Waterdale. In the same way that Doncaster Gallery Library & Museum preserved the original façade of the historic Doncaster Girls High School, we need to think of similar ways to reimagine these key city assets. It would be unforgivable if they were lost forever. We also need to incorporate the River Don more effectively into the cityscape. In most river cities, the river is a focal point, but the River Don is comparatively inaccessible from the centre of Doncaster, blockaded behind both the Frenchgate Centre, the East Coast Mainline, and Doncaster's railway works. There are no waterside bars or eateries, no readily accessible riverbank walkways, no celebration of the Victorian wharfs and warehouses. And we need a campaign to elevate St. George's Minister to become a cathedral. It already has the scale and historic pedigree. This would ultimately be a decision for the Church of England, but it goes without saying that cathedral cities have an additional visitor pull.

We need a signature investment. The Yorkshire Wildlife Park proves that Doncaster can sustain an attraction of regional, if not national, visitor significance. But why have just one? Morecambe in Lancashire has recently secured £50 million in public money to help build the Eden Project North, mirroring the hugely successful original Eden Project botanical garden in Cornwall. Eden Project North will directly employ 400 people, with a forecast of a further 1,500 regional jobs, injecting £200 million annually into the North West economy. Why can't Doncaster match that? Many of Doncaster's best heritage opportunities, such as coal and rail, have already been hijacked by our irritating neighbours. The National Coal Mining Museum opened in Wakefield in 1988, whilst The National Railway Museum (which also filched both the Mallard and the Flying Scotsman from Doncaster) has been in York since 1975. And, before you ask, the National Horse-racing Museum was bagged by Newmarket in Suffolk in 1983. Well, in the nicest possible way, they can all go and shove it. Doncaster needs instead to find its own gamechanger; a big, hairy, audacious, new, head turning, point of interest. If Morecambe can do it, then I am certain that Doncaster can do it too.

The cherry on the cake, however, would be a university. Britain's leading cities all have one. I acknowledge here that Doncaster College, like many other further education colleges, now has a university centre offering degree courses, and that's a positive thing. But a standalone, campus university defines a city in so many more ways. It has the potential to attract bright minds to the city and, in many cases, keep them in the local workforce. By establishing a student population, the city's relevance for all young people broadens. The belief that you can only get ahead in life by moving to Sheffield or Leeds is put in check. If you're a young person with a job in Doncaster, you can choose to live here too, rather than preferring to commute in from one of our seemingly more youth-centric neighbouring cities. A local youth economy would blossom. If Doncaster can attract funding for a new hospital, there are plans to integrate a new health university within it. That's a smart idea. As much as I would advocate for a University of Doncaster, the courses it offers need to be relevant, leading to careers with both prospects and opportunity, and the health sector is one such industry.

This wish list is neither prescriptive nor exhaustive. None of what I am advocating is easy. There are no silver bullets or quick fixes. Everything I have suggested here will take time and money. Lots of time and lots of money. And guess what too; the government (whether that be the Tories or Labour) aren't going to give Doncaster all that money. Sure, the government recently awarded Doncaster a £20 million endowment-style fund over 10 years, as one of 55 "left-behind town" to invest in local people's priorities, but that's just a drop in the ocean (and referring to anywhere as a left-behind town couldn't be any more patronising). We would likely as not have to find the real money ourselves. We would need to beg and borrow, crowdfund, win lottery grants, doff our caps to philanthropic millionaires, and do a whole manner of other crazy things. We would need an imaginative cocktail of creative workarounds, disruptive thinking, light bulb moments, social financing, and good old fashioned Yorkshire thriftiness. You may say it's impossible, all jam tomorrow and pie in the sky. And maybe you'd be right. But let's channel a little bit of our inner Brian Blessed, the big lad from Mexborough who would grow up to star in Hollywood movies, train as a cosmonaut in Russia, and attempt to climb Mount Everest three times. I wonder if anyone has ever dared to tell Brian that something might be impossible? I somehow doubt it. A little bit of Doncaster's grit and determination really can go a long way. When my great, great, great grandchildren visit Doncaster, I would really hate it if the first words they mutter when they step off the train are 'is that it?' We must do better than that.

There are glimmers of hope and optimism. Assuming plans don't drift sideways, the expected reopening of the airport speaks for itself. Alongside this, a new, second University Technology College will open in 2025, focused on health science and green technologies. There are noises too that the NCATI building could be repurposed and re-open with a new role in the local railways sector. Doncaster should also benefit from its position within South Yorkshire's Advanced Manufacturing Investment Zone, announced in 2023, the first of its kind in the UK. And love it or loathe it, the distribution and logistics sectors continue to thrive in and around Doncaster, with new facilities continuing to come online. These are all good news stories, but all this is arguably happening despite city status, rather than because of it. This should all be the baseline of our aspiration, not the peak.

I hope Doncaster goes on to do bigger, better, and bolder things. I really do. But for now, I'll step down from my soap box and sign off. Writing this bid, and indeed this book, has been my absolute privilege. My head is swelling with a library of new information which wasn't there before (and I worry a little about which critical, body function controlling datasets have been permanently deleted from my cerebrum to make room for all this new trivia). This has been a big chapter in my own story, but its time now to get back to writing other proposals for other things. I couldn't really think of a perfect sentence to end the book, a fitting way to finish my tribute to

Doncaster, so I pinched one instead. John Parr's lyrics sprung to mind again, eulogising about new horizons and blazing skies. I think though that the pilot who flew the last plane out of Doncaster summed up everything quite nicely and had already come up with the perfect words. So, Doncaster, I will simply just say goodbye and wish you good luck.

God speed and tailwinds all the way!

Roll of Honour

A host of remarkable people contributed to Doncaster's successful city status campaign. Their contributions ranged from those who gave just a few moments of their time to those who were hands on and did a lot of heavy lifting, but every contribution counted. I have done my best to list as many of these wonderful people as I can below, but there are so many that it's very probable that I have missed somebody out, and if I have, I apologise. A personal thank you to you all from me. I'll also take the liberty of saying thank you on behalf of the City of Doncaster for everything you have all done. You were all simply amazing!

Dani Adams, Damian Allen, Dean Asher, Gavin Baldwin, Paul Bareham, Karen Beardsley, Suzy Brain-England OBE, Suzy Broadhead, Glyn Butcher, Tom Bywood, Anne Carley, David Chorlton, Charlotte Coupe, Karen Creed, Steph Cunningham, John Davis, Matthew Davis, Georgia Deith, Charlotte Dimond, Charlotte Dinsdale, Chris Dungworth, Jade Dyer, Dan Fell, Samuel Finn, Nick Fletcher, Nick Fromont, Carl Hall, Warren Hands, Joe Harrigan, Courtney Helsby, Andy Hibbitt, Dan Hill, Liam Hoden, Stephen Houghton, Tim Hume-Smith, Yvette Ireland, Lindsy James, Dan Jarvis MBE, Ros Jones CBE, Alison Jordan, Lord Graham Kirkham KCVO, Ian Leech, Carl Les, Ginny Lindle, Ian Mayer, Owen Marshall-Dungworth, Ian Martin, Scott McFarlane, Dan McLaughlin, Ed Miliband, Ashleigh Milner, David Milnes,

John Minion, Akeela Mohammed, Andy Morley, Riana Nelson, Emma Norton, Alan Ogle, Gemma Parkinson, John Parr, Ian Pearson, Martin Peppard, Gemma Peters, Kevin Pritchard, Deborah Rees, Dave Richmond, Lorna Reeve, Bobbie Roberts MBE, Jennifer Rodrigues, Kev Rogers, Chinwe Russell, Mitchel Salter, Tariq Shah OBE, David Shaul, Kathryn Singh, Gemma Smith, Karen Staniforth, Chris Stephenson, Revd David Stevens, Paul Stockhill, Lee Tilman, Jessica Touhig, Adi Turnpenny, Graham White, Kim Wilkins, Cheryl Williams, Allan Wiltshire, Dame Rosie Winterton DBE, Cath Witherington, and Jill Wood.